canoe and
kayak routes
of **Northwest Oregon**
including Southwest Washington

canoe and
kayak routes
of Northwest Oregon
including Southwest Washington

Third Edition
Philip N. Jones

THE MOUNTAINEERS BOOKS

THE MOUNTAINEERS BOOKS
is the nonprofit publishing arm of The Mountaineers Club,
an organization founded in 1906 and dedicated to the exploration,
preservation, and enjoyment of outdoor and wilderness areas.

1001 SW Klickitat Way, Suite 201, Seattle, WA 98134

© 2007 by Philip N. Jones

Third edition: first printing 2007, second printing 2010. Second edition printed in 1997, first edition published in 1982 under the name *Canoe Routes: Northwest Oregon*

Manufactured in the United States of America

Project Editor: Elizabeth Cromwell/Books in Flight
Copy Editor: Brenda Pittsley
Cover and Book Design: Peggy Egerdahl
Layout: Elizabeth Cromwell/Books in Flight
Cartographer: Paul Christenson
Photographer: Philip N. Jones

Cover photograph: *Sunrise on the Columbia River* © Dan Gavere/Aurora Photos
Frontispiece: *Cowlitz River (Trip 45)*

Library of Congress Cataloging-in-Publication Data
Jones, Philip N.
    Canoe and kayak routes of northwest Oregon / by Philip N. Jones.—3rd ed.
    p. cm.
    Includes bibliographical references and index.
    ISBN 1-59485-032-1 (ppb)
    1. Canoes and canoeing—Oregon—Guidebooks. 2.
Kayaking—Oregon—Guidebooks. 3. Oregon—Guidebooks. I. Title.
GV776.O7J66 2007
797.1'0979—dc22
                        2006037994

ISBN (paperback): 978-1-59485-032-5
ISBN (ebook): 978-1-59485-246-6

contents

THE WILLAMETTE RIVER

TRIBUTARIES OF THE WILLAMETTE

THE CASCADES

COLUMBIA GORGE

SOUTHWEST WASHINGTON

Early morning at Hosmer Lake (Trip 31)

COLUMBIA RIVER

THE COAST

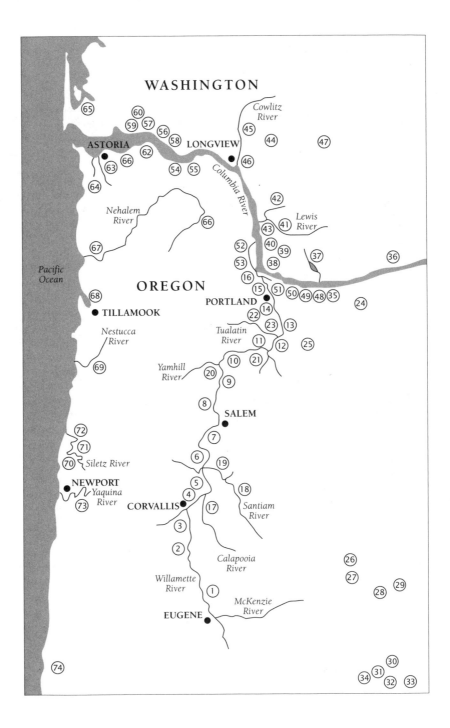

acknowledgments

The preparation of the first edition of *Canoe and Kayak Routes of Northwest Oregon* was made possible largely through the able assistance of David Puls, Holly Mitchell, and Jack Holmgren, all of whom helped paddle many of the fifty trips that were described in that edition. The second edition expanded the geographic scope into the Columbia Gorge and the Cascades. My wife, Holly Mitchell, and sons, Mitchell Jones and Alex Jones, helped paddle many of the trips described in this and prior editions. Many others, including employees of various public agencies and members of local paddling clubs, helped in countless ways. Paddlers who frequent various Internet mailing lists devoted to Northwest canoeing and kayaking provided considerable information.

MAP KEY

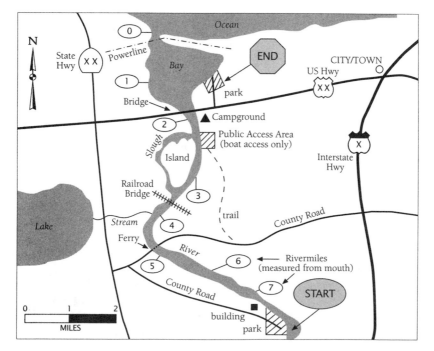

updates and corrections

I would appreciate hearing from readers who spot errors or have suggestions or updated information to offer. Many changes from earlier editions resulted from readers who were kind enough to offer their suggestions and corrections. Please write to me either in care of the publisher, or directly—my address and phone number can be found in the Portland phone book—or send me an email at *philipnjones@yahoo.com*.

Updates and corrections to this book will be posted on the websites of the Lower Columbia Canoe Club at *www.l-ccc.org/routes* and of the Oregon Ocean Paddling Society at *www.ooopskayak.org/routes*.

Little Deschutes River (Trip 33)

safety considerations

Safety is an important concern in any outdoor activity. No guidebook can alert you to every possible hazard or anticipate the abilities or limitations of every reader. The descriptions in this guidebook are not representations that every trip is safe for you or your party. If you decide to take one of these trips, read both the information block and the entire trip description carefully before beginning the trip. You assume all risks and you assume full responsibility for your own safety. River channels frequently change due to flooding and other natural forces. Water conditions, weather conditions, logjams, changes in riverbeds and shorelines, and the capabilities of your party and your selected craft cannot be predicted by the author or the publisher, who disclaim any representation concerning the accuracy of the material contained herein or that any of the described trips are suitable for you or your party.

Waldo Lake (Trip 34)

introduction

This guide is an attempt to catalog some of the flatwater paddling opportunities on rivers and lakes in northwestern Oregon; a few trips spill over into southwestern Washington. The area covered is roughly the Willamette Valley from Eugene north to Portland, the north and central Oregon Cascades, the Columbia Gorge and southwest Washington, the lower Columbia River and its tributaries, and the coast from Willapa Bay in Washington south to the Siltcoos River on the central Oregon coast. Most of the flatwater rivers in the region are covered, but only a few of the hundreds of lakes are included.

All of the trips can easily be paddled in one day or less. The Willamette River, for example, has been divided into sixteen trips of a few hours each, although the trips can be combined into tours lasting several days. Some of the trips are sufficiently short that two can be paddled in a single day.

Most of the trips are suitable for novice paddlers equipped with an open canoe or a sea kayak and some common sense, but some are on swift streams or open waters that require paddling skills not possessed by a beginner; read the trip descriptions carefully when selecting a trip. Also keep in mind that conditions often change, and a trip described as flat may become difficult due to changes in riverbeds, weather, water level, and other factors.

When the first edition of this guide was published in 1982, the title was *Canoe Routes: Northwest Oregon*, even though the author paddled most of the trips using sea kayaks. While the text discussed both canoes and kayaks, and the illustrations displayed an assortment of both types of boats, the title was chosen to avoid the widely held connotation that kayaks were exclusively whitewater craft. At that time, sea kayaks were relatively uncommon. Today, sea kayaks are as popular as canoes, particularly here in the Pacific Northwest. As a result, the title for the second edition was changed to reflect the wide use of both canoes and sea kayaks (many of which never venture out into salt water). The text, however, retains its original theme: canoes and kayaks each have their advantages and disadvantages, and each is particularly suited to different conditions, different uses, and different users. The important thing is to select the craft that best meets the conditions and the cargo, keeping an open mind toward both types of boats. Advice on selecting either a canoe or a kayak is included later in this introduction.

Trip Descriptions

For each trip described in this book, the following information is summarized in capsule form at the beginning of the description:

Location: A general indication of the area in which the trip is located is given, usually by reference to a nearby city or town.

Distance: For most of the trips, an estimate of the distance to be covered is given in miles. For river trips, the mileage should be quite accurate because it is usually based on the rivermiles shown on U.S. Geological Survey (USGS) topographic maps. In some cases, however, the distances to be covered may be approximate due to changes in riverbeds. In other cases, significant changes in riverbeds may make the official rivermiles very inaccurate and an estimate of the distance is provided. For trips on lakes or bays, only a distance range, such as "from 2 to 6 miles," is given if no specific route is described.

Time: The estimate of time is a rough guess of how much time will be spent on the water, but keep in mind that the type of boat, ability of the paddlers, and water level all affect speed. These estimates are on the generous side; you may be able to paddle some of the trips in half the estimated time, particularly if water levels are high and currents swift. The estimates allow enough time for a leisurely pace and a relaxing lunch, but they do not include driving time or time spent shuttling cars.

Maps and charts: The U.S. Geological Survey topographic maps and the National Oceanographic and Atmospheric Administration (NOAA) charts for each trip are indicated. References are made to the 7.5-minute series (7.5") USGS maps, but not to the older 15-minute series (15"), because the 15-minute maps are generally out of print and out of date. The 7.5-minute maps are available for all of the trips described, although in some instances four or five sheets are necessary for complete coverage of a particular trip. The NOAA charts are available only for the coast, the Columbia River, and the Willamette River north of Newberg. Thus, for trips on lakes, coastal rivers, portions of the Willamette, or tributaries of the Columbia or Willamette, either no chart is listed, or the indicated chart covers only a portion of the trip. A more detailed discussion of available maps occurs later in this introduction.

Season: The majority of the trips described in this book may be paddled all year. Trips on the coast, the Columbia, and the main channel of the Willamette are in this category. Some of the trips, however, are not suitable for year-round paddling due to seasonal fluctuations of water levels or snow in the mountains. Some of the smaller rivers and backwater sloughs are in this category. Some of the trip descriptions provide detailed information about river levels measured by various gauges. Current river levels can be found in local newspapers or sources listed at the end of this book. Lakes in the Cascades are often either snowbound or frozen until spring or summer. "Season" gives an indication of when the water level on a particular trip should (in an average or normal year) be high enough to allow paddling, or when a lake is accessible. This indication may be of little value during periods of unusually heavy rainfall, of severe drought, when water is being released from upstream reservoirs, or when winter snowfall is higher or lower than normal. "Season" is an indication of when each trip is at its best for navigation, rather than other purposes, such as wildlife observation. In most cases, the text of each trip points out the best times for such opportunities, or it may point out the best times to avoid other watercraft, such as powerboats and jet skis. Paddlers should also be mindful of fishers and hunters. Waterfowl hunting season generally runs from early October to mid-January, and during that time paddlers should avoid popular hunting areas,

Best Trips in Winter
37—Lacamas Lake and Round Lake
51—Smith and Bybee Lakes

particularly wildlife refuges where (despite the name) hunting is usually permitted. The rest of the year, paddlers looking for solitude should keep in mind that the fishing season usually runs from the third week in April to the end of October, although anglers are usually unobtrusive compared with water-skiers and jet skis. Prohibitions on the use of motors on particular waters are usually noted in the text, as are speed limits, which usually prevent waterskiing. If particular waters allow waterskiing and jet skis, paddlers should try to visit them in the fall, winter, or spring, not in the summer.

Rating: Each trip is rated for difficulty according to the following rating system:

Class Characteristics

A   Still water or rivers with less than a 2-mile-per-hour current; suitable for novices if the weather is favorable.

B   Rivers with a current between 2 and 4 miles per hour; some maneuvering skill required.

C   Rivers with a velocity above 4 miles per hour, or with rapids or turns that require significant maneuvering skill.

The use of a rating system has many advantages; principally, it brings a degree of standardization to describing difficulties that might be encountered on a particular river. However, no rating system can be completely accurate or free from subjective considerations, nor can a rating system predict changes in conditions.

When using this book, the ratings should not be relied upon exclusively, but should be viewed as a general description of the type of water to be encountered and the speed of the water in particular. For example, an A rating has been assigned to several trips on the open waters of the Columbia River because the current is usually fairly slow, but on stormy days these particular trips can be dangerous. Examine the entire trip description and take into account the effects of weather, flooding, tides, low water conditions, spring freshets, potential logjams, and other hazards before embarking on any of these trips. If the reader relies exclusively on the assigned rating, an incomplete view of the trip is obtained.

In some cases, the trips described in this book involve short portages around rapids, waterfalls, dams, or small logjams. Whenever possible, these obstacles are mentioned within each trip description, although the author cannot predict every logjam that might form. Obstacles are generally not taken into account in the ratings because it is assumed that the reader will not attempt to paddle through them. Although these obstacles are sometimes mentioned in parentheses after the assigned rating, they are described in detail only in the trip description itself. Once again, the assigned rating, by itself, does not fully inform the reader of these obstacles, some of which may be dangerous. Read the entire trip description carefully before selecting a trip, and always be on the lookout for hazardous conditions, even on trips described as easy. Large bodies of open water and swift rivers demand respect at all times.

For those same reasons, some of the trips in this book are unsuitable for children, either as paddlers or as passengers. Children should never be taken on trips where a capsize is likely or difficulties such as rapids, logjams, or strainers are possible. Again, read the entire trip description before starting a trip, and play it safe.

Equipment

Your most important piece of equipment (after your PFD) is the boat you select. A flatwater paddler has two basic choices of boats: a canoe or a kayak. Native peoples have used both for centuries. In North America, Indians from the east coast to the Pacific Northwest and western Canada built bark canoes. Here in the Pacific Northwest, a few cedar or spruce bark canoes were used by natives, but the cedar dugout canoe was much more common. In the arctic regions, where trees were scarce, natives built kayaks covered with animal skins.

Today, canoes and kayaks are made in a variety of sizes and shapes to suit every intended use. Often the two types of boats seem to merge, as in a decked canoe or a large open touring kayak. Two basic differences remain, however. First, the canoe paddler sits near the level of the gunwales, or sometimes kneels. The kayaker, on the other hand, sits low in the boat with legs outstretched. Second, the canoeist uses a relatively short, single-bladed paddle, whereas the kayak paddler uses a longer paddle with blades at each end.

Every canoe or kayak is a compromise: maneuverability versus tracking, weight versus durability and size, seaworthiness versus speed, and price versus quality. From reading some sales brochures, one would think that manufacturers have solved the age-old trade-offs. Brochures describe every boat as tracking like an arrow while capable of turning on a dime, light as a feather but capable of rough whitewater use, fast to paddle but capable of carrying large loads. Do not believe them. Be grateful if you find a manufacturer or dealer who is honest about his or her boats, enabling you to choose one that meets your particular skills, needs, and intended uses.

If you are not sure what you want, study the catalogs of several manufacturers, read paddlers' magazines, visit more than one dealer, rent or borrow a few boats to see what they are like, and seek out more experienced paddlers for advice on particular models. If possible, talk to someone who already owns the

Best Trips with Children

25—River Mill Lake
51—Smith and Bybee Lakes
60—Brooks Slough and Skamokawa Creek
74—Siltcoos River

On Quinn Creek, north of Hosmer Lake (Trip 31)

model you are thinking of buying. A local canoe or kayak club is an excellent place to talk to other paddlers.

Some general recommendations can be made, however. If you have a family or bulky equipment, or prefer sitting higher off the water, a canoe may be the wisest choice. If you plan to paddle on salt water or other open, windy waters (such as the Columbia River), buy a kayak. If you have a regular paddling partner, consider a canoe or a double kayak. A folding kayak is essential if you are interested in flying into remote areas, or simply need to store it in a spare closet.

In any event, make sure you are getting a quality boat, not a poorly designed toy. With proper care, it should be an investment and a pleasure for a lifetime. In contrast, a cheap toy will frustrate you every time you paddle it.

Canoes
Canoes come in a variety of lengths, the most common being 16 to 18 feet. The shorter boats, while highly maneuverable and easy to carry, have a smaller capacity and are frequently unsuitable in rough water due to a low freeboard (the distance between gunwales and waterline). Larger boats are heavier and

somewhat less maneuverable, but have greater capacity and (due to their longer waterlines) are generally faster to paddle. If you have a lot of gear to carry, or children to take along, or both, consider a 17- or 18-foot boat. If you prefer to travel light, a 16-foot model may be just the ticket. For most paddlers, however, a 16-foot boat is slightly too small, an 18-foot model is slightly too large, and a 17-foot model is the best compromise, depending on other design criteria.

The shape of the hull can radically alter the above characteristics. A deep canoe (said to have a high freeboard) deflects waves and increases the volume of cargo the boat can carry, but has the disadvantage of catching the wind

Hosmer Lake (Trip 31)

when the paddler wishes it would not. A high bow or stern has similar trade-offs: waves are less likely to spill into the boat, but a crosswind is difficult to deal with.

Another trade-off occurs when a canoe is designed to either track (travel in a straight line) or to turn quickly. No boat can do both well. A boat designed for lakes should track well, while boats designed primarily for swift rivers should turn quickly.

A small keel helps improve a canoe's ability to track, but the keel often catches on rocks. Most canoes built today lack a keel. The primary exceptions are aluminum canoes, which often have a 1-inch keel running the length of the boat, or perhaps they compromise the keel issue by using a shallow "shoe keel." Almost all fiberglass and plastic canoes lack a keel, but other design characteristics (such as a sharp bow and stern) are used to achieve good tracking. In fact, the presence of a keel often indicates poor design: if the canoe is properly designed, a keel is unnecessary.

The rocker has a similar effect: a canoe with a flat bottom is stable and holds its course well, but will not turn as easily as one with a keel line shaped like a rocker on a rocking chair. Canoes specifically designed for flatwater have little or no rocker, while whitewater boats usually have a slight (or even pronounced) rocker.

Construction materials are as varied as hull designs. The first canoes in the Pacific Northwest were dugout cedar logs or wood frames covered with bark or animal skins, whereas Indians in other parts of North America were using bark canoes almost exclusively. A tiny handful of craftsmen still make birch bark canoes for the purist trade. Canvas-covered wood boats were developed in the late 1800s and dominated the market for many years. Still available in limited quantities, they are beautiful if properly maintained, but they are expensive and somewhat heavy.

Next came the three modern materials that have become the most popular by far: fiberglass, aluminum, and plastic. Each has its advantages and its staunch advocates. Of the three, aluminum was the first to appear when, in 1945, Grumman Aircraft sought a peacetime product to replace its declining aircraft sales. The resulting aluminum canoes were hailed as very durable, and Grumman and other manufacturers sold thousands and thousands over the next fifty years. Disadvantages of aluminum, however, are that it is difficult to repair if ever damaged, and it tends to "stick" to rocks. Aluminum is also somewhat noisy to paddle. Aluminum has fallen out of favor with most buyers, although many canoe liveries (who rent canoes) and guide services still buy aluminum boats for their durability. If you are interested in an aluminum boat, buy a well-known brand because quality can vary widely.

Fiberglass, on the other hand, while somewhat less durable, can be repaired relatively easily at home or in the field. Because fiberglass is easier to mold than aluminum, it is available in a wider selection of hull designs suitable for use on flatwater or whitewater, or in racing. Fiberglass is also quieter than aluminum as it moves through rough water.

Manufacturing techniques used for aluminum and fiberglass vary to suit particular needs, and the quality of the resulting boat can vary considerably. Aluminum boats can vary in the type of aluminum used, the gauge of the sheet metal, the riveting technique, and the number of reinforcing ribs. Fiberglass hulls range widely in weight, primarily due to the construction techniques and types of resin and fabric used. For example, recreational canoes are available in superlight fabrics such as Kevlar or carbon fiber, which can reduce the weight of a boat from seventy-five pounds to forty pounds. Weight is particularly important in areas where portages are common, such as the Boundary Waters Canoe Area in northern Minnesota.

Plastic boats have become popular in recent years, for good reason. One of the first combinations of plastic materials involves a plastic and foam sandwich known as Royalex, consisting of several layers of ABS (acrylonitrile-butadiene-styrene) plastic covered by vinyl, with a core of ABS plastic foam. Manufactured by Uniroyal, Royalex is used by many canoe manufacturers. It is extremely durable due to its puncture resistance and its "memory" (ability to return to its original shape after deformation). Though Royalex boats are not particularly light, the other advantages make up for that disadvantage. The only drawback may be the price of a Royalex boat, which is moderately high.

The price problem has resulted in additional materials being brought to the market. Mid-priced boats are now available that employ polyethylene in a plastic and foam sandwich, such as the Discovery line of canoes from Old Town. Such boats combine many of the desirable features of ABS/vinyl and foam sandwiches, at a much lower price, with only a slight increase in weight. As a result, polyethylene sandwich boats have become very popular.

Even less expensive are boats made entirely of single-layer polyethylene. Single-layer polyethylene boats rarely offer many advantages other than price, however. Most require metal stiffeners in order to maintain structural integrity. Even worse, one of the design criteria of some models is the ability to stack several boats together in order to minimize shipping costs. That feature helps keep the price low, but does little to improve the handling of the boat. In general, serious paddlers should avoid single-layer polyethylene canoes.

Lastly, canoes made from wood strips (usually cedar) and covered with clear fiberglass are also available. They are beautiful and lightweight, but fairly expensive due to the labor required to build them. To help solve the cost problem, plans and materials are available for the home boatbuilder to build a cedar-strip canoe.

Most canoe manufacturers offer a variety of models and materials, each designed for a particular use. The trick is to determine what each boat is designed to do because the manufacturer or dealer may claim that every boat can do everything well. Such claims are simply not true, so you should try to decide for yourself which model is best suited for your intended use. If you plan long trips in the wilderness, or plan to carry extra passengers, look for a wide, long, deep boat with a large capacity. A 17- or 18-foot boat, 14 or 15 inches deep, with a 37-inch beam might fit the bill, but keep in mind that a large-capacity boat may be slower than other boats. If you plan trips involving long or numerous portages, your boat should probably be built with an ultra-light fabric such as Kevlar. If you prefer a fast boat for smooth lakes, look for a medium-length, narrow boat. A 16- or 17-foot boat with a 34-inch beam and a 13-inch depth might meet that criterion, but remember that its load-carrying capacity is somewhat less than that of a larger boat. If you need a whitewater boat, look for a medium-length boat with a pronounced rocker and a high gunwale. A 16-foot boat with a 15-inch gunwale and a definite rocker may be your choice. If you plan to use your boat principally for fishing or photography, a shorter, beamier (and thus more stable) boat may do nicely. If you want to be able to pack your boat into remote lakes, a short, light boat is needed. A solo pack canoe may be as short as 12 feet and may weigh only thirty pounds.

Kayaks

Although canoes were once the only choice for flatwater paddling, kayaks now rival their popularity. To most people, the word kayak is synonymous with whitewater, but many models of flatwater touring kayaks are available. In order to track better and to accommodate cargo carried on overnight or multiday tours, the flatwater kayaks are longer, higher, and wider than their smaller whitewater counterparts. Flatwater kayaks have become known as sea kayaks, even though many users never set their paddles in salt water.

The primary advantage of a kayak is its ability to deal with rough water or windy weather. Due to its covered decks, a kayak is much less likely to take on water in rough situations than a canoe. Because a kayak presents a lower profile (and the paddler sits lower), a kayak is much less susceptible to wind than a canoe.

To a beginning paddler, a kayak with a rudder is somewhat easier to paddle than a canoe. Even on flatwater, paddling a canoe in a straight line requires some skill. However, once a canoe paddler learns the J stroke (see Canoe Paddling, below), neither craft is particularly difficult to paddle on flatwater.

Kayaks have disadvantages, too. Although some sea kayaks can carry food and gear for a two-week trip, careful packing is required. In contrast, a canoe can carry bulky items with ease. Families have a hard time squeezing children into a kayak as extra passengers, but a canoe is ideal for carrying two adults and two children.

Sea kayaks are available as both one-person models and those designed for two. The latter (known as double kayaks) are equipped either with a single large cockpit or two smaller ones; the double-cockpit configuration is more common, particularly on boats intended for serious use on open waters. Kayaks designed for two paddlers almost always employ a rudder, which is controlled by foot pedals, while many single kayaks omit the rudder. Double kayaks generally have the advantages of speed and stability over single kayaks, but single kayaks carry more gear per paddler than double boats. The reason is simple: a paddler in a single kayak has both a bow and a stern to load with gear, while each paddler in a double has only the bow, or the stern, but not both.

Native peoples built the first sea kayaks using animal skins and wood frames. With modern sea kayaks, fiberglass is normally the material of choice, although plastic models are becoming popular. The plastic boats tend to be less expensive, but some plastic boats have the disadvantage of being generally less rigid than fiberglass models.

One-person whitewater kayaks need not be ruled out for flatwater use, but the beginner should be aware that they are difficult to paddle in a straight line, although they are very maneuverable. And most whitewater kayaks are tipsy.

Inflatable kayaks are also available, but they have limited appeal to the flatwater paddler. While compact, lightweight, and relatively inexpensive, they track poorly and move slowly. Storage space for gear is limited or nonexistent. For the serious paddler, their use is best restricted to whitewater trips, particularly when gear can be carried in an accompanying inflatable raft.

Also available are short, wide kayaks designed for casual recreational use. Such boats are fine for short trips on small lakes or rivers with a steady current, but they are generally inefficient for paddling long distances on flatwater.

Like canoes, the hull design of a kayak is critical. In the case of a single kayak, a narrow boat (perhaps 21 to 22 inches wide) is faster than a beamier 23- or 24-inch model, but the narrow boat is less stable and carries less gear. Longer boats (17 or 18 feet) track better, paddle faster, and carry more gear than shorter boats (15 or 16 feet). The same rules apply to double kayaks, although the dimensions are different. Most doubles are between 18 and 20 feet in length and are about 30 inches wide. Recreational doubles are somewhat wider.

Some models of double and single kayaks are available in more than one volume size. The difference is often accomplished by using an upper deck that is more highly domed, in order to accommodate larger loads for longer trips.

The most incredible of the sea kayaks are the folding kayaks, which were invented in Europe nearly a hundred years ago. In 1929, a German folding kayak was used to run the Columbia, long before the dams were built. Folding kayaks are now available from several manufacturers in either single or double models. Using fabric hulls and collapsible wooden or aluminum frames, these boats are desirable when storage space is at a premium, or, more importantly, when access to wilderness water is only by light aircraft. These folding boats are considered de rigueur for flying into remote country. They tend to be somewhat beamier (and thus slower) than their fiberglass cousins, but they may carry more gear. The nature of these boats and their high cost generally preclude their use on whitewater or other situations where their hulls or frames may be damaged, but where transport is difficult, there is no substitute for a good folding kayak. Folding boats include the German Klepper, the French Nautiraid, the Canadian Feathercraft, and others. Quality varies considerably. A good quality folding boat is a major investment, but it will last a lifetime.

As in the case of canoes, make sure you get a kayak model that will meet your needs, regardless of whether you are buying a rigid boat or a folding one. Shop around, study the sales literature, and talk to other paddlers about particular manufacturers and models.

Assembling a folding kayak

Canoe Paddles

Canoe paddles are usually made of wood, fiberglass, or aluminum and plastic. Most serious paddlers opt for light, high-quality wood paddles. In selecting a wood paddle, look for a light paddle made of laminated wood, possibly reinforced with a layer of fiberglass cloth. Paddles made entirely from fiberglass are also very good. Aluminum/plastic combinations are also available. They can be less expensive than laminated wood or fiberglass, but they may be somewhat lower in quality. Regardless of the material chosen, the two primary criteria are light weight and high strength.

For the paddler who insists on the latest, lightest equipment, paddles are also available in Kevlar, carbon fiber, or graphite, for a price.

Most canoe paddles are available in sizes that range from about 52 inches to 62 inches, in order to fit paddlers of different sizes. Many different formulae have been developed to determine the proper length for each paddler. One simple formula: when you stand on a level surface, your paddle should reach from the floor to within 2 inches of your chin, although some paddlers select a paddle that reaches as high as their nose.

Canoe paddles with bent shafts deliver more power with each stroke than straight-shafted paddles, but they may be more difficult to get accustomed to, and they should be avoided in whitewater, where quick action may not allow the paddler time to worry about which way the shaft is bent. Bent-shaft paddles are usually a little shorter than straight-shafted paddles.

Kayak Paddles

Kayak paddles are available in the same materials as canoe paddles: wood, fiber-glass, and aluminum/plastic combinations. As in the case of canoe paddles, the primary considerations are light weight and high strength. The fiberglass paddles are generally light and high quality, and thus they are often the first choice of serious paddlers. Wood paddles range from mediocre to very good. In general, paddles with plywood blades attached to wood shafts are not as light or well constructed as ones made from laminated wood.

Kayak paddles are also available in Kevlar, carbon fiber, or graphite, for those willing to pay a high price for the lightest possible paddle.

Kayak paddles are double-ended and much longer than canoe paddles. Many kayak paddles are sold in metric sizes, although some manufacturers use inches. The overall length depends on the type of paddling that will be done. For most flatwater paddlers, an 8-foot (245 cm) paddle is considered the norm, but tall paddlers with wide boats (or short paddlers with narrow boats) may prefer a longer (or shorter) paddle. For flatwater, a relatively long (7.5 to 8.5 feet, or 220 to 260 cm) paddle is preferred, especially in a beamy two-person folding boat, while a shorter paddle (about 7 feet, or 215 cm) is used for whitewater.

When selecting a kayak paddle, notice that the blades are available in several widths, from about 4 to 8 inches. Most paddlers use the wider blades. Some paddlers, however, believe the wider blades are best for stronger paddlers and other paddlers should use the narrow blades which are thought to produce a smoother, less stressful paddling stroke. The narrower blades are generally longer than the wider blades, and the shaft is thus shorter. As a result, if you plan to use narrow blades with a beamy double kayak, or an even beamier folding double kayak, a longer paddle will be required.

Kayak paddles are available as one-piece or take-apart models. The one-piece paddles may be somewhat stronger, but they are more difficult to trans-port and store. In addition, they must be purchased as either feathered (offset) or nonfeathered, and the feathered models can be purchased as right-hand or left-hand control, while the take-apart models can be adjusted instantly, both for feathering and for right/left control. As a result, most flatwater kayak pad-dlers buy take-apart models. The question of feathered paddles is discussed below under "Kayak Paddling"; if you are not sure whether you want to use a feathered paddle, buy or borrow a take-apart and try it both feathered and nonfeathered before deciding. The distinction between a right-hand feathered paddle and a left-hand feathered paddle is not crucial; most lefties can learn to feather right-handed quite easily.

Clothing

The seasons clearly dictate what clothing is appropriate, and what is not. On those rare occasions when bad weather is unlikely, tee shirts and shorts are fine, as long as extra dry clothing is carried for each person in the boat. If a capsize is remotely possible (and it usually is), the extra clothing should be placed in waterproof containers and securely attached to the boat. A wet suit or dry suit is a good idea in cold weather or when rough water may be encountered.

In summer, light cotton clothing that covers the arms and legs is invaluable for sunburn protection, but during the rest of the year the best fabrics are either wool or synthetics due to their ability to maintain warmth even when wet. In cool weather, cotton should always be avoided.

Paddling in rainy weather is not nearly as unpleasant as it sounds, if proper precautions are taken. Impervious fabrics keep out the rain, but keep in an equal amount of perspiration. Loose-fitting garments provide adequate ventilation—too much, in fact, during windy periods. In cold, wet weather, many paddlers use breathable fabrics such as Gore-Tex over synthetic fleece clothing and polypropylene long underwear. Others wear dry suits or wet suits for the highest level of protection against hypothermia in the event of a capsize.

Footwear should be considered carefully. In warm summer weather, almost anything will work. Old tennis shoes, worn without socks, are good, particularly on shallow waters where frequent exits are required. Sandals may be worn for the same reason. In cool, wet weather, waterproof boots or wet-suit booties are a good investment. Rubber-bottomed boots with leather uppers are a popular choice, but insulated models should be used on cold trips.

A hat is important in all seasons, to fend off sun in summer and rain in the other eleven months of a Pacific Northwest year. A wool brimmed hat does both, but a stocking cap is warmer.

Gloves are essential in cold weather. Wet suit gloves are often used. In warm weather, bicycle gloves help avoid blisters while maintaining ventilation.

Safety Equipment

Both federal and state laws require life jackets (personal flotation devices, or PFDs) to be carried for every person aboard a boat. The PFDs must be wearable, rather than the seat cushion style of PFD, and children age twelve and under must actually wear their PFDs. Although the law does not require that PFDs be worn by adults, common sense dictates that PFDs should be worn at all times by everyone while on the water, not sat on or stowed in the bottom of the boat to be lost in a capsize. If you don't believe in wearing your PFD at all times while on the water, make a regular habit of reading every newspaper article that describes a local drowning. The single most common factor: failure to wear a PFD. According to the Oregon State Marine Board, eighty-five percent of Oregonians who drowned in boating accidents would have survived had they been wearing their PFDs.

Prices, sizes, styles, and comfort of PFDs vary considerably, so shop around to find one you will be comfortable wearing all day. Size is not just a comfort factor: the PFD must be snug enough that the wearer (especially children) cannot slip out of it. Also, the boat itself should be equipped with flotation devices (if not already built-in) for the safety of crew, cargo, and boat.

An extra paddle should be tied to the boat, but not so securely as to delay its use in an emergency. Grab loops or painters should be installed at the bow and stern, and a bailing scoop should always be handy. An inexpensive scoop can be made from a large plastic container such as a bleach bottle: cut off the bottom at an angle, but leave the cap on; tie the scoop to the boat with a long cord to prevent it from being lost in a capsize.

An important item of equipment to consider in rainy weather or rough water is a spray skirt. Used on either a kayak or a canoe, a spray skirt not only keeps rain off the paddler's legs, but also keeps the interior of the boat and any cargo dry. If a ready-made spray skirt is not available for your boat, a home-made version can usually be sewn out of waterproof fabric.

A length of rope should be carried on every trip. It can be used for tying up boats, for lining boats through rough or shallow areas, and for rescuing people or swamped boats. A pulley extends the rope's usefulness. On any trip involving a river current, every boat should carry a throw rope for rescuing swamped boaters. A throw rope is a length of rope (usually polypropylene, which floats) in a specially designed bag, permitting it to be thrown to swamped boaters. Even if the current is a gentle one, a throw rope should be considered essential.

Sparks Lake (Trip 30)

Best Trips with Mountain Views

24—Lost Lake
30—Sparks Lake
31—Hosmer Lake

Paddlers should also carry a boat repair kit, for use in event of damage by rocks or other obstructions. The contents of the kit depend, of course, on the type of boat being used. Some paddlers try to get by with just a roll of duct tape, but a more extensive kit should be considered.

Always take along the Ten Essentials. In a survival situation, such as a capsize in cold weather, these small items of equipment can make a big difference:

1. Extra clothing (carried in a waterproof "dry bag").
2. Food or extra food.
3. Extra water.
4. Sun protection (sunglasses and sunscreen). Sunglasses should be carried year-round to protect against not only direct sunlight, but also the glare off the water's surface. For the same reason, sunscreen should be used regularly.
5. Illumination, such as a flashlight or headlamp.
6. A first-aid kit
7. Fire starter (waterproofed matches and/or a lighter and a chemical firestarter should be carried on every trip, and always in waterproof containers).
8. A repair kit and tools, such as a pocketknife.
9. A map of some kind in addition to the sketch map from this book—a USGS topographic map or a NOAA chart (both discussed in more depth in the next section)—should always be carried, along with a compass and/or a GPS unit. Those with limited experience in the use of a map and compass should consult a good reference book on the subject.
10. Emergency shelter.

Maps and Charts

The sketch maps included in this book have been drawn to scale, although the width of rivers has often been exaggerated for clarity. For those wishing more detailed maps, each trip description includes references to U.S. Geological Survey (USGS) topographic maps and (where applicable) National Oceanographic and Atmospheric Administration (NOAA) charts.

The rivermiles marked on the sketch maps, the USGS maps, and the NOAA charts can be confusing. The mile distances are measured from the mouth of each stream. For example, the point where the Luckiamute River joins the Willamette River is rivermile 0 of the Luckiamute. The same point, measured from the mouth of the Willamette, is that river's mile 108.

USGS topographic maps are the most detailed land maps available. They are printed in several scales, but the most useful are the 7.5-minute series. The USGS maps are available from map stores, some nautical dealers, and most outdoor stores or through the mail from the USGS (see the appendix at the back of this book). Free order forms and indexes are available for each state.

NOAA charts provide extremely detailed data on water features such as depths, bridges, powerlines, obstructions, and shorelines, but are available only for major navigable waters. In Oregon, the charts are available for the Willamette River north of Newberg, the Columbia River, and the coast. The charts are available at nautical supply houses, or by mail from the Distribution Division of National Ocean Survey (see the appendix at the back of this book). An index to Pacific Coast charts is available free of charge.

The Oregon State Marine Board publishes a brochure entitled "Oregon Boating Facilities Guide" which shows the location of every public boat ramp in the state, plus the location of commercial boating marinas and moorages. Facilities located at each site are described as well. The Marine Board also publishes pamphlets on boating safety, "Boating Guide to the Lower Columbia and Willamette Rivers," and "Oregon Boating Regulations," which list every body of water that has restrictions on powerboats. Free copies of these publications are available from the Marine Board, and many of their publications are available on their website. See the appendix at the back of this book for addresses.

Overnight Equipment

Oregon has many areas where paddlers can enjoy trips lasting two or more days. The Willamette is an excellent example. Depending on your pace, two, three, or four of the trips on the Willamette could be combined for a pleasant weekend outing, or all could be combined into a strenuous five-day trip or a relaxing weeklong excursion. Overnight trips, and equipment to be taken, should be planned carefully. Don't count on covering distances as fast, or maneuvering as easily, with a loaded boat as with an empty one.

In addition to the usual overnight equipment one would take for a hike, keep these considerations in mind for paddling overnighters. A large collapsible plastic water jug enables you to carry water to campsites that have none, and it takes up little room when not being used. A two-and-a-half-gallon jug should easily be adequate for two persons on an overnight trip. In wet weather, careful thought should be given to sleeping gear. A synthetic sleeping bag is a bit bulkier and heavier than a down-filled one, but it is less expensive and has the advantage of being warm even when damp.

Best Multi-day Trips

1–16—Willamette River, Eugene to Portland
54—Lower Columbia River Water Trail
55—Columbia River Heritage Canoe Trail

Some Basics of Paddling

A comprehensive discussion of paddling techniques is beyond the scope of this book, and probably beyond the ability of the author, but the following two sections are an introduction to the basic strokes used in flatwater paddling. The beginner should be warned, however, that a reading of the following few paragraphs will not qualify one to safely paddle all of the trips listed in this book. While most of the trips described here are suitable for the inexperienced, several of the trips, as noted in the trip descriptions, require a skill level that can only be acquired by on-the-water practice, preferably with the help of a more experienced paddler. Local paddling clubs offer classes in canoe and kayak paddling, and are far better than attempting to learn from a book. What follows, then, is more of a warning of some of the complexities of paddling techniques than a full discussion of them.

Also keep in mind that paddling is not the exclusive method of propelling a canoe or kayak. Canoes can also be poled. Both types of craft can be equipped with a simple sail, often of homemade design. Tarps, ponchos, and paddles can often be combined for temporary use, and even sleeping pads can be used to catch the wind when traveling downwind. Some paddlers even use an umbrella to catch the wind, hooking the umbrella handle on the cockpit coaming of a kayak or on the grab-handle of a canoe near the bow. A kite is particularly useful as a sail. Many paddlers carry a Jalbert parafoil kite because it develops considerable pull. The parafoil design uses no rigid members, so it can be stowed easily and quickly. A kite also has the advantage of permitting better forward visibility than a sail or an umbrella.

Sails of any kind should be used with caution. They are best used in a steady, moderate wind. They should not be used in high winds or when the wind direction might change suddenly, nor should they be used if sudden course changes may be needed.

Canoe Paddling

A two-person canoe is propelled using two single-bladed paddles, usually on opposite sides of the boat. The stern paddler, who has greater available leverage, performs the primary steering of the boat. Much of the time, the bow paddler provides propulsion only.

Having considerably more influence on the direction the boat travels, the stern paddler must use the paddle to counteract the effect of his or her own paddling on one side of the boat. The principal stroke for this purpose is the J stroke: when nearing the end of the stroke, the stern paddler rotates the paddle slightly and strokes away from the boat for a few inches. When paddling on the left side of the boat, the path of the paddle forms a J in the water; when paddling on the right side, the J stroke produces a mirror image of a J. The relative strengths of the paddlers determine whether the J strokes made by the stern paddler are slight or exaggerated. Meanwhile, the bow paddler is usually paddling a normal straight stroke.

The importance of the J stroke for flatwater paddling cannot be overemphasized. Many a marriage has ended in divorce because the stern paddler never learned this simple stroke, and thus the couple could not paddle in a straight line. The stern paddler can make the boat turn in either direction without changing sides by using either stronger or less pronounced J strokes, or the draw stroke discussed below. For quick turns, the bow paddler paddles on the opposite side of the boat from the direction to be turned, using a sweep stroke that begins close to the bow and travels in an arc away from the bow, and ending with the paddle perpendicular to the canoe. Meanwhile, the stern paddler is paddling on the same side, or J stroking on the opposite side.

Another technique to make a turn, or to move the canoe sideways, involves paddling at right angles to the keel line of the boat. When paddling toward the boat, the stroke is called a draw; when paddling away from the boat, it is a pry. When two paddlers both pry or draw on the same side of the boat, the boat moves sideways, a useful technique for avoiding a midstream obstacle or when approaching a dock or shore. When one paddler pries and the other draws on the same side (or pries on the opposite side), the boat rotates on its center, which is useful for turning in constricted places.

All of these strokes can be performed reasonably well while sitting upright on the seat of a canoe. However, many situations require the paddler to kneel, with the knees braced against the hull and the buttocks placed against the front edge of the seat or a thwart (one of the braces running across the top of the canoe, from gunwale to gunwale). In rough water, or when making a sharp turn, the added stability from kneeling is essential. Kneeling also reduces the surface area affected in windy weather. Some paddlers point out that canoes built by Native Americans were never equipped with seats, and that the use of modern seats is a major cause of capsizes. Although that view may be in the minority, paddlers should not hesitate to kneel in rough water, windy weather, or anytime a capsize is a possibility.

Kayak Paddling

Whether a one- or two-person boat, a kayak is propelled with one or two pairs of long double-bladed paddles. Most flatwater kayak paddles are detachable at the midpoint of the shaft for storage and transport. The same connection is also used to adjust the angle between the two blades. While the beginner may think that the blades should be parallel, the most popular (and most efficient) use of the paddle involves "feathered" or offset blades, where one blade is rotated up to ninety degrees from the other. The primary advantage of a feathered paddle is the reduced drag or wind resistance of the airborne blade. The use of feathered paddles is not unanimous: some paddlers prefer an nonfeathered paddle, which is easier on the wrists.

Although it may at first glance seem unnecessarily complex, using a feathered paddle is quite easy to learn. Most right-handed paddlers adjust their paddles so that the left blade faces up, away from the water, when the right blade is being stroked. At the completion of the right stroke, the paddler flexes the right wrist backwards while allowing the shaft to rotate in the left hand. At this point, the left blade is at a right angle to the water, ready to enter the water and be stroked. The right blade is parallel to the water, facing down toward the water, and passes through the air with little resistance.

Left-handed paddlers do the opposite, using their left hand to rotate the blades and allowing the shaft to rotate in their right hand. However, many lefties paddle the same as a right-hander, particularly if their paddle is not adjustable.

In the past, the blades on feathered paddles were offset a full ninety degrees: the blades were perpendicular to each other. A full ninety-degree offset is now considered to cause wrist problems for some paddlers, and many feathered paddles are now manufactured with a reduced offset of only forty-five, sixty, or seventy-five degrees.

Once the feathered paddle is mastered, the next two most common mistakes are closely related: paddling too deeply and at too steep an angle. The paddle blade should not be submerged beyond the point where the blade meets the shaft, and the shaft should be held at a relatively shallow angle.

In some of the shorter two-person boats (particularly the folding boats), the stern and bow paddlers must coordinate strokes to avoid striking their paddles together; the stern paddler is usually responsible for staying in sync. In longer double boats, the distance between the two cockpits makes such coordination unnecessary.

If your kayak is equipped with a foot-operated rudder, and you plan to visit only the quietest of flatwater, you may skip the next few paragraphs; but if you ever venture out on fast-moving streams (several are described in this book), you will discover that a rudder is no substitute for knowledge of a few basic steering strokes. In fact, a rudder can be a liability in fast current, because it inhibits backpaddling. And in rough water, a rudder is sometimes not even in the water when the stern of the boat is exposed. Many serious paddlers avoid boats with rudders; they prefer to learn to control their boats with paddle strokes. If you plan to learn to paddle in rough, open waters, you should consider buying a boat without a rudder. As a compromise, you might consider a boat with a retractable skeg (a small fin near the rear of the boat).

Several techniques are available for turning a kayak that lacks a rudder. The simplest is called the stern rudder: the rear paddler simply places one end of the paddle in the water and holds it against the force of the moving kayak. The kayak reacts by turning toward the side on which the rudder was made. Obviously, this technique works only when the boat is moving faster than the water in which it is floating.

The stern rudder produces a relatively abrupt change in course. More subtle adjustments can be made by continuing to paddle as normal, but making more forceful strokes on one side than the other.

Another technique involves paddling on one side of the boat only. In a double kayak, that technique can be combined with your partner backpaddling on the other side, but close coordination between the paddlers is necessary in shorter boats. If these strokes are made in wide arcs rather than parallel to the hull, they become highly effective sweep strokes similar to the sweep strokes used in a canoe.

Kayak paddles can also be used for other purposes besides forward momentum. Sideways travel can be accomplished by draw strokes as described above for a canoe. Backpaddling is another important stroking method, particularly on swift waters when "ferrying" from one side of the channel to the other to avoid obstacles.

Capsizes can be prevented by using the paddle in an outrigger position. Place the face of the paddle on the surface of the water in the direction which the capsize may occur. If the paddle is held firmly (or slapped forcefully), the resistance of the water against the blade may prevent a capsize (or arrest one in progress). This technique is known as bracing, and its use is essential in rough water. Never venture out into the open ocean or other potentially rough water without proper training in bracing and self-rescue skills.

Kayak sailing near Sauvie Island (Trip 16)

Best Trips Close to Portland

48–50—Columbia Slough
51—Smith and Bybee Lakes
52—Sauvie Island

Safety Techniques

Flatwater canoeing is a relatively safe activity if approached in an intelligent manner with a reasonable amount of caution. Even so, every year several people in Oregon manage to drown themselves, often in placid waters and only a few feet from shore.

Compliance with a few simple rules would prevent most or all of these accidents. First, a life jacket should be worn at all times while on the water. Modern life jackets provide insulation in cool weather and are quite comfortable; any slight inconvenience is more than compensated for by the margin of safety provided. You should also remember not to wear any heavy or bulky objects such as hip boots or a backpack that might add to your weight or detract from your swimming ability.

Equally important is a realistic appraisal of your own skills as a paddler and as a swimmer. When planning a trip, gather as much information as possible about the length of the trip and the type of paddling involved, and if you have any doubts about whether your skills are evenly matched with the trip, look for an easier one or perhaps seek more skilled companions. While most of the trips described in this book are suitable for beginners, some are not. When selecting a trip, read the entire description prior to launching, and be aware of unusual conditions (such as flood stages or high winds) that may turn calm waters into turbulent ones.

Paddlers on moving water must keep a careful lookout for obstructions ahead, so that obstructions can be recognized before it is too late to react properly. Many of the small rivers described in this book are prone to logjams and other blockages. Larger rivers are often lined with wing dams, which are rows of pilings intended to direct the current of the river. All of the rivers are subject to strainers, which are trees that have fallen into the river. The primary problem with logjams, wing dams, and strainers is that the river's current continues to flow through such obstructions, while your boat cannot. Thus the current can pull your boat up against the obstruction, often resulting in a capsize in a very dangerous place. The solution is to exercise extreme caution whenever in the vicinity of a logjam, wing dam, or strainer. If possible, give such obstructions a wide berth. If it is not possible to keep clear of them, land well upstream and portage.

Weather is another important factor that can create dangerous conditions. Do not attempt to cross large open areas if bad weather is likely to arrive, and always carry enough rain gear and warm clothing to allow you to function when it does. If in doubt, stay close to shore rather than crossing open lakes and bays. Close to shore is also the best place to be in the event of a capsize.

Upper Columbia Slough (Trip 48)

Unfortunately, other boaters occasionally present a hazard due to large wakes, excessive speed, failure to watch for other craft, or even the influence of alcohol. Using common sense can minimize the risk to small craft (such as yours). Avoid areas where commercial craft or powerboats are common, or minimize the time you spend in such areas. If possible, paddle in such areas at times or in seasons when powerboats are less likely to be present. Avoid water-skiers, keeping in mind that the operator of the towboat is probably paying more attention to the skier and other ski boats than to small canoes and kayaks. Stay close to shore, where larger boats are less likely to be.

On the Columbia, stay out of the commercial shipping lanes, which are marked on NOAA charts. If you must cross the main channel of a large river, do so quickly, keeping a constant lookout for approaching craft, which usually have the right of way. Learn how to deal with the wakes produced by large ships. Some paddlers prefer to stay close to shore as ships pass by, but the wakes of large ships are most pronounced in shallow water and often ricochet off the shore. Large wakes are particularly difficult to deal with if you are paddling on a narrow tributary of the Columbia because the wake will often travel some distance up the tributary; don't linger in such places if large ships are nearby. Because of the difficulty of dealing with large wakes near shorelines, many paddlers prefer to keep well away from shorelines as ships pass. If in doubt, beach your boat when a ship appears. And drag your boat well up the beach whenever you visit the shore of the Columbia; a wake from a large ship can toss your boat around like a toothpick.

The most obnoxious of all watercraft are jet skis, partly because of the dangerous manner in which some people operate them. The good news is that they are prohibited on nearly every river in Oregon, with some notable exceptions. For example, they are permitted on the Columbia and Willamette, but they are prohibited on nearly every tributary to the Willamette. For detailed information on where they are allowed, ask the Oregon State Marine Board to send you a copy of their administrative rules, or visit their website. The bad news is that jet skis have become popular, and during warm weather they can be ubiquitous. Stay as far away from them as possible.

As a matter of courtesy, also stay away from anglers. Whether fishing from a boat or from the bank, they deserve to be disturbed as little as possible. Give them a wide berth, do not paddle across their lines, do not make a lot of noise or splash around unnecessarily, and they will treat you with similar respect.

In the event serious misfortune does strike, you will want someone to come looking for you and your companions. In order for this to happen, a responsible friend should be told exactly where you are going, where you plan to leave your car, when you plan to return, and who to call if you do not return. A cell phone can be carried in a waterproof container, but don't rely on a cell phone as a substitute for common sense and caution.

What If You Capsize?

If you do tip over, here are some safety suggestions:

Most boats are equipped with built-in flotation, so you should not instinctively abandon your craft. First, in moving water determine whether you are in any personal danger from downstream logs or rocks. If you are being carried downstream, try to float feet first, to cushion any impact. If possible, stay upstream from your boat. A boat loaded with gear and filled with water could easily crush a paddler against a log or a rock.

If you are in no immediate personal danger, determine the status of your companions, and help them as much as possible. Only then should you worry about your swamped boat or the paddle that just disappeared around the next bend. Your life, and that of your fellow paddler, is much more valuable than any boat or equipment.

If swimming to shore presents any problems due to distance, poor swimming skills, or lack of a life jacket, stay with the boat, except perhaps in swift water. You cannot control the path of a swamped boat being carried rapidly downstream, but on calm waters you may be able to remove much of the water by bailing or other techniques. One such technique for reentering a swamped canoe involves dragging the canoe across the midsection of a second canoe. A detailed description can be found in many paddling books. It is difficult to perform in rough water, but it is otherwise effective if practiced in advance. When performing such a rescue, you will appreciate the fact that you have previously attached your gear to the boat in a manner that kept it inside the hull of the boat, rather than dangling over the side. If the water is cold, remember that a swamped boat will usually float close to the surface of the water, allowing the paddlers to sit in it (or on it) and stay out of the water to a large extent.

Remember the old adage: a swimmer has only a fifty/fifty chance of surviving fifty minutes in fifty-degree water. Get everyone out of the water as soon as safely possible, and make sure in advance that you and all of your paddling friends can recognize the symptoms of hypothermia and know how to treat it. This writer owes his life to one such friend.

But the most important thing to do is probably the hardest to remember: do not panic. Common sense is your best friend.

Transporting Boats

Canoes and kayaks are awkward items to carry on a car. Numerous roof racks are on the market; their suitability depends on the type of both boat and car involved, although most of the popular brands offer adapters to fit almost any car or craft. Racks can also be homemade, using brackets that are available separately. Combined with 2x4 crossbars, some old carpet scraps, and some ingenuity, a strong set of racks can be made quite cheaply.

When putting a boat on a rack, make certain that the boat is securely attached to the car, not just to the rack. Freeway speeds and sudden stops can be disastrous for a poorly attached boat. On long trips, the straps should be checked frequently.

Shuttling Cars

Because many of the paddle routes described here are one-way river trips, another transportation problem occurs: how to get back to the launching point, where your car is waiting. With large groups of paddlers, extra cars and drivers are usually abundant, and shuttles are easily accomplished, especially when some of the cars are capable of carrying more than one boat. But for a pair of paddlers, the solution to the car shuttle question is often the use of two cars and a lot of needless miles driven and gasoline consumed, particularly when only one of the cars is equipped with a roof rack.

On long trips, a third person who shuttles the cars but does not paddle is tremendously helpful, but friends like that are hard to find. Hitchhiking sometimes works, especially if you meet up with other paddlers, but hitchhiking in remote rural areas is often disappointing, if not dangerous, although some paddlers claim that a hitchhiker wearing a life jacket and carrying a paddle invokes such a degree of curiosity that a ride is guaranteed.

On short trips, a bicycle is an excellent solution to the shuttle problem. The bike (preferably an old rusty one) is left at the destination, either carefully hidden in the brush or securely locked, or both. At the conclusion of the trip, one of the paddlers then pedals the bike back to retrieve the car. Because the rider does not need to carry the lock while pedaling the bicycle back to the car, an entire arsenal of heavy locks and chains can be used to make sure the bike stays put.

Most paddlers don't relish the thought of a tiring bicycle ride at the end of the day, but they can usually cover 10 miles or so of flat terrain in less than an hour. And with luck, the same person will not have to pedal after every trip; the appropriate way to begin the bike ride is with the flip of a coin to determine which paddler has the privilege of pedaling back to the car.

One other tip may make your canoe trip and car shuttle more enjoyable: don't leave anything of value in your car while paddling. Covering valuables with an extra item of clothing simply invites a break-in. If enough people follow this simple rule, perhaps someday thieves will tire of breaking into cars only to find an empty interior. Leave most valuables at home, and carry the rest in the boat.

Paddling on the Willamette River
Sixteen of the trips described in this book cover the Willamette River from south to north, from the Eugene area to Kelley Point, where the Willamette joins the Columbia north of Portland.

The trips are presented as short segments, each of which can be paddled in a day or less. Most involve only about five hours of paddling. Although paddling time and time spent driving and shuttling cars, making side trips, birdwatching, etc., usually consume the bulk of a day for most river travelers, some ambitious paddlers are able to paddle two or more adjacent trips in a single day. The trips in the Eugene-Corvallis area cover up to 20 rivermiles, but due to the slow current downstream, the mileage of each of the trips decreases dramatically as the river approaches sea level at Oregon City.

Public land along the Willamette can be divided into two types. The first includes boat ramps and public parks accessible by automobile. Each of the trips described here begins and ends at such a park or boat ramp. The second type consists of public land acquired as part of the Willamette Greenway project. These areas are not accessible by car, but for that reason make excellent lunch spots or campsites.

Some of the greenway access areas are equipped with picnic tables, outhouses, and, occasionally, fireplaces, while others are completely undeveloped. Some sites that were improved with facilities were destroyed in the flood of 1996. Drinking water is rare and should either be carried from home or found in some of the towns or parks along the river.

The State of Oregon has published an excellent map of the Willamette that shows the facilities available at each park and access area. The map, called the "Willamette River Recreation Guide," is updated from time to time, thus showing the current status of the greenway acquisition program. For a copy, write to the Oregon Parks and Recreation Department (see the appendix at the back of this book), or view the guide online at *www.oregonstateparks.org/images/pdf/will_river_guide.pdf.*

The greenway program also provided for posting the banks of the Willamette with occasional rivermile markers (see photo on following page). The signs appear sporadically, usually on public access land, but rarely exactly at the mileage they purport to mark. While they are fortunately unobtrusive, binoculars are often necessary to read them from midstream. Occasionally, vandalism or natural forces may carry them off, so don't rely on always spotting a rivermile marker to chart your progress downstream. For example, the flood of 1996 washed away many, perhaps most, of the signs.

In 2005, a consortium of public agencies and nonprofit groups began development of a Willamette River Water Trail from Eugene to the Columbia. The upper section of the river, from Eugene to Buena Vista, and the middle section, from Buena Vista to Wheatland, have now been marked with Willamette River Water Trail signs to identify public lands and public parks, and maps to the upper and middle sections have been published and also placed on the Internet. The maps similarly show the location of parks and other public lands. Signs are expected to be placed on the lower section in the future, and a map of the lower section will be produced. For additional information, visit *www.willamettewatertrail.org.*

The main channel of the Willamette can be paddled year-round, but some of the channels behind islands (for example, Lambert Slough, described in Trip 9, Wheatland Ferry to St. Paul) become quite shallow after midsummer. Spring and summer are the most popular seasons for boating, while fall is perhaps the prettiest. But don't overlook winter paddling. When you are properly equipped (i.e., good rain gear and several layers of wool or synthetics, or a wet suit or dry suit), a winter day spent on the Willamette can be very rewarding.

Although much progress has been made in recent years, the Willamette is still not a completely clean river. For example, the storm drain systems in both Corvallis and Portland are combined with the sanitary sewer system, and both systems overflow into the Willamette during rainy periods. This overflow (known as combined sewer overflow, or CSO) is hazardous. During those periods, don't let water contact your mouth or eyes, and wash your hands with soap and clean water before eating lunch.

At three points on the Willamette, small ferries carry auto traffic across the river. These ferries, operated by the counties in which they are located, cross at Buena Vista (north of Albany), Wheatland (north of Salem), and near Canby (south of Oregon City). Parks located near or adjacent to these ferry landings are designated as starting or ending points for several trips on the Willamette and on tributaries that enter the Willamette just upstream from the crossings.

A Willamette River rivermile marker

To a large extent, these ferries are holdovers from earlier times when bridges were uncommon. They remain as quaint reminders that travel once moved at a much slower pace than it does today. The Wheatland Ferry, for example, has been operating since 1844, and the Buena Vista Ferry made its first crossing in the early 1850s.

When planning a trip, keep in mind that ferry operations may be unpredictable. Their current schedules are described in the trip descriptions, but those schedules can change or water levels may prevent the ferries from operating. When driving to or from a trip, or making a car shuttle, don't depend on using one of the ferries; but if the ferry is running, take the few extra minutes for a ride into the past.

One other caution about the ferries: when paddling across their short routes, give them a wide berth. The Canby and Wheatland ferries use underwater cables to control their course, and the Canby and Buena Vista ferries use overhead powerlines. The Wheatland ferry also uses an overhead cable as an additional guide. As a result, the ferries are not capable of maneuvering quickly, and the operator might not see your small boat before it is too late.

Tides and Tidal Currents

Several of the trips described in this book are on tidal waters. Obviously, the coastal bays and rivers are tidal, but most people are unaware that the Columbia and the Willamette rivers as far south as Oregon City and as far east as Bonneville Dam are also influenced by ocean tides.

Two high tides and two low tides occur each day. One of the high tides is higher than the other, and one of the low tides is lower than the other. The four tides are referred to as higher high water, lower high water, higher low water, and lower low water. The height of the tides is measured in feet above mean lower low water, which is referred to as zero. Thus, a higher high water of 7 feet followed by a lower low water of minus 2 feet produces a total fluctuation, or tidal range, of 9 feet.

Tides must be distinguished from tidal currents. High tide and low tide indicate the high and low points of the vertically rising and falling water. Tidal currents represent the horizontal movement of the water past a given point. Ebb is the seaward flow of water, and flood is the inward flow. Slack water occurs at the moment between ebb and flood when the horizontal movement of the water is zero. In theory, slack water should occur precisely at each high tide and low tide, but in practice the highs and lows rarely coincide with slack water. Both tide tables and tidal current tables are necessary to determine the exact time of slack water, maximum ebb, and maximum flood.

The National Ocean Survey publishes detailed tide tables and tidal current tables annually. They are available for purchase at most nautical supply stores. Tide and current tables are also available on the Internet. These tables should be consulted on waters close to the Pacific, such as coastal bays and the lower portions of coastal rivers, especially the Columbia.

The small tide table booklets given out by boating and fishing stores do not include data on tidal currents, such as the velocity of the currents or when they reach their maximum, nor do they indicate the times of slack water. But they are better than nothing because the hours and height of the tides are listed.

Paddlers should consult a tide table before (and during) every trip on tidal waters in order to avoid paddling against the tidal current. But tides present two serious dangers, other than making paddlers work hard to overcome their currents.

The first danger is created when the ebb tide on a coastal bay or river meets the resistance of the ocean. Rough water usually results, particularly in river mouths, when river flow adds to the velocity of the ebb tide. Shallow areas accentuate the problem. Even on windless days, rough conditions can result. The danger is greatest at maximum ebb. There is a moral to this story: avoid the mouths of coastal rivers and bays. If you must pass through an area near the mouth of a river or bay, do it only at slack tide; the time of slack water can be determined only by consulting a tidal current table, not a tide table.

The second danger is more insidious. Never paddle on a shallow slough or other body of water when the tide is going out, or you may be stranded in mud until the next high tide, twelve hours later. Even worse, if you enter a shallow channel on the higher high tide and become stranded as the tide falls, the next high tide (the lower high tide) may not be sufficient to float your boat, and you may be stranded for twenty-four hours. Oftentimes, the mud is too soft and too deep to support a person's body, and walking to higher ground or deeper water is both impossible and dangerous.

An aluminum canoe and a folding kayak on Long Island (Trip 65)

Paddling Ethics

When traveling by canoe or kayak along a river or lake, certain basic "streamside manners" should be observed out of consideration for paddlers who follow and for neighboring landowners. The purpose of these manners is to leave no trace of your passing. Most are just plain common sense, but sometimes people need to be reminded of them. Here are a few suggested rules:

1. Do not litter. Pack out all garbage. Do not leave extra food for the chipmunks; it only encourages them to concentrate at popular sites.
2. Keep noise to a minimum. People do not go into the woods to listen to other people shouting or playing boom boxes.
3. Use a small backpacking stove rather than building a fire. The era of the campfire ended long ago. If you must build a fire, use an established fireplace, keep the fire small, and use only dead and down wood from outside the camp area. In an emergency, if you must start a fire in a new location, don't build it up against a large boulder or a log, and do your best to return the ground to its natural state afterwards (after making sure the coals are well drowned). Don't try to burn cans or foil.

4. Bury human waste at least 200 feet from all water sources and at least 100 feet from any possible campsites or trails.
5. Do not trespass or camp on any private property.
6. Camp at least 200 feet from the water. Most shorelines are fragile.
7. Leave your pets at home.

Conservation

People who use rivers and lakes for any purpose have a moral obligation to leave the waters in the same condition in which they found them. In fact, boaters should do their best to leave the waters in better condition than they were found. So not only should you refrain from littering and polluting, you should pick up after those who are not quite as considerate. Don't let bottles and cans float by; pick them up and improve the scenery a little for the next person.

In the same vein, if only out of a selfish desire to preserve one's own recreation, you should join with other environmentally inclined individuals who are working to protect local rivers and lakes from pollution and destruction. Dues to local or national environmental groups are only a few dollars a year and serve the dual purpose of helping fund their activities and keeping members informed of environmental problems through magazines and newsletters. Several local groups have been formed for the specific purpose of protecting local rivers. For example, the Tualatin Riverkeepers and the Willamette Riverkeeper organizations have been formed to protect those two rivers.

Consider joining a local paddling club to meet other paddlers, to join organized paddling trips, and to keep informed of conservation issues. The flatwater paddling clubs located in northwest Oregon and southwest Washington are listed in the appendix at the back of this book. A few of the clubs are small and have no permanent address; ask at local paddling shops or other clubs to find a current contact.

The Oregon State Marine Board regulates boating on bodies of water in Oregon. It decides when and where powerboats and jet skis (legally known as "personal watercraft") may be used in Oregon. Don't hesitate to speak up for the rights of paddlers by contacting the Marine Board or attending its hearings when issues affecting paddlers are on the agenda.

Private Property

The rivers, lakes, and bays described in this book are generally considered to be publicly owned, based on a history of public use for commerce and recreation. The same rule, however, does not apply to their shores. Paddlers should assume that the banks of all fresh water are in private ownership, with the exception of public parks, boat ramps, and highway bridges.

Paddlers cannot indiscriminately select sites for launching, lunching, or lounging without regard for the rights of private property owners. The long-term solution is the acquisition of additional parkland, but the disregard of private property rights by paddlers can only increase local landowners' opposition to new parks.

Best Trips for Wildlife Viewing
40—Ridgefield National Wildlife Refuge
61—Aldrich Point

In this book, public parks and access areas along each route are usually marked on the sketch maps. All other land should be assumed to be private.

Public Facilities and User Fees

The parks, boat ramps, and other access points described in this book are maintained by a variety of government agencies, which can be contacted for more detailed information or updates (see the appendix at the back of this book).

Many parks in Oregon and Washington are subject to user fees, and the list of such parks grows each year as government budgets continue to shrink. For some reason, voters seem more interested in cutting their taxes than maintaining their park systems.

In Oregon, many state parks are subject to entrance fees of a few dollars. Parks personnel often collect the fees during the summer months. At other times, a day-use permit can be purchased at vending machines located at the parks, or visitors can buy an annual permit in advance. The annual permit is particularly valuable if you plan to visit state parks more than a few times each year.

Washington state parks are also subject to admission fees. Both daily and annual passes are available.

Other launching facilities in Washington are maintained by the Department of Fish and Wildlife, which was created when the Washington Department of Fisheries was merged with the Department of Wildlife. The department maintains many boat ramps and public access areas on Washington's rivers and lakes. Hunters and anglers are the principal users of the facilities; they effectively pay for maintenance of the facilities by purchasing hunting and fishing licenses. Other users (such as paddlers) are allowed to park cars and launch boats at the Fish and Wildlife facilities if they help pay their way by purchasing an annual Vehicle Use Permit (also known as a Stewardship Access Decal) and displaying it on their vehicles. Hunters and fishers receive a free permit when they buy a hunting or fishing license, but other users are charged $10. There has been considerable confusion as to which facilities are subject to the law, but tickets have been issued to paddlers who failed to display the permit on their vehicles. A current list of the sites where permits are required can be found at the Washington Fish and Wildlife Department website. According to the statute (RCW 77.32.380), the program applies to clearly identified land owned by the Department of Fish and Wildlife. So if a boat ramp or public access area is posted as owned by the department (or by either of its predecessor agencies), buy a Vehicle Use Permit and put it in your car window. The permits can be purchased wherever fishing licenses are sold in Washington, or by mail or Internet order. The permits are not sold in Oregon. For more information, visit *www.wdfw.wa.gov/wlm/vup.*

The U.S. Forest Service charges user fees at some day-use areas, such as Lost Lake near Mount Hood. The Forest Service also requires cars parked at some trailheads to display an annual Northwest Forest Pass or a daily National Forest Recreation Day Pass, available for a few dollars at ranger stations and many outdoor outlets. A few of the trips described in this book begin at those same trailheads. Passes usually must be purchased prior to arrival at the trailhead; unlike state park passes, forest service passes cannot be purchased on-site, except at a few trailheads where "iron ranger" vending stations have been installed. Call a local ranger station for a current list of affected trailheads, or buy an annual pass and don't worry about it. Another option, for convenience, would be to purchase several daily permits in advance, then date one of the permits (in ink) before each use. (Permits purchased at iron rangers require the date and location of use to be inserted at the time of purchase.)

Sites operated by the National Park Service also charge user fees. For example, a user fee is required at the Mount St. Helens National Volcanic Monument. The Forest Service offers a single pass that satisfies the fee requirements of all Forest Service and National Park Service sites in Oregon and Washington.

Many county parks also charge user fees, in both Oregon and Washington.

As you paddle the trips in this book, notice that many of the modern boat ramps with paved parking lots and restroom facilities display signs noting that the facilities were built with funds from the Oregon State Marine Board, which collects boat registration fees from owners of powerboats and sailboats. The dirty, grungy, unimproved launch sites display no such signs. Paddlers do not contribute financially to the Marine Board. Yet paddlers are the first to scream when user fees are imposed or boat registration fees are proposed for kayaks and canoes.

The bottom line: expect to pay user fees at almost any city, county, state, or federal park or access area. Carry a few extra dollars (or buy annual permits where available), and do your share to help maintain the parks and access areas that you utilize. Because policies regarding user fees (and the amounts charged) vary as time goes by, paddlers should keep abreast of current regulations and user fees by contacting the agencies listed in the appendix at the back of this book. Again, carry money or annual permits at all times, and don't complain when an agency is forced to charge for providing decent facilities for paddlers.

THE WILLAMETTE RIVER

1 Armitage Park to Harrisburg

Location: North of Eugene
Distance: 18 miles
Time: 4 hours
Maps: USGS Eugene East, Coburg, Junction City, and Harrisburg 7.5"
Season: Year-round
Rating: C

This is a fast-moving section of the Willamette and the last few miles of the McKenzie. It begins a few miles north of Eugene and ends at the tiny town of Harrisburg.

Begin by leaving a car at the Harrisburg City Park boat ramp near the north end of Harrisburg, at the corner of First and Monroe Streets. This sleepy town was once a busy port of call for steamboats plying the Willamette. It was founded in the early 1850s, and the first steamboat called in 1856. The importance of the river commerce to the town diminished in the 1870s when the railroad arrived.

The launching point is Armitage Park, a Lane County park located where Coburg Road and Interstate 5 cross the McKenzie north of Eugene. It can be reached from Harrisburg by following River Road South to Coburg Road. A day-use fee is charged from May through September. A season pass is also available.

An alternative launch is available on the north side of the river near Armitage Park. From the north end of the bridge on Coburg Road, turn east on McKenzie View Drive and drive 50 yards to a right turn leading down a gravel road to an informal launch site under the bridge.

The McKenzie and the Willamette in the Eugene area are not slow backwater sloughs. While encountering no whitewater, paddlers must do more than drift along enjoying the view. Wear your life jackets, and carefully watch the currents and channels. New islands and channels are constantly being created, only to be eroded away or abandoned later.

The McKenzie enters the Willamette at approximately rivermile 175 of the Willamette. This same point is considered to be rivermile 0 of the McKenzie because rivermiles are measured from the mouth of each river. The area near this intersection is a maze of islands, and paddlers are not likely to know exactly when one river becomes the other. Unless you are particularly observant you will probably still be looking for the intersection 10 miles after you pass it. Watch for occasional rivermile markers. Although Armitage Park is officially located at rivermile 7 of the McKenzie, changes in the riverbed over the years have shortened the distance to the Willamette to about 3 miles.

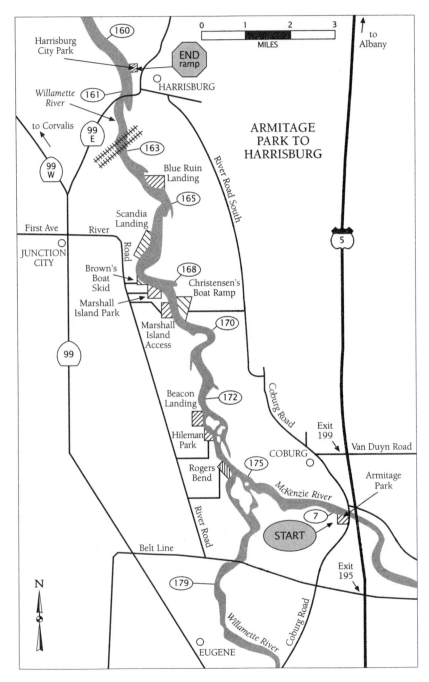

Harrisburg City Park

160

0 1 2 3
MILES

to Albany

END ramp

HARRISBURG

Willamette River 161

to Corvalis

99 E

163

99 W

ARMITAGE PARK TO HARRISBURG

Blue Ruin Landing

River Road South

165

First Ave

River

Scandia Landing

JUNCTION CITY

Road

Brown's Boat Skid

168

Christensen's Boat Ramp

Marshall Island Park

99

Marshall Island Access

170

5

Beacon Landing

172

Coburg Road

Hileman Park

Exit 199

Van Duyn Road

COBURG

Rogers Bend

175

Armitage Park

McKenzie River

River Road

START

7

Belt Line

Exit 195

N

179

Coburg Road

Willamette River

EUGENE

The numerous parks and public landings along the way make good stopping points if you would like to plan a shorter trip. For lunch or exploring, however, the public landings (Beacon Landing, Scandia Landing, and Blue Ruin Landing) are preferable because they have no auto access.

Two railroad bridges are reached at rivermile 163. Note that both are lift spans, built in the days when commercial boat traffic used this part of the river. Also note that the lift portions of both bridges are now over dry land, evidence of the changing course of the river.

Harrisburg appears just after you pass under the US Highway 99E bridge. Several islands and gravel bars may be found in this area. Watch for swift currents. The right side of the channel is generally the best course under the highway bridge and past the town. This crossing was first served by a ferry in 1848, and then by a bridge in 1923.

The boat ramp, not easily seen from upstream, is on the right bank, at the north end of town. If the current is strong, stay close to the bank, or you will miss the ramp.

2 Harrisburg to Peoria

Location: North of Eugene
Distance: 20 miles
Time: 5 to 6 hours
Maps: USGS Harrisburg and Peoria 7.5"
Season: Year-round
Rating: B

The paddle between Harrisburg and Peoria is a fast one. Although the Willamette River winds its way around numerous large bends and past several islands, the current is strong, even late in the year.

Begin the trip by leaving an extra car at Peoria Park just north of Peoria. If driving from the north, take Interstate 5, exit 228, and drive west to Tangent, then south on US Highway 99E to Shedd. If driving from the south, take Interstate 5, exit 216, drive west to Halsey, and then north on US Highway 99E to Shedd. From Shedd, drive west on Fayetteville Drive to Peoria Park. Before leaving the park, take a good look at the river just off the boat ramp, so you will recognize it from the water. In recent years, a gravel bar just offshore from the ramp has slowly turned into a sizable island and then joined the mainland. To land at the boat ramp, stay close to the right bank and at the downstream end of the island turn into the inlet behind the island.

Before the railroad attracted most of the business to neighboring Shedd and Halsey, Peoria was an important river port. The town is said to have been founded by members of the Peoria Party of 1839, a group of Illinois pioneers who had more than their share of difficulties in their journey to Oregon.

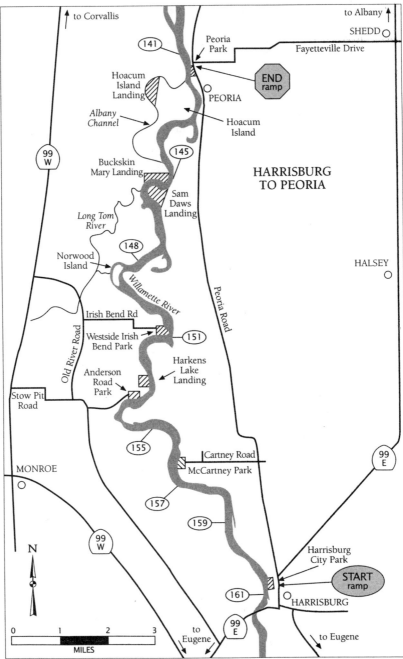

to Corvallis

to Albany

SHEDD

141

Peoria
Park

Fayetteville Drive

Hoacum
Island
Landing

END
ramp

PEORIA

*Albany
Channel*

Hoacum
Island

99
W

145

Buckskin
Mary Landing

**HARRISBURG
TO PEORIA**

Sam
Daws
Landing

*Long Tom
River*

148

Norwood
Island

HALSEY

Willamette River

Peoria Road

Irish Bend Rd

Old River Road

Westside Irish
Bend Park

151

Harkens
Lake
Landing

Anderson
Road
Park

Stow Pit
Road

155

Cartney Road

99
E

MONROE

McCartney Park

157

159

99
W

Harrisburg
City Park

N

START
ramp

161

HARRISBURG

0   1   2   3

to
Eugene

99
E

to Eugene

MILES

The launching point is reached by driving south on Peoria Road to Harrisburg. Launch at the Harrisburg City Park boat ramp at the north end of town, at the corner of First and Monroe Streets.

Between Harrisburg and Peoria, the river has a consistent pattern of S curves as it flows north. If you are in a hurry or just tired of paddling, keep to the faster water on the outside of each curve; but if you are looking for a more leisurely trip, keep to the inside shore.

Watch for strainers. As the faster water on the outside of each turn erodes the riverbank, trees frequently fall into the river. Considerable hazard is presented to paddlers because the current can often pull a boat under the logs.

Numerous islands (both small and large) in this section of the river give paddlers opportunities for decision making. The safest course is usually to stay in the main channel because the side channels can be difficult to navigate. Either way, keep a lookout for debris and shallow spots.

Watch for rivermile markers along the way. At rivermile 149, Norwood Island marks the mouth of the Long Tom River. As of this writing, a logjam had formed against a bridge over the channel behind the island. The current behind the island can be strong, and reversing direction after you have started down the channel can be difficult or impossible, so avoid using that channel unless you have scouted it in advance. Shortly after passing Norwood Island, the river begins to slow down somewhat, as the river channel levels out and widens.

At rivermile 144.5, just past two public access areas (Sam Daws and Buckskin Mary Landings) marked by several rivermile markers, the Albany Channel exits to the left, behind Hoacum Island. This side streambed was once the main channel of the river. It rejoins the main channel at Peoria, 0.25 mile upstream from Peoria Park, the ending point for this trip.

Between rivermiles 144 and 143, the right bank has historically been known as Snag Boat Bend. It is now part of the William L. Finley National Wildlife Refuge.

3 Peoria to Corvallis

Location: South of Corvallis
Distance: 10 miles
Time: 4 hours
Maps: USGS Peoria, Riverside, and Corvallis 7.5"
Season: Year-round
Rating: B

As the Willamette approaches Corvallis from Peoria, it begins its transformation from a fast-moving river with rapidly eroding banks to a slower, wider, and straighter channel. But it still moves along quickly; this 10-mile section takes only a few hours.

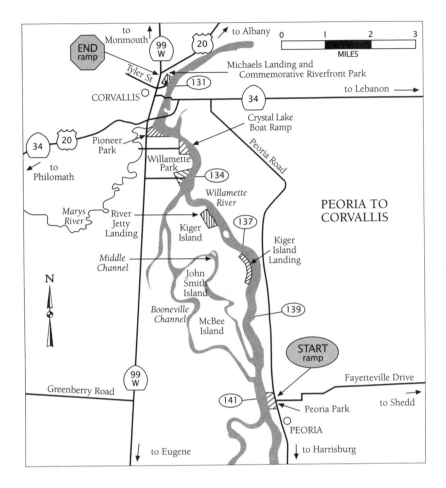

Start this trip by leaving an extra car or a bicycle in Corvallis at Aquathusiasts Boat Ramp at Michaels Landing at the north end of Commemorative Riverfront Park. In downtown Corvallis, drive north on Second Street, then turn right onto Tyler Street. At the foot of Tyler Street, turn north to the boat ramp.

Then proceed to Oregon Highway 34 and drive east about a mile. Turn right onto Peoria Road, and follow it about 8 miles to Peoria Park just north of Peoria.

About a mile after launching, you will reach a fork in the river. The main channel keeps to the right, while the Booneville Channel and Middle Channel exit on the left. The navigability of both of these side channels is questionable, particularly in summer or early fall. Booneville Channel is reported to be navigable through June in most years, or when the Corvallis gauge is at 1.7 feet or above. If you feel adventurous, you might give one of them a try, with the understanding that portages may be required.

Even if you stay in the main channel, this section of the Willamette is noted for snags and strainers in the river. Keep a lookout for any obstructions ahead, and give them a wide berth.

This section of the river has only one sizable park, Willamette Park at river-mile 134. Unfortunately, landing at Willamette Park is difficult due to the strong current and the relatively steep bank.

The Willamette River near Corvallis

Just past Willamette Park, on the east side of the river, is the mouth of East Channel. According to some reports, it can be paddled about four miles east and south to Muddy Creek, which can then be paddled another 1.5 miles south to Peoria Road, or three miles south to Church Drive, near the community of Oakville. A small riffle will be found just above Church Drive.

Marys River enters the Willamette at the southern edge of Corvallis, at rivermile 132. If you decide to venture into its mouth (Pioneer Park and a public dock are a few yards upstream), be careful, as the entrance can be shallow and rocky late in the year. At other times, it is a pleasant diversion from the Willamette, but be careful of the current and trees in the river if you are not accustomed to maneuvering your boat in a strong current.

The Corvallis area is popular with boaters, particularly in speedboats. Do your best to stay out of their way; they are in too much of a hurry to watch out for you, much less look back at the effects of their wakes.

Other types of boaters use the area, too. If you see a funny-looking canoe with eight oarsmen, it is the Oregon State University crew out for a practice session. Their crew house is located just across the Willamette from downtown Corvallis.

As you approach Corvallis, the takeout is at Michaels Landing boat ramp, a few blocks north of the bridges in downtown Corvallis, at about rivermile 131.

4 Corvallis to Albany

Location: Corvallis–Albany area
Distance: 12 miles
Time: 2 to 4 hours
Maps: USGS Corvallis, Riverside, Lewisburg, and Albany 7.5"
Season: Year-round
Rating: A

Most Oregonians associate Albany with the view they get as they roar past on the freeway. They do not look beyond the industrial section of the town to its numerous historic buildings, much less notice that the Willamette flows through Albany and past those factories north of town.

Like many Oregon towns, Albany was named for an eastern city. At one point, its name was changed to Takenah, an Indian word describing the deep channel where the Willamette is joined by the Calapooia River; but some people interpreted the word as meaning "hole in the ground," so the name Albany was reinstated.

This is a relatively short trip. Some paddlers may wish to combine it with Trip 3, Peoria to Corvallis, or Trip 5, Albany to Buena Vista.

Start this trip by leaving an extra car at Bowman Park in Albany, at the foot of Geary Street, just east of downtown Albany. (From downtown Albany, drive

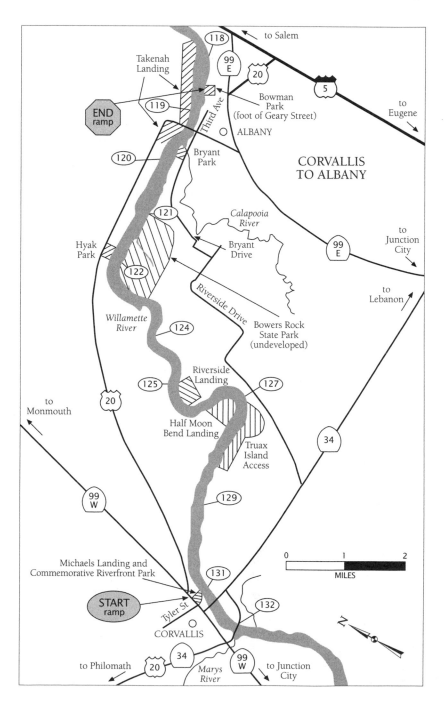

to Salem

Takenah
Landing

118

99
E

20

5

to
Eugene

END
ramp

119

Third Ave

Bowman
Park
(foot of Geary Street)

O ALBANY

120

Bryant
Park

**CORVALLIS
TO ALBANY**

121

*Calapooia
River*

to
Junction
City

Hyak
Park

122

Bryant
Drive

99
E

Riverside Drive

to
Lebanon

*Willamette
River*

124

Bowers Rock
State Park
(undeveloped)

Riverside
Landing

125

127

to
Monmouth

20

Half Moon
Bend Landing

34

Truax
Island
Access

99
W

129

Michaels Landing and
Commemorative Riverfront Park

131

0   1   2

MILES

START
ramp

Tyler St

132

N

O
CORVALLIS

to Philomath

20

34

*Marys
River*

99
W

to Junction
City

east on Water Avenue, then turn left onto Geary.) Leave your car in the parking lot near the dock and boat ramp.

Then drive to Corvallis either on the west side of the river (use US Highway 20) or on the east side (follow Bryant Drive south to Riverside Drive and Oregon Highway 34).

Launch your boat at Aquathusiasts Boat Ramp at Michaels Landing, just north of Commemorative Riverfront Park in Corvallis. The ramp is just north of the foot of Tyler Street, a few blocks north of the two bridges into downtown Corvallis. Be wary of speedboats in the Corvallis area.

The river is slow and wide north of Corvallis, but there is no real reason to be in a hurry. Sit back and enjoy the pastoral surroundings, or watch for wildlife. In spring and summer ospreys can be seen soaring overhead, hovering over the river, or diving feet first for fish. These birds can be seen with some frequency along the Willamette in this area.

Three public access areas (Truax Island Access, Half Moon Bend Landing, and Riverside Landing) between rivermiles 129 and 125 offer excellent lunch spots or campsites, but none offers drinking water. You should carry your own, but if you run out, it is available at Hyak Park at rivermile 122.

Bowman Park is on the right bank, about a mile downstream from the two bridges in downtown Albany.

5 Albany to Buena Vista

Location: North of Albany
Distance: 14 miles
Time: 6 hours
Maps: USGS Albany, Lewisburg, and Monmouth 7.5"
Season: Year-round
Rating: A

The town of Buena Vista, or what is left of it, is a classic example of a town whose economic life has always been centered on the river. No main roads or highways have ever passed through it. It has never been served by a railroad, although tracks have passed within a few miles on either side of the town. Yet it was a thriving industrial center in the late nineteenth century, when its kilns were the region's only source of clay pipe and cooking ware.

Today the kilns, lumber mills, gristmills, hotels, and saloons are gone, and a small community is all that remains. Its only distinction is the site of the southernmost of the three remaining ferries on the Willamette. First operated by the town's founder, Reason B. Hall, the ferry has now been crossing the Willamette for more than 140 years.

To paddle from Albany to Buena Vista, start by leaving an extra car at Buena Vista Park, on the west bank of the river at Buena Vista, just south of the ferry landing. Buena Vista can be reached by driving west from Interstate 5, exit 242. If the ferry is not running, you'll need to drive north to the bridge at Independence, or south to the bridge at Albany because boats are not permitted to use the ferry landing on the east bank of the river. The ferry currently runs Wednesday through Sunday, from April through October.

If the ferry is not running and you are parked on the west side, drive south on Buena Vista Road and Spring Hill Road to Albany. From the east side, return to Interstate 5 and proceed south to Albany.

In Albany, drive to Bowman Park, at the foot of Geary Street, about a mile east of the downtown bridges. Launch your boat from the boat ramp or the adjacent dock.

As you pass through Albany, the left (west) bank of the river is all publicly owned. Because this portion of Takenah Landing is not accessible by car, river travelers have the area to themselves, without any screeching tires or blaring

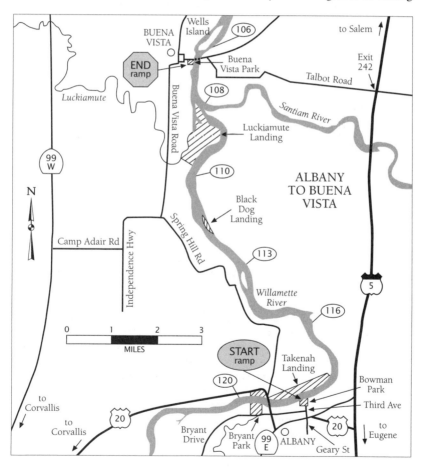

car stereos. Unfortunately, not all river travelers are as quiet as canoeists and kayakers. Expect to see plenty of powerboats and jet skis in the Albany area on warm days.

Luckiamute Landing, another greenway area, with campsites, occupies a 2-mile-long bank between rivermiles 110 and 108. At rivermile 108, the Luckiamute enters from the west and the Santiam from the east (see Trip 19, Santiam River). What a contrast these rivers present! The Santiam, draining two thousand square miles of foothills and mountains, enters wide and strong. By comparison, the entrance of the small and lazy Luckiamute is easy to miss. Because the current of the Luckiamute is nil, its mouth can easily be explored by canoe or kayak.

Below the mouth of the Santiam, huge white cliffs tower over the newly strengthened Willamette. Ospreys and turkey vultures circle overhead, while herons stand erect and silent on the banks.

In summer, a small floating dock on the west bank near the head of Wells Island marks Buena Vista Park, a Polk County park. Landing is not permitted on the east bank, in order to keep the area clear for the ferry.

6 Buena Vista to Independence

Location: Between Albany and Salem
Distance: 11 miles
Time: 4 hours
Maps: USGS Monmouth and Sidney 7.5"
Season: Year-round
Rating: B

The Willamette River carves a 5-mile arc between Buena Vista and Independence around an area containing much history, as evidenced by its name, American Bottom. The name derives from the days when the residents of the Oregon region were evenly divided between Americans and French-Canadians. The Canadians were concentrated in "French Prairie" near St. Paul, while the Americans had "American Bottom."

Independence seems relatively untouched by the passage of time. Named for a Missouri river town, its historic architecture is clearly visible even as one approaches by water. A new riverfront amphitheater was completed in 2005. Immediately to the west is the town of Monmouth, the last dry town in Oregon. Alcohol could be purchased in Monmouth for the first time starting in 2002.

Start this trip by leaving an extra car in Independence at Riverview Park at the foot of South C Street. Independence can be reached from Salem by following River Road south. Independence can be reached from the south by driving from Buena Vista up the east side of the Willamette on Buena Vista Road and then Sidney-Independence Road.

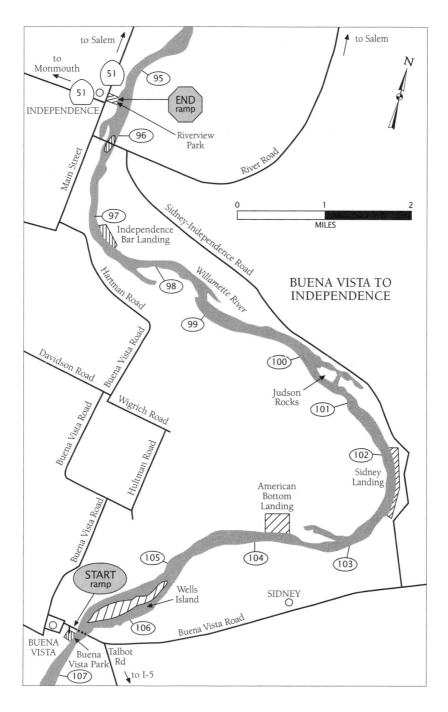

to Salem

to Salem

N

to
Monmouth

51

95

51

INDEPENDENCE

END
ramp

96

Riverview
Park

River Road

0   1   2

MILES

97

Independence
Bar Landing

Sidney-Independence Road

Hartman Road

98

Willamette River

BUENA VISTA TO
INDEPENDENCE

99

Davidson Road

Buena Vista Road

100

Judson
Rocks

101

Wigrich Road

Buena Vista Road

Hultman Road

102

Sidney
Landing

American
Bottom
Landing

Buena Vista Road

105

104

103

START
ramp

Wells
Island

SIDNEY

106

Buena Vista Road

BUENA
VISTA

Buena
Vista Park

Talbot
Rd

to I-5

107

Buena Vista Ferry

After leaving your car at one of two boat ramps in Riverview Park, drive south from Independence on Main Street. About a mile out of town, turn left onto Hartman Road, and follow it (and several signs) to Buena Vista. Launch your boat at Buena Vista Park, just south of the ferry landing. The ferry currently runs Wednesday through Sunday, from April to October. (Boats are not permitted to use the ferry landing on the east bank of the river.)

Wells Island lies in the river just north of the ferry route. A mile long, the island is a county park with facilities for camping and picnicking. Water is not available on the island, but can be brought over from Buena Vista Park. The main channel of the river is to the east of Wells Island. The channel west of Wells Island is not reliable; it may be choked with debris, have some rough water, or both.

Below Wells Island, the Willamette is usually wide and smooth, but some tight corners can be encountered in some years. Near the east bank lies the community of Sidney. Under the name of Ankeny's Landing, the Sidney area was once the major fuel yard of the upper Willamette, where steamboats could lay in a fresh supply of cordwood. Just east of here lies Ankeny National Wildlife Refuge, a large federal reserve devoted primarily to the preservation of wintering grounds for a subspecies of Canada geese, the dusky Canada goose.

After passing one more large island, the river turns north, and the Independence bridge comes into view. A large floating dock on the left bank marks the end of the trip.

7 Independence to Salem

Location: South of Salem
Distance: 12 miles
Time: 4 hours
Maps: USGS Monmouth, Rickreal, and Salem West 7.5"
Season: Year-round
Rating: A

Between Independence and Salem, the Willamette makes several wide bends around Hayden Island, Browns Island, and Minto Island, none of which are true islands. As the Willamette has changed its course over the last 150 years, the channels behind islands named by early settlers dried up and left only disconnected sloughs, crescent-shaped lakes, and large nonislands.

The trip from Independence begins in Salem when you leave an extra car or bicycle at the boat ramp in Wallace Marine Park in West Salem. Although the ramp is located under the west end of the Oregon Highway 22 bridges, the entrance to the park is 0.4 mile north of the bridges; drive north on Wallace Road (Oregon Highway 221), then turn right onto Glen Creek Road to enter the park.

Then drive, with your boat, south to Independence. The west side drive is probably the fastest (follow Oregon Highway 22 west to Oregon Highway 51 and turn south), but the east side is more scenic. In Independence, launch from one of the two boat ramps in Riverview Park at the foot of South C Street.

Shortly after the launching, the river makes a broad S curve toward a large unnamed island at rivermile 92. The tiny community of Halls Ferry is located behind the island on the right bank. Watch carefully for rocks as you pass this island. The site of the former ferry landing is located downstream near rivermile 91 and is today a small public access area. Watch for rivermile markers. The owner and operator of the ferry in the 1880s was B. F. Hall, son of the founder and ferry operator of Buena Vista, 15 miles upstream.

The closer you get to Salem, the more likely will be the presence of powerboats. Keep an eye open for them, and do your best to stay out of their way.

Two of the largest "nonislands," Browns Island and Minto Island, occupy the right bank and are now part of nine-hundred-acre Minto-Brown Island Park, operated by Marion County and the city of Salem. The park offers more than 12 miles of trails, most of which are paved.

The only bridges on the trip, the dual bridges of Oregon Highway 22 in Salem, mark its end. Wallace Marine Park, under their west ends, is extremely popular with powerboats, so be careful when landing.

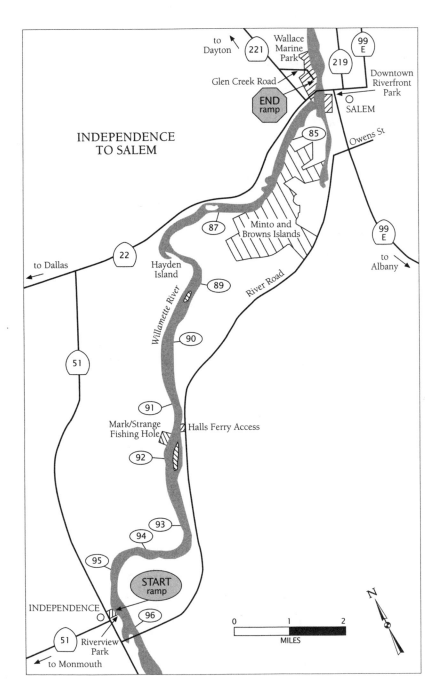

8 Salem to Wheatland Ferry

Location: North of Salem
Distance: 12 miles
Time: 4 hours
Maps: USGS Salem West and Mission Bottom 7.5"
Season: Year-round
Rating: A

The 12-mile paddle from Salem to Wheatland is a particularly pleasant trip. It offers smooth paddling, a gentle current, several public access areas to explore, and some interesting history.

Originally named Atchison, Wheatland was first settled in 1844 by Daniel Matheny, who took up the noble professions of farming, operating a ferry, and selling property in his future town. The current ferry, as of this writing, the *Daniel Matheny V*, was christened in 2002. It carries nine cars and runs seven days a week, except on Thanksgiving and Christmas or when water levels are too high for safe operation.

Across the river on the east bank was the site of Jason Lee's Methodist Mission, which Lee abandoned in 1840 in favor of a site 12 miles upstream. The Indians had named the new site Chemeketa, but in 1844, the same year Wheatland was settled, the missionaries renamed the town Salem and began marketing lots.

To paddle through this historic area now known as Mission Bottom, leave an extra car on either side of the river at the Wheatland Ferry crossing. (The east side features a state park boat ramp a short distance north of the ferry landing. The west side has a boat ramp known as Ediger Landing.) The ferry can be reached from Interstate 5 by driving west from exit 271 (Woodburn) or 263 (Brooks).

Then drive south to Wallace Marine Park in West Salem. On the east side, follow Wheatland Road or Matheny Road to Oregon Highway 219 and continue south to Salem. In Salem, turn west onto Oregon Highway 22 (Marion Street) and cross the river. If starting from the west side of the Wheatland Ferry, drive to Oregon Highway 221 and turn south to West Salem.

The launching point is the public boat ramp at Wallace Marine Park, under the west end of the Oregon Highway 22 bridges. The entrance to the park can be reached by turning east onto Glen Creek Road off Wallace Road (Oregon Highway 221), 0.4 mile north of the Oregon Highway 22 bridges into Salem.

The river passes several islands at rivermiles 83 and 80. At rivermile 79.5, where the river turns sharply north, beware of Rice Rocks, which may be hidden just below the surface of the water near the left bank; the right bank is much safer.

At rivermile 77, the west bank is (or perhaps was) known as Lincoln, while the east bank is named Spongs Landing, after a ferry operator of the late 1800s. Today the landing is a county park.

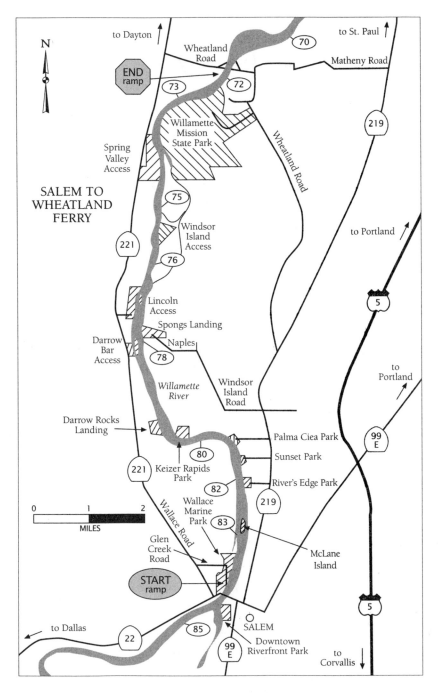

N

to Dayton

Wheatland Road

70

to St. Paul

Matheny Road

END ramp

73

72

219

Willamette Mission State Park

Wheatland Road

Spring Valley Access

SALEM TO WHEATLAND FERRY

75

Windsor Island Access

to Portland

221

76

5

Lincoln Access

Spongs Landing

Darrow Bar Access

Naples

78

to Portland

Willamette River

Windsor Island Road

Darrow Rocks Landing

Palma Ciea Park

99 E

80

Sunset Park

221

Keizer Rapids Park

River's Edge Park

82

Wallace Road

219

0   1   2

MILES

Wallace Marine Park

83

McLane Island

Glen Creek Road

START ramp

5

to Dallas

22

85

SALEM

Downtown Riverfront Park

99 E

to Corvallis

Windsor Island lies along the east bank between rivermiles 76 and 74. The main channel once passed on the east side of this island, but today the main channel is on the west side, and the east channel is all but abandoned.

A similar nonexistent "island," Beaver Island, occurs between rivermiles 73 and 72. On the east bank of the former channel, now known as Mission Lake, is the former site of Jason Lee's mission, now the large Willamette Mission State Park. Just past rivermile 72 is the Wheatland Ferry crossing and the end of this trip. A piling just downstream from the ferry crossing marks the state park boat ramp, where you may have left your extra car.

9 Wheatland Ferry to St. Paul

Location: St. Paul area
Distance: 15 miles
Time: 4 to 6 hours
Maps: USGS Mission Bottom and Dayton 7.5"
Season: Year-round
Rating: A

The Willamette River from Wheatland to St. Paul provides one of the area's most popular canoe trips. The current is steady and the scenery pleasant as the river winds its way past several interesting islands. The largest of these is Grand Island, nearly 5 miles long. On its west side is Lambert Slough, an adventurous variation to this trip.

Lambert Slough

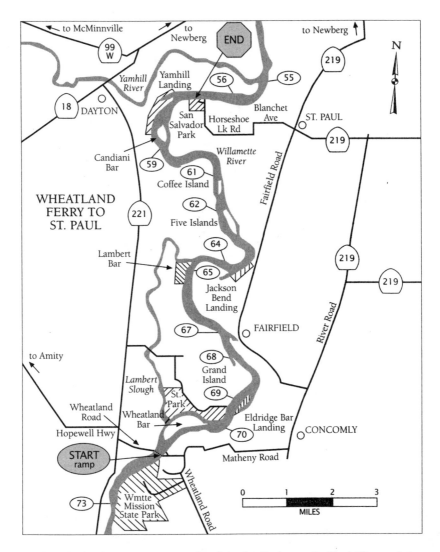

Start by leaving an extra car at San Salvador Park near St. Paul. To get there, drive west from St. Paul on Blanchet Avenue, which becomes Horseshoe Lake Road before it reaches the park. Then drive south from St. Paul through Fairfield and turn right (south) onto Oregon Highway 219. A quarter mile past the community of Concomly, turn right onto Matheny Road and follow it 4 miles to the Willamette Mission State Park boat ramp just north of the ferry landing. The ferry runs seven days a week, except on Thanksgiving and Christmas. (The Ediger Landing boat ramp is available on the west side of the river, if you prefer.)

The Lambert Slough variation leaves the main channel of the Willamette almost immediately after the launch. Look for a row of pilings on the left bank, then paddle through an opening in this barrier to a slough behind Wheatland Bar. A half-mile later (including some shallow spots), the Lambert Slough can be reached by portaging over Wheatland Dam at a low point near its north end. This variation is not recommended except early in the year, and only to those willing to put up with numerous shallow spots and some brushy paddling. The reward, as you might guess, is a shady, secluded journey. The slough has numerous passages that require lining the boats through shallow areas or fighting your way through brush or reeds and grasses. One or two parts require a portage. The effort is worth it, but you might not agree. If it sounds to your liking, choose a warm spring day and bring an old pair of sneakers and an adventurous friend.

For the less adventurous, stay in the main channel or, after paddling through the pilings near the Wheatland Ferry, stay in the 2-mile slough behind Wheatland Bar until it rejoins the main channel at about rivermile 70.

The Willamette has been active in this part of its journey north, carving numerous islands and sloughs only to abandon them, leaving crescent-shaped lakes, inlets, and gravel bars. At several points, dikes and dams have been built to minimize the wandering tendency. Dams at the southern ends of Wheatland Bar, Grand Island, Five Islands, Coffee Island, and Candiani Bar are all examples of such preventive construction, and the sloughs behind them make attractive detours, although the navigability of the sloughs is not always dependable.

At rivermile 60, the river curves to the west around Weston Bar, where the Spruce Goose was brought ashore in 1993 after its ocean and river journey from southern California to its new home at the Evergreen Aviation Museum in McMinnville.

Beware of strong currents and log debris near Candiani Bar. The takeout at San Salvador Park appears on the right at rivermile 56.

10 St. Paul to Champoeg State Park

Location: Newberg area
Distance: 12 miles
Time: 5 hours
Maps and chart: USGS Dayton, St. Paul, and Newberg 7.5"; NOAA chart 18528
Season: Year-round
Rating: A

This 11-mile section of the Willamette curves around the northwest corner of French Prairie, a one-hundred-square-mile area of small towns and farmland that has played a central role in Oregon's history. First inhabited by Kalapooian Indians, its current name is derived from the French-Canadians who settled in the area after retiring from Hudson's Bay Company. Today, its small towns have retained much of their charm, and many of the Victorian farmhouses of the area have survived their first century.

Start this trip by leaving an extra car or bicycle at Champoeg State Park, reached from Interstate 5 by driving west from exit 278 or 282 (see map for Trip 11, Champoeg State Park to Canby). After entering the park, follow the signs to the Oak Grove Day Use Area. Shortly after leaving the main road and entering the day use area, turn right (north), following signs pointing to the Group Tent area. Follow the paved road as it turns to dirt and crosses a large field. Leave your extra car near a fence on the far side of the field, a short stroll from the boat dock.

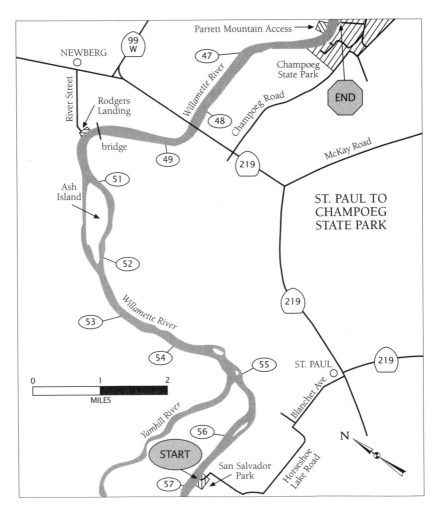

Then drive west from the park to Oregon Highway 219, and follow it south to St. Paul. In St. Paul, turn right onto Blanchet Avenue, but slow down to admire the imposing St. Paul Catholic Church, and try to imagine what French Prairie was like in 1846 when the church was built to replace a log chapel. Follow Blanchet Avenue through hop fields as it becomes Horseshoe Lake Road and eventually ends at the launching point, the boat ramp at San Salvador Park.

The river, wide and smooth, is joined by the sluggish Yamhill River (Trip 20, Yamhill River) 2 rivermiles after launching. (For a detour, paddle up the Yamhill.) At rivermile 52, Ash Island divides the river. Both channels are navigable, but if powerboats are out in force, as they usually are on summer weekends, take the relatively secluded left channel. Depending on the water level, a row of pilings may cross the entrance to the left channel; paddle through (or over) the pilings carefully.

In the right-hand channel, a private ferry at rivermile 51.5 shuttles farm equipment and crops between the island and the east bank. The island is private property.

A mile downstream, near the public boat ramp at Rodgers Landing in Newberg, local industry and a large pipeline bridge dominate the skyline.

The western end of Champoeg State Park is reached near rivermile 46, but the boat dock is still a mile away, at the east end of the park. Your car is a short walk from the dock.

For a longer trip, consider using Champoeg State Park as an overnight stop. The park offers campsites, cabins, and yurts for overnight stays. A group campsite is particularly convenient because it is located adjacent to the boat dock. Reservations are usually required.

11 Champoeg State Park to Canby

Location: Wilsonville area
Distance: 10 miles
Time: 5 hours
Maps and chart: Newberg, Sherwood, and Canby 7.5"; NOAA chart 18528
Season: Year-round
Rating: A

This is a straightforward section of the Willamette, but one filled with history and wildlife. Unfortunately, this section is crowded with powerboats on warm summer weekends. Try it in the off-season to avoid water-skiers and jet skis.

The trip starts at the site of the former town of Champoeg, now a state park. The trip also ends at a state park. Leave an extra car near the boat ramp at Molalla River State Park on the south side of the Willamette, 0.5 mile west of the Canby Ferry. From Canby, the park can be reached by driving north on Ferry Road. Then drive south on Ferry Road to Canby, and from there southwest on

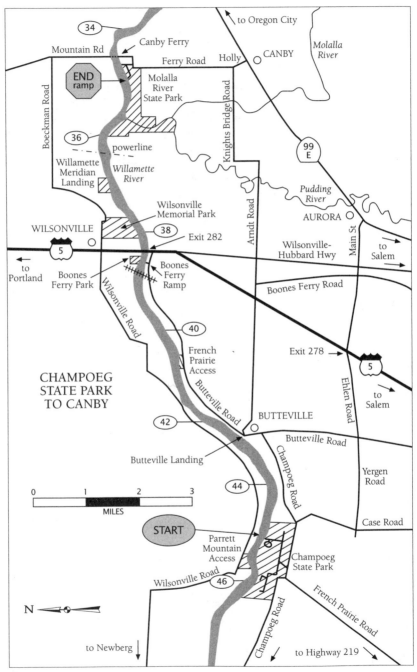

US Highway 99E to Aurora. Turn right onto Main Street, and follow it as it becomes Ehlen Road after crossing under Interstate 5, then Yergen Road after crossing Butteville Road. Turn right onto Case Road, and go to Champoeg Road. Turn left, then enter Champoeg State Park and follow the signs to the Oak Grove Day Use Area. Shortly after leaving the main road and entering the day use area, turn right (north), following signs to the Group Tent area. Follow the paved road as it turns to dirt and crosses a large field. Park near a fence on the far side of the field, and carry your boat a short distance to the boat dock.

In the early 1800s, Champoeg was the main port for the area south of it known as French Prairie. By 1843, when 102 settlers met to form a government for the Oregon Territory, Champoeg was a sizable cluster of buildings centered on a street named Napoleon Boulevard. The names of the 52 men who voted for the creation of an American government are now inscribed on an obelisk in the park. Their town, however, was twice destroyed by floods, first in 1861 and then in 1890. Today, a marker shows the level of the 1861 flood a dozen feet up the side of the memorial pavilion. Things haven't changed much since then: the level of the 1996 flood is shown on one of the pilings at the boat dock.

From Champoeg, the Willamette travels east in a slow path toward Wilsonville and the huge bridges of Interstate 5. Just west of these bridges is the former site of Boones Ferry, marked by a small park on the left and a large marina on the right. This part of the river is referred to as "the Newberg Pool"; don't count on much current.

Just after passing under the Interstate 5 bridge, the Charboneau development appears on the south bank and a park (with a public boat dock) is on the left bank.

Watch for wildlife, particularly near the mouth of the Molalla River around rivermile 36 (see Trip 21, Pudding River, a tributary of the Molalla). One of the largest heron rookeries in the state is located on the east side of the Molalla's mouth. Unfortunately, powerboats in this area often mar the tranquility of the scene. Take out at the boat ramp at the Molalla River State Park, 0.5 mile west of the Canby Ferry landing.

12 Canby to West Linn

Location: Canby–Oregon City area
Distance: 7 miles
Time: 3 hours
Map and chart: USGS Canby 7.5"; NOAA chart 18528
Season: Year-round
Rating: A (Warning: Avoid Willamette Falls)

The 7-mile stretch of the Willamette between the mouths of the Molalla and Tualatin Rivers is a pleasant reminder that portions of the river, even close to industrial centers such as Oregon City, can still be secluded. This is a short

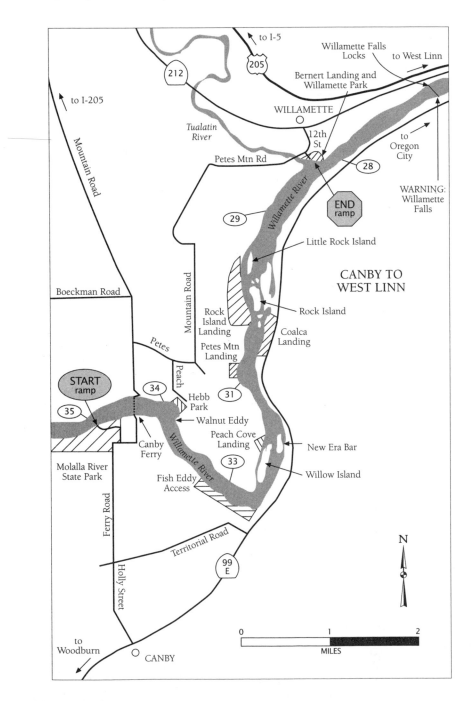

to I-5

Willamette Falls Locks

to West Linn

212

205

Bernert Landing and Willamette Park

to I-205

WILLAMETTE

Tualatin River

12th St

to Oregon City

Petes Mtn Rd

28

Mountain Road

Willamette River

29

END ramp

WARNING: Willamette Falls

Little Rock Island

CANBY TO WEST LINN

Boeckman Road

Mountain Road

Rock Island Landing

Rock Island

Coalca Landing

Petes

Petes Mtn Landing

Peach

START ramp

34

Hebb Park

31

35

Walnut Eddy

Canby Ferry

Peach Cove Landing

New Era Bar

Willamette River

33

Willow Island

Molalla River State Park

Fish Eddy Access

Ferry Road

Territorial Road

Holly Street

99 E

N

to Woodburn

CANBY

0   1   2

MILES

section, which could conceivably be paddled in a long summer's evening, although a more leisurely trip is justified.

Leave an extra car at Willamette Park at the foot of 12th Street in the Willamette section of West Linn, which is located 2.5 miles southwest of West Linn on Oregon Highway 212, or at Interstate 205, exit 6. Your car can be left either at the Bernert Landing boat ramp, just north of the mouth of the Tualatin River, or near a gravel beach between Bernert Landing and the mouth of the Tualatin. (The large parking lot at Bernert Landing is reserved for vehicles with boat trailers.) Then cross the Tualatin River on the nearby bridge, and drive south on Petes Mountain Road to the Canby Ferry.

Cross the ferry, and launch your boat at the boat ramp at Molalla River State Park 0.5 mile west of the ferry landing. (The ferry runs year-round, unless water levels are very high. If the ferry is not operating, launching at the ferry landing or Hebb Park would save driving to the Wilsonville or Oregon City bridges.)

Shortly after your launching, the river turns to the southeast at Walnut Eddy, then abruptly north at Fish Eddy. The river is quite deep at each of these turns, but it is relatively shallow in between and near Willow Island.

Willow Island and nearby New Era Bar are excellent spots to watch for wildlife, particularly herons that feed in shallow areas. If the water level is high

Willamette Narrows

enough, try paddling behind these islands. Just downstream, the proximity of US Highway 99E makes this area a popular fishing spot.

More islands are encountered near rivermile 30, where the current picks up speed in an area known as Willamette Narrows. Once again, the channels behind the islands are interesting to explore. On the east shore, the first island is Rock Island. Logs and other debris might block the entrance to the channel behind it; if so, try one of the entrances just downstream, although they might be too shallow during low water.

Just downstream on the west shore is Little Rock Island; the channel behind it is usually clear and wide, a welcome sight if powerboats plague the area. Little Rock Island itself is twelve acres, part of a thirty-two-acre preserve owned by the Nature Conservancy.

Soon the Tualatin enters from the left, under the bridge to Petes Mountain Road. If you have time to spare, venture (carefully) up the Tualatin (you will not get very far) or downstream toward the Willamette Falls Locks, but stay close to the west bank in order to avoid dangerous Willamette Falls.

Take out just downstream from the mouth of the Tualatin River, either at the Bernert Landing boat ramp or at the gravel beach between Bernert Landing and the mouth of the Tualatin.

13 West Linn to Lake Oswego

Location: West Linn area
Distance: 7 miles
Time: 5 hours
Maps and chart: USGS Canby, Oregon City, Gladstone, and Lake Oswego 7.5"; NOAA chart 18528
Season: Year-round
Rating: A (Warning: Use locks to avoid Willamette Falls)

The installation of the Willamette Falls Locks was a major event in the history of commerce and transportation on the Willamette River. Previously, shipments of grain, lumber, and livestock were portaged around the falls at Oregon City, but since 1873 traffic has been barged through the locks with little delay.

The first step in making this trip is to call the Willamette Falls Locks (503-656-3381), or visit *www.nwp.usace.army.mil/op/wfl/home.asp*, to determine if they will be open for small pleasure craft. Although the locks have historically been open from 9:30 AM to 8:00 PM seven days a week, operations have recently been curtailed for budgetary reasons. In recent years, the locks have been open Thursday through Monday during summer months only. Also, during weekdays and some weekends, barge and log raft traffic may preclude recreational traffic. The locks operate free of charge to all boats.

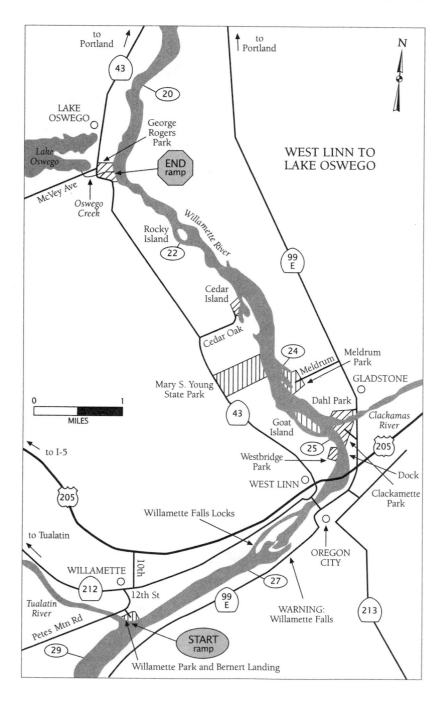

to Portland

43

20

LAKE OSWEGO

George Rogers Park

Lake Oswego

END ramp

McVey Ave

Oswego Creek

Willamette River

Rocky Island

22

Cedar Island

Cedar Oak

24

Meldrum

Meldrum Park

GLADSTONE

Mary S. Young State Park

Dahl Park

Clackamas River

to I-5

43

Goat Island

25

205

MILES

0   1

to Tualatin

Westbridge Park

WEST LINN

Dock

Clackamette Park

205

Willamette Falls Locks

10th

to Portland

N

WEST LINN TO LAKE OSWEGO

99 E

OREGON CITY

WILLAMETTE

212

12th St

27

99 E

WARNING: Willamette Falls

213

Tualatin River

Petes Mtn Rd

29

START ramp

Willamette Park and Bernert Landing

Willamette Falls Locks

The next step is to leave an extra car in Lake Oswego at the lower parking lot of George Rogers Park. The park is near the intersection of McVey Avenue and State Street (Oregon Highway 43). Glance at the huge chimney from the old blast furnace so you will know when to stop paddling.

Start the trip at the mouth of the Tualatin River at Willamette Park at the foot of 12th Street in the community of Willamette, 2.5 miles south of West Linn on Oregon Highway 212, or at Interstate 205, exit 6. Launch at either the Bernert Landing boat ramp or the gravel beach between Bernert Landing and the mouth of the Tualatin River. (The large parking lot at Bernert Landing is reserved for vehicles with boat trailers.)

Once in the river, stay near the left bank and watch carefully for other boat traffic, both large and small, that may be entering or leaving the locks. As you approach the locks, look for the pull cord to let the locks operator know a customer has arrived. Or use a cell phone to call the locks. Also keep an eye on the red and green traffic light. If the red light is on, stay clear of the entrance of the locks to give exiting craft plenty of room. Proceed through the locks only when instructed to do so by the loudspeaker or when the green traffic light is on.

From south to north, the locks consist of six chambers: a guard lock, a long canal basin, and four lock chambers. Depending on water levels, not all of the locks will be needed to lower your boat from the upper pool to the lower river. For example, in the summer the guard lock is left open whenever the level of the upper pool is within 4 feet of the lip of the falls. The lowest chamber has a vertical lift of 15 feet, while the other chambers each involve about 10 feet of lift. The lift of the guard lock varies from season to season, from 10 feet to only a few inches. The total lift of the entire set of locks is usually about 45 feet.

In each of the lower chambers, you will be handed a rope to hold onto as the water level falls. Don't tie your boat to the rope, unless you want to end up hanging high and dry. The operator can adjust the speed with which the water leaves each chamber, in order to lower the turbulence for small boaters. Passing downstream through the locks usually takes about thirty minutes, while the upstream passage takes about fifteen minutes more.

After the locks, the river passes under two bridges, one historic and the other modern. After the second bridge, a large public dock has been built on the east bank near a motel, and then the Clackamas River joins the Willamette from the east, and Goat Island lies near the west bank. To avoid powerboat traffic, paddle into the channel behind Goat Island, except late in the season when the channel may be shallow or even dry. A mile later, Mary S. Young State Park is on the left near a rocky outcropping. After another mile are Cedar Island (which is neither an island nor populated by cedars) and a public boat ramp near its north end.

At rivermile 22 is an island appropriately named Rocky Island, and a mile farther the Oswego blast furnace is visible next to Oswego Creek. Land at the boat ramp in George Rogers Park just past the mouth of Oswego Creek.

14 Lake Oswego to Willamette Park

Location: Portland area
Distance: 5 miles
Time: 2 to 3 hours
Map and chart: USGS Lake Oswego 7.5"; NOAA chart 18528
Season: Year-round
Rating: A

The paddle from Lake Oswego's George Rogers Park to Portland's Willamette Park is short but scenic, and Elk Rock Island (a park halfway along) is worth at least a short layover. This entire section of the Willamette is narrow in places and is also popular with powerboats and jet skis. Stay close to one bank or the other to avoid them.

Start by leaving an extra car at Willamette Park, the entrance to which is at the intersection of Southwest Nebraska Street and Macadam Avenue (Oregon Highway 43). Or consider returning to the starting point by bus. Tri-Met bus line 36 runs south along Macadam Avenue to the put-in spot, George Rogers Park, at the intersection of McVey Avenue and State Street (Oregon Highway 43) in Lake Oswego.

From the George Rogers Park lower parking lot, portage your boat a short distance to the river. (Unfortunately, a paved road to a boat ramp is usually gated.)

The town of Oswego (now Lake Oswego) had its beginnings on this site in 1850 when a water-powered sawmill was built on the banks of what was then called Sucker Creek. The creek was dammed, turning part of the creek into a millpond. A decade later, iron deposits were found in the neighboring hills, and in 1867 ironworks were erected. Eventually the pond was enlarged to become Lake Oswego, and a canal was dug to allow steamboats to travel from the Tualatin River to the lake. Eventually low iron prices and low water on the Tualatin put an end to both the steamboats and the smelter.

One mile past the launching site, the river passes under a railroad bridge, and another mile later it narrows as it passes Elk Rock Island. An island only at high water, this peninsula is a city park accessible only by boat or (at low water) by foot. A tiny beach in a small cove on the west side of the island makes an excellent landing spot for lunch, exploration, or napping on the rocks. A primitive trail circles the island, and an old shelter stands near the east side.

Powers Marine Park, on the left bank at rivermile 17, sees heavy use in the summer, as does Sellwood Riverfront Park, on the right bank at rivermile 16.5.

Oaks Bottom, on the east side of the river just north of the Sellwood Bridge, is an example of the flood plains that once lined the Willamette. Most of the flood plains have been diked, drained, and developed, and are no longer

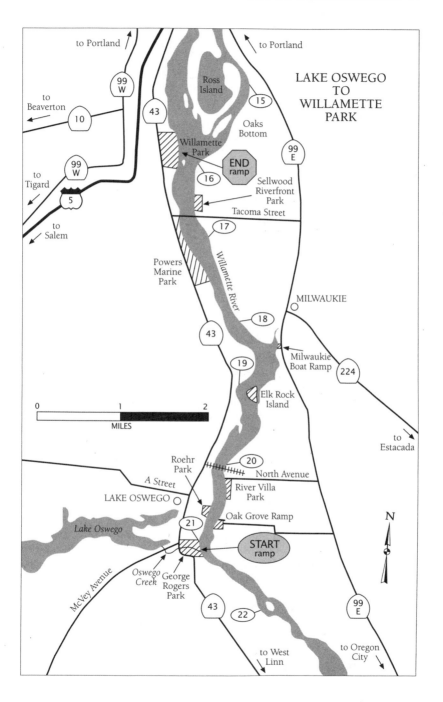

available to reduce the severity of spring floods. Although separated from the river by an amusement park, Oaks Bottom is one of the few flood plains that continues to serve its natural purpose.

The takeout point for this trip is the boat ramp at Portland's Willamette Park. On a spring or summer day, you can expect Willamette Park to be swarming with people, cars, and boat trailers.

15 Willamette Park to Swan Island

Location: Portland
Distance: 9 miles
Time: 5 hours
Maps and chart: USGS Lake Oswego and Portland 7.5"; NOAA chart 18526
Season: Year-round
Rating: A

The Willamette River undergoes dramatic changes as it passes through the city of Portland. On the southern edge of town, it is almost rural in character, thanks to wooded banks and extensive parks such as Powers Marine Park and Oaks Bottom. After passing through the city, however, the river is almost entirely industrialized, with huge grain elevators, public wharfs, and containerized shipping terminals.

This trip paddles under eight bridges. From south to north, they are the Ross Island, the Marquam (Interstate 5), the Hawthorne, the Morrison, the Burnside, the Steel, the Broadway, and the Fremont (Interstate 405) Bridges. Of the eight, the huge arches of the Fremont are the most grand and the piers of the Marquam are the ugliest, but the most intricate is the Steel Bridge, with its double-deck auto and railroad draw spans that can be operated independently.

A new 170-foot dock for human-powered craft has been built just south of the east end of the Hawthorne Bridge, between Clay and Market Streets, built by the city and the Portland Development Commission. A nearby warehouse has been converted into a new home for various rowing clubs, dragon boat clubs, Willamette Riverkeeper, and a paddling store. Parking is also provided. Portland Boathouse, a nonprofit organization formed by those groups, operates the boathouse.

The ending point, where you should leave an extra car, is the public boat ramp at Swan Island, easily reached by driving west on Going Street from Interstate 5, exit 303. After Going Street drops down onto Swan Island (actually a peninsula these days), turn right onto Basin Avenue and follow it to Emerson Street, then turn left into the parking lot for the Swan Island boat ramp.

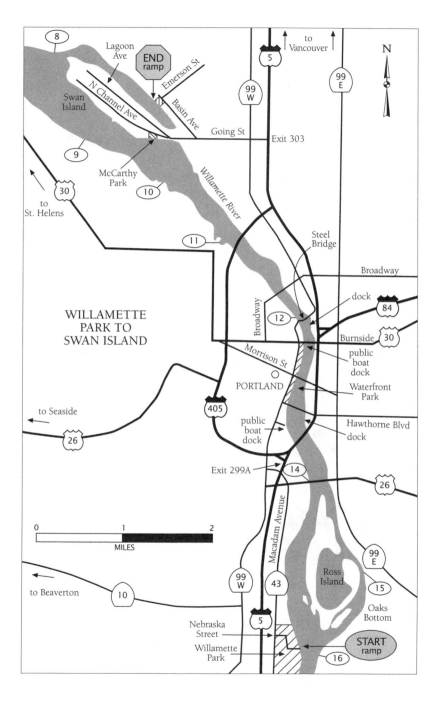

Portlandia arrives at the Portland waterfront

The trip could be shortened slightly by landing at tiny McCarthy Park, in the 4600 block of North Channel Avenue (near the intersection with Anchor Street), where a cement walkway leads down to the water.

The launching point for this trip is the city's Willamette Park, the entrance to which is at the intersection of Southwest Nebraska Street and Oregon Highway 43 (Macadam Avenue). To reach Willamette Park from Swan Island, return to Interstate 5 and drive south. Then take exit 299A and follow the signs to Oregon Highway 43, southbound. Turn left at Nebraska Street to enter the park. On a spring or summer day, you can expect Willamette Park to be filled with people, cars, and boat trailers.

After launching from Willamette Park, you might consider paddling around the east side of Ross Island to avoid some of the powerboat traffic. If you stay in the main channel, just west of Ross Island the Johns Landing area has been redeveloped. Once the domain of lumber mills and furniture factories, the west bank is now built up with condominiums, apartments, restaurants, and office buildings. The area to the north, near the Ross Island Bridge, is undergoing similar changes. With each new development, the city has been requiring the developers to build public bicycle and pedestrian paths along the river. Someday the paths will link Willamette Park and Powers Marine Park with the downtown waterfront.

On the east side of the river, the Eastbank Esplanade stretches from the Hawthorne Bridge to the Steel Bridge. This bicycle/pedestrian path includes connections to sidewalks on the Hawthorne, Morrison, Burnside, and Steel Bridges, a lengthy floating section near the Burnside Bridge, and a public dock, the Convention Center Dock, at rivermile 12.3.

The endpoint for this urban paddle is the Swan Island public boat ramp, on the east side of the Swan Island Lagoon, which can be entered at rivermile 8 near the dry docks. Be careful of industrial boat traffic in the Swan Island area.

16 Swan Island to Kelley Point

Location: North of Portland
Distance: 9 miles
Time: 5 hours
Maps and chart: USGS Portland, Linnton, and Sauvie Island 7.5"; NOAA chart 18526
Season: Year-round
Rating: A

Swan Island has always played an important role in the development of Portland. In the 1850s, when several embryonic towns were competing for the role of the regional center of shipping and commerce, difficulties in crossing the Swan Island sand bar during periods of low water were downplayed by Portlanders, while downstream rivals exaggerated the hazards of crossing the bar.

Swan Island even played a role when the age of air travel began. In the 1920s, Swan Island was selected as the site of a municipal airport, and a causeway was built to the east shore out of dredgings from the west channel, which had the additional benefit of deepening the west channel for ship traffic. The airport was barely completed in time to host a 1927 visit by Charles Lindbergh.

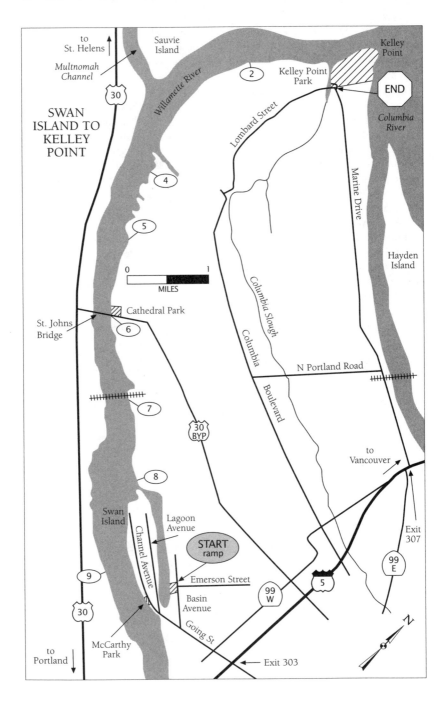

St. Johns Bridge

The trip described here starts at the public boat ramp on the former east channel of the river and paddles 9 miles downstream to the mouth of the Willamette at Kelley Point. The park at Kelley Point, where an extra car should be left, can be reached from Interstate 5, exit 307, by driving west on Marine Drive. A canoe launch is maintained on Columbia Slough, just inside the entrance to the park.

From Kelley Point Park, return to Interstate 5 and drive south to exit 303. Drive west on Going Street, and turn right onto Basin Avenue to the boat ramp near the intersection of Basin Avenue and Emerson Street. If you would rather not paddle in the Swan Island Lagoon, the trip could be started at tiny McCarthy Park in the 4600 block of North Channel Avenue (near the intersection with Anchor Street), where a cement walkway leads down to the water.

On entering the main channel of the Willamette, the first major landmark consists of the huge Port of Portland dry docks on the north end of Swan Island, among the largest on the West Coast. Keep them in mind next time your boat needs repairs.

Speaking of large craft, keep a lookout for large ships (and their wakes) throughout this trip because they will often not see you and your tiny craft.

The University of Portland stands on the bluff just north of the dry docks, and across the river is the port tanker basin, home of several petroleum depots. Only two bridges cross this section of the river, a railroad bridge at rivermile 7 and the St. Johns Bridge at rivermile 6.

The St. Johns Bridge stands as a model of what bridges ought to look like. Built in 1929–1930 at a cost of $4 million, its 1000-foot suspension span was for years the longest and highest (205 feet) of its type. The beautiful gothic towers inspired the naming of a city park under the bridge's east end, Cathedral Park.

The upstream end of Sauvie Island is reached at rivermile 3, where Multnomah Channel (see Trip 53, Multnomah Channel and Scappoose Bay) exits on the left. The Willamette ends its long journey to the Columbia River at Kelley Point Park. The canoe launch is located a short distance up the Columbia Slough (see Trip 50, Lower Columbia Slough), which enters the Willamette on the east side, near a large grain elevator about 0.5 mile south of Kelley Point.

17 Calapooia River

Location: Albany
Distance: 9.5 miles
Time: 4 to 5 hours
Maps: USGS Riverside, Tangent, Lewisburg, and Albany 7.5"
Season: Winter to spring
Rating: A (B–C in summer)

The Calapooia River is a small tributary of the Willamette, originating on the western slopes of the Cascades between the Santiam and the McKenzie Rivers. It joins the Willamette at Albany and was named for a group of Indians that inhabited the region. A relatively narrow and flat river, it is best paddled in winter or spring. As summer approaches, a few riffles and rapids develop.

The trip is started by leaving an extra car in Bryant Park in Albany. From downtown Albany, drive west on Third Avenue, cross the Calapooia River bridge, and turn right into the park. As you cross the bridge, look to see if any rocks or rapids are present under the railroad bridge just downstream. Leave your car at the northeast corner of the park, near the mouth of the Calapooia, where you will find an informal landing.

When leaving the park, turn right and drive west, then south, on Bryant Drive to Riverside Drive. Turn left, then turn right onto Oakville Road. About 4 miles farther, turn left onto Oregon Highway 34. Shortly after crossing the Calapooia, turn right and park next to the bridge. In recent years, concrete barriers have blocked vehicle access to the launching area under the bridge, leaving room for parking only a few cars, and requiring a 150-foot carry to the river.

As the crow flies, your launching point under the bridge is only 5 miles from Albany, but the Calapooia River follows a leisurely, undulating course of almost twice that distance. Even so, the river never seems content with its existing channel. The current may seem slow, but it constantly works on its banks, devouring pastures in directions it wants to travel, while leaving gravel bars in places it has been. Neighboring farmers have fought erosion by depositing old car bodies in a few strategic locations; a course in identifying cars of the '40s and '50s could easily be taught from a canoe on the Calapooia.

As is typical for small rivers in Oregon, the Calapooia is prone to logjams and other obstructions. For example, the section of the Calapooia upstream from this section has had a 7-mile-long logjam for many years. If you paddle this lower section, you may encounter occasional small logjams and strainers. One such logjam was reported in 2005 to be located just below the Oregon Highway 34 bridge; it was barely passable next to the left bank.

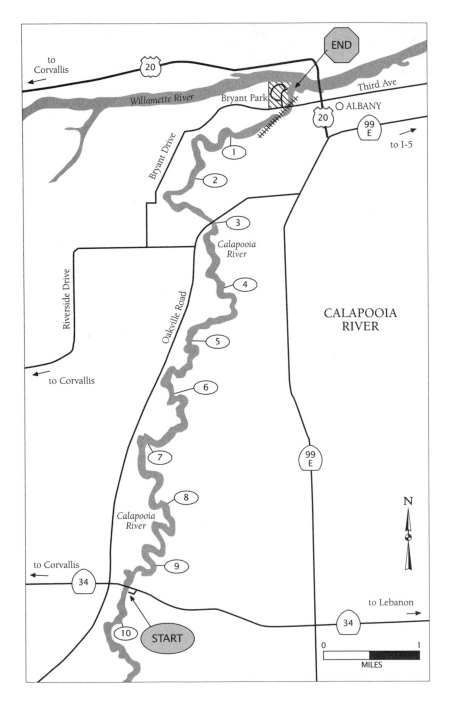

My most memorable experience on the Calapooia began one January day when I sighted two nutria on a muddy bank. (Similar in appearance to a muskrat, but about twice as large, nutria became residents of western Oregon after escaping from financially unsuccessful fur farms.) Upon closer examination, the animals modestly hid in a clump of branches and twigs at the water's edge. In an attempt to prompt them into posing for the camera, I gently applied a canoe paddle to their refuge. The response was immediate. Two furry projectiles, each consisting of not less than fifteen pounds of airborne nutria, exploded from the brush. In the style of a berserk torpedo, the first collided with the side of the canoe well above the waterline. The second landed in shallow water near the bow of the boat with the grace of a depth charge. It has yet to be determined who was more frightened, the two nutria or the two paddlers.

Two railroad bridges and an auto bridge mark the end of the trip at Bryant Park. Under the latter, the man-made Albany-Santiam Canal enters the Calapooia via a sizable waterfall. Watch for rocks or rapids under the second railroad bridge. Your car is about 100 yards downstream on the left, about 200 feet before the confluence with the Willamette River. Stay close to the left bank to find the landing.

18 South Santiam River

Location: East of Albany
Distance: 20 miles
Time: 4 to 5 hours
Maps: USGS Lebanon, Crabtree, and Albany 7.5"
Season: Year-round
Rating: C

Boating on the South Santiam is usually associated with the whitewater sections of the upper river, where kayaks and rafts are essential equipment. The lower part of the river, however, while too tame for most whitewater enthusiasts, provides an excellent canoe trip in fast water. Although the lower river is not considered whitewater, its current is strong, and choppy sections are abundant. You may also encounter a strainer or two. If you are looking for placid waters, this trip is not for you.

Start by leaving an extra car in Jefferson, a tiny town northeast of Albany. It can be reached from Interstate 5 by driving east from exit 238 or 242 (see also the map for Trip 19, Santiam River). Park your car near the public boat ramp in downtown Jefferson at the foot of Ferry Street, at the corner of Ferry and Mill Streets, a block north of the bridge, on the east bank of the river.

Then drive across the bridge and continue west from Jefferson about a mile. Turn left onto Scravel Hill Road, and follow it to US Highway 20. Turn left

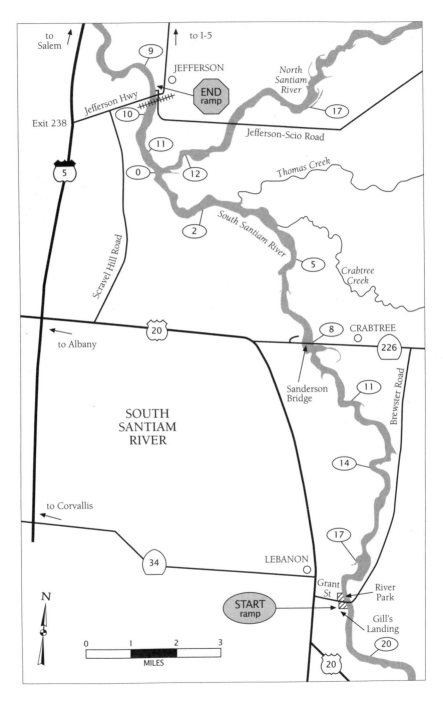

again, and follow US Highway 20 into Lebanon. Turn left onto Grant Street, following the signs to River Park. When you see the park on the left and the bridge over the South Santiam, turn right at a sign marking Gill's Landing, a large parking lot and a public boat ramp.

The river current is fast. In the first 10 miles, the channel drops almost 100 feet. This section has few landmarks other than islands and river bends; you probably will not be sure of your exact location until you reach Sanderson Bridge at Crabtree. If you are accustomed to paddling on slower water, you will be amazed when you realize that you have just paddled 10 miles in much less than two hours.

Winter is a good time to enjoy this river, if you dress properly and are lucky with the weather. Spring and late fall are also good, but in summer and early fall you have to be careful to avoid shallow sections.

The second 10 miles of this trip, from Sanderson Bridge to Jefferson, is similar to the first section, but a bit slower and smoother. Along the way, Crabtree Creek and Thomas Creek enter from the east, but they are both small and you may miss them. The North Santiam, however, is hard to miss when it enters from the same direction. This junction is considered to be rivermile 0 of the South Santiam, but it is rivermile 11.75 of the North Santiam and the main branch Santiam River.

Just 2 miles downstream are the two railroad and highway bridges at Jefferson. The boat ramp is on the right bank, a few hundred feet past the bridges. If the current is strong, stay close to the right bank to make your landing.

19 Santiam River

Location: Northeast of Albany
Distance: 11 miles
Time: 4 to 5 hours
Maps: USGS Albany, Sidney, Monmouth, and Lewisburg 7.5"
Season: Year-round
Rating: B

The Santiam River is not a typical Willamette River tributary. Unlike the motionless waters of the Luckiamute, the Yamhill, or the Pudding, the Santiam River is nearly as big and as wide as the Willamette itself. This trip starts near the confluence of the North Santiam and the South Santiam Rivers and travels down the main branch Santiam River to the Willamette. An exploration of the quiet Luckiamute is an optional side trip.

Begin the trip by leaving an extra car or bicycle at the Buena Vista Ferry. The ferry is reached from Interstate 5 via Talbot Road, exit 242. Drive west through the small town of Talbot to the ferry landing a few miles beyond. Take the ferry to Buena Vista Park, with its boat ramp and floating dock, on the west

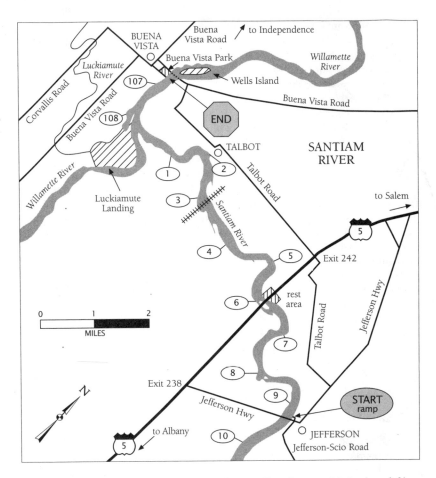

bank. (The ferry does not run on Mondays or Tuesdays, and it is closed from November through March.) Boat launching is not allowed on the east bank.

Then drive east, back over the freeway, to the town of Jefferson. When you reach Jefferson, stay on the main street as it curves toward the river. But do not rush through Jefferson without at least looking around a little; some of the advantages of a town that has been bypassed by the freeway are obvious in Jefferson. A slow, small-town pace of life and more than a few architectural gems are just two of the benefits. Just before the bridge, turn right. At the foot of Ferry Street, a block north of the bridge, is a public boat ramp.

The Santiam is wide, with a strong current. The island near rivermile 8 can be passed on either side, but the left channel seems the deepest. Just downstream is a feature aptly named "The Cliff."

Two miles downstream are the huge twin bridges of Interstate 5, where a large rest area on the north bank straddles the freeway. The bridges are new, built in 1995. A boat ramp was located under the old bridges, but it was destroyed in the construction of the new bridges. As of this writing, it has not been replaced. Small boats can still land under the bridges, but the current can be strong. If you feel like stopping, consider landing on the right bank well upstream from the bridges.

An island sits under the south end of the bridges. During the summer, when the water is low, the channel behind the island may be too shallow, even for canoes. In the winter, it may be rough, so the best choice is to stay in the main channel as you pass under the bridges.

The Willamette Valley is home to numerous birds of prey. Watch for red-tailed hawks, kestrels, and the large northern harrier with the telltale white patch on its rump. Ospreys can also be seen scouting the river for fish.

A railroad bridge appears near rivermile 3. Downstream, large cliffs mark the junction of the Willamette from the south and the Luckiamute from the southwest. The Willamette seems smaller than the wide Santiam, and both dwarf the Luckiamute. If you have some extra time, explore the mouth of the Luckiamute. Its quiet waters offer considerable contrast to the two torrents it joins.

From the mouth of the Luckiamute, Buena Vista Park is just 1.5 miles downstream, near the head of Wells Island.

South Santiam River

20 Yamhill River

Location: Near Newberg
Distance: 12 miles
Time: 4 to 5 hours
Maps and chart: USGS Dayton, St. Paul, Dundee, and Newberg 7.5";
NOAA chart 18528
Season: Year-round
Rating: A

It is difficult to believe that large steamboats once cruised the lazy waters of the Yamhill River, but a huge set of locks was built for their use just outside the town of Lafayette. This trip begins at the locks, travels 7 miles down the Yamhill to the Willamette, then goes 5 miles farther on the Willamette to Newberg.

Begin by leaving a car in Newberg, which is southwest of Portland on US Highway 99W. After entering Newberg on US Highway 99W, turn left onto River Street, just past Herbert Hoover Park, then follow River Street to its foot at the Rodgers Landing boat ramp, where you park your shuttle car. A day-use fee is required to use the boat ramp. An older ramp at the downstream end of the park has been closed to vehicles, but it can still be used by paddlers who would like to avoid the trucks and trailers at the upstream end of the park.

Then drive southwest on US Highway 99W toward Lafayette. Look for a left turn marked Yamhill Locks Park, and follow it to the park. If you reach Lafayette, you have driven too far on US Highway 99W. The locks, some 275 feet long, were built between 1897 and 1900, along with a 16-foot dam, to facilitate boat traffic up the Yamhill to McMinnville. Today the dam is gone, but the locks still stand next to the rapids known as Yamhill Falls. In winter and spring, the falls are under several feet of smooth water.

Launch your boat below the falls. Launching at this park is sometimes difficult, depending on the water level. The best launching is just below the old locks, close to the parking lot. (For better launching, and a shorter trip, try using the boat ramp in Dayton, as shown on the sketch map.)

The trip downstream is smooth and lazy. You might see a few anglers with outboards, but not enough to really disturb this tranquil river. At Dayton, the river crosses under Oregon Highway 18 and a footbridge.

The Yamhill has little current to it, so you will be glad when it joins the faster Willamette. From the mouth of the Yamhill, Newberg is 5 miles downstream. Watch for red-tailed hawks and great blue herons. Also watch for the ski boats and jet skis that will not be watching for you.

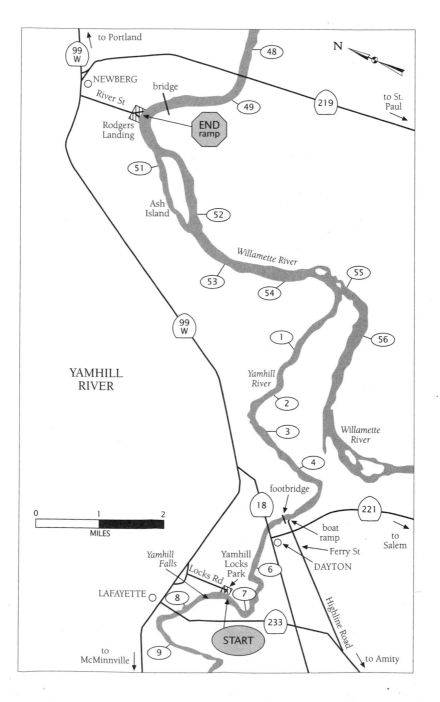

Two miles from Newberg, look for a row of pilings on the left bank, indicating the entrance to the slough behind Ash Island. The slough has less current than the main channel of the river, but also a lot fewer motorboats, so it is a wise choice.

The island is private property (as evidenced by the private ferry used to cross the main channel). The Rodgers Landing boat ramp is just a mile downstream from Ash Island.

A touring kayak at Yamhill Locks Park

21 Pudding River

Location: Aurora–Canby area
Distance: 9 miles
Time: 4 hours
Maps and chart: USGS Yoder, Woodburn, and Canby 7.5"; NOAA chart 18528
Season: Winter to spring
Rating: A

The Pudding River has its origins in the foothills east of Salem, but it flows north to join the Molalla and the Willamette Rivers near Canby. Its name originates from pioneer days when a group of tired and wet settlers prepared elk blood pudding on its banks.

Begin the trip by leaving an extra car near the boat ramp at Molalla River State Park on the south side of the Willamette River, 0.5 mile west of the Canby Ferry.

From the takeout, drive south on Ferry Road and Holly Street to Canby, then turn right onto US Highway 99E and follow it toward Aurora. In Barlow, turn north onto Barlow Road, then west onto Anderson Road. Follow Anderson Road to a railroad bridge near Aurora. Launch under the railroad bridge; limited parking is available on the shoulder of the road. (The south end of Anderson Road is blocked to traffic.)

Unless the river has been doing some major excavation work on its banks, the trip is uneventful. Watch for beaver, muskrat, and birds such as kingfishers and green herons. Slack water pools off to the sides indicate former oxbows abandoned by a river that could not make up its mind. Because of frequent changes in the channel, the rivermiles marked on USGS maps (and the sketch map printed here) are not particularly accurate.

Immediately north of the Arndt Road Bridge (rivermile 4.5), the river demonstrates its indecisiveness. In 1980 it broke through a large oxbow and occupied two separate channels around the resulting island. The right channel was faster and shorter, while the left was more leisurely. In 1981 the property owner built a causeway to his newly created island, and the new causeway even survived the flood of 1996. As a result, the river now occupies its original channel to the west.

From about rivermile 1.5 to the takeout point, the waters flow through Molalla River State Park. Eventually, the muddy waters of the Pudding join the relatively clear waters of the Molalla and 1 mile later reach the Willamette. A major heron rookery is located on the right bank in the cottonwood trees along this mile of the Molalla. In the winter, when the leaves are off the trees, the nests are clearly visible. In the summer, look for the euphemistic "whitewash."

Turn right onto the Willamette, and watch for the small state park boat ramp on the right bank about 0.5 mile downstream. Also keep a careful eye on the powerboats that swarm the area.

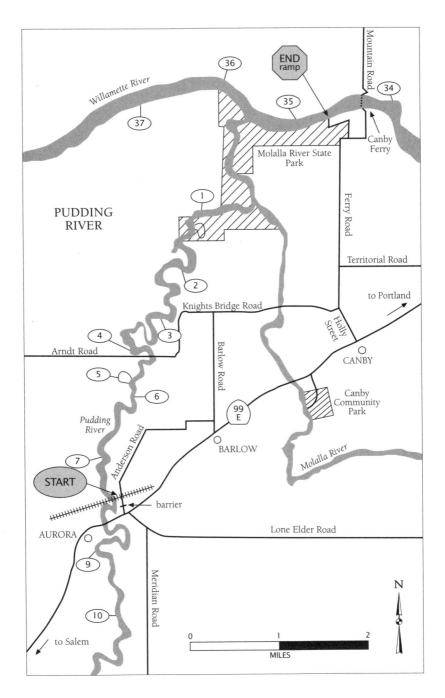

22 Tualatin River— Schamberg Bridge to Lake Oswego

Location: Near Tualatin
Distance: Up to 11 miles
Time: Up to 5 hours
Maps: USGS Beaverton and Lake Oswego 7.5"
Season: Year-round
Rating: A (Warning: Do not paddle below Shipley Bridge)

This trip covers the 11-mile section of the Tualatin River from Schamberg Bridge near Sherwood to Shipley Bridge near Lake Oswego. Although the Willamette River is just 5 miles below Shipley Bridge, those 5 miles include some dangerous sections and should be avoided by ending the trip at Shipley Bridge. (Those last 5 miles involve a portage around a small dam, some shallow rocky stretches during low water, and some rough and dangerous stretches during high water.)

Three other cautions: First, this 11-mile trip might be long and tiring for some paddlers, particularly late in the summer when the water level is low and the current nonexistent. Second, launching at Schamberg Bridge is very difficult, involving a steep descent down a dirt bank. Third, logjams can form on this section of the river, particularly between Schamberg Bridge and US Highway 99W. The solution to all three problems is to launch at one of the many public parks shown on the sketch map (and described below) at rivermiles 11.5, 10.8, 9.8, 8.9, or 7.4, and then paddle down to Shipley Bridge.

Or simply launch at one of the parks, paddle in either direction, and then paddle back to your car, eliminating the need for a car shuttle, particularly in the summer when the Tualatin has little or no current.

To do the entire 11-mile paddle, begin by taking Interstate 205 to exit 3 and following Stafford Road north past Wankers Corner to Shipley Bridge. Just north of the bridge, turn east onto Shadow Wood Drive and follow it 0.25 mile to a small landing. Leave your extra car here.

To reach the starting point from Wankers Corner, drive west on Oregon Highway 212 through Tualatin to US Highway 99W. Turn left and drive 2.7 miles to Six Corners. Turn right there, and drive north on Roy Rogers Road to Schamberg Bridge. Parking space is limited and access is not the best because the trails to the river are very steep and muddy; try launching at the south end of the bridge, close to the river, on either the west or east side of the road. Stay close to the bridge in order to avoid private property.

Watch for occasional rivermile markers, small blue signs indicating the distance to the mouth of the Tualatin at the West Linn community of Willamette.

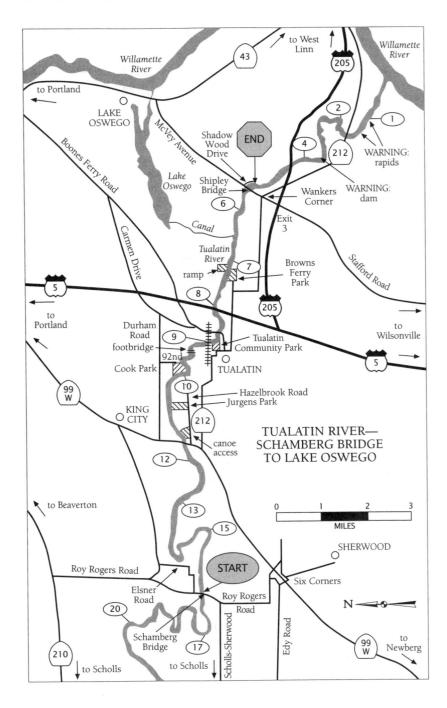

TUALATIN RIVER—
SCHAMBERG BRIDGE
TO LAKE OSWEGO

The markers were placed by the Tualatin Riverkeepers, a local conservation group. At rivermile 11.5, the river passes under US Highway 99W. Taylors Ferry operated at this site for many years, and during the 1920s the crossing was served by a huge covered bridge. On the right bank, just under the US Highway 99W bridges, the City of Tualatin has developed a public canoe access, which can be reached from Hazelbrook Road. Less than a mile later, the river passes Jurgens Park, also on Hazelbrook Road.

The river soon approaches two city parks. Cook Park, a Tigard city park, is located at rivermile 9.8, and Tualatin Community Park is at rivermile 8.9, marked by the second of two railroad bridges. Both parks offer boat ramps and picnic facilities. Beware of a shallow rocky area in late summer near the first railroad bridge at rivermile 9.3. It's not dangerous, but it may require a short portage or a bit of wading.

After passing under Boones Ferry Road and Interstate 5, the river passes Browns Ferry Park, marked by a public dock on the right at rivermile 7.7. This Tualatin city park, built in 1997, features a canoe/kayak dock, restrooms, amphitheater, trails, bike paths, birding blinds, and interpretative kiosks.

Kayaks on the Tualatin River

An obscure public boat ramp can be found on the left bank at rivermile 7.4. It is located in the community of Rivergrove, on Dogwood Drive, between Tualamere and Merlin Streets, across the street from Bryant Woods Park.

At rivermile 6.7, watch for an opening on the left bank, leading to a large dam which regulates the flow of water into a "canal" to Lake Oswego. The canal was hand-dug by Chinese laborers in the 1870s to allow steamboats to bypass the unnavigable lower portion of the Tualatin. Included in the same scheme were plans for locks at the lower end of the lake to allow water traffic from Portland to Hillsboro without interruption. Although the locks were never built, steamboats used the canal for several years. Today, overgrown and unnavigable, the only purpose of the canal is to maintain the water level of Lake Oswego. The modern dam now standing at the head of the canal was built in 1996 after the Tualatin flooded over the top of the old dam, resulting in Lake Oswego overflowing its banks. For safety reasons, stay well away from the dam.

The takeout is on the left bank, just past Shipley Bridge at rivermile 5.3. Don't even consider paddling past the takeout. The dam at rivermile 3.5 is very dangerous, and the stretch of the river below the dam is rocky and rough, with the exception of one short flat section, which is described in Trip 23, Tualatin River—Fields Bridge.

23 Tualatin River—Fields Bridge

Location: West Linn
Distance: 2.5 miles
Time: 1 hour
Maps: USGS Canby 7.5"
Season: Late spring or early summer
Rating: A (Warning: Do not paddle below Fields Bridge)

Most of the lowest portions of the Tualatin River are rocky and rough, in contrast to its flat, meandering course through Washington County. But one section of the lower Tualatin is flatwater paddling. Although this section is short, it offers a pleasant escape from civilization. Try it one day after work for a quick diversion.

To reach the put-in (and the takeout), start in downtown Willamette, just south of West Linn, off Interstate 205 at exit 6 (Tenth Street). Drive west on the main street (Oregon Highway 212, Willamette Falls Drive) 1 mile to Fields Bridge. Just before crossing the bridge, turn right onto Dollar Road, then park on the left shoulder near a dirt road leading down to the river. The launch site is at the foot of the dirt road under Fields Bridge. (An alternate launch site is on Johnson Road, at rivermile 2.6, at the south end of a guardrail.)

Warning: This trip paddles upstream from Fields Bridge, not downstream. Below the bridge are several rapids rated class II or possibly III. Don't paddle below the bridge unless you're capable of handling those rapids.

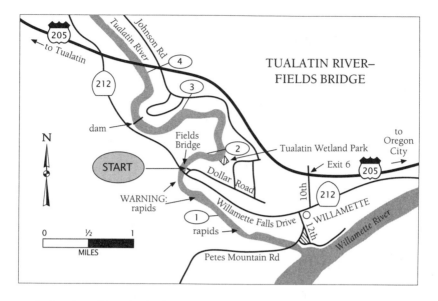

Before launching, look closely at the current and make sure that it is sufficiently gentle that you'll have no trouble paddling upstream against it, or making a landing under the bridge. If in doubt, wait for another day when flow is less.

If conditions are right, launch under the bridge and paddle upstream as far as the water level and current permit. Ideally, you should be able to paddle for a mile, or possibly a mile and a half, nearly to the dam at rivermile 3.4.

Although a few homes are visible from the river, this section has a secluded feel to it, and you can expect to see considerable wildlife. Great blue herons, green herons, kingfishers, osprey, ducks, and nutria are likely to be seen during a paddle lasting an hour or less.

The riverbank is marked with occasional rivermile markers, installed by a local environmental group, the Tualatin Riverkeepers. At rivermile 2.1 is Tualatin Wetland Park, marked by a fishing platform. Near rivermile 2.9, you'll probably encounter your first rapid. Try paddling up through the rapid, but only if your boat-handling skills are up to the task. Above rivermile 3, you'll likely encounter rapids you can't paddle through. Turn around and drift back to Fields Bridge. Along the way, you may notice a small island or two. The channels behind the islands might be navigable, or they might be blocked by logs. Don't try paddling down a blind channel if the current is so strong as to make a U-turn difficult.

As you approach Fields Bridge, stay close to the left bank to make your landing. Don't even think about paddling below the bridge unless your white-water skills are adequate.

24 Lost Lake

Location: Northwest of Mount Hood
Distance: Up to 3 miles
Time: 4 hours
Map: USGS Bull Run Lake 7.5"
Season: Summer through fall
Rating: A

Lost Lake is well known. Chances are, you have been picnicking or camping there before. If not, everyone else has. Its popularity is entirely justified: A small, beautiful lake with a campground, picnic area, and resort, it offers a dramatic close-up view of the north and west faces of Mount Hood.

Lost Lake is the largest lake in the Mount Hood National Forest on which powerboats are prohibited. It is also crystal clear and deep. At 175 feet, it is the deepest lake in the Mount Hood National Forest. (Bull Run Lake, just over the ridge from Lost Lake, is both larger and deeper, but Bull Run Lake is neither in the Mount Hood National Forest nor is it open to public access because it is in the Bull Run Reserve, the source of Portland's water supply. Try not to think how nice the paddling must be.)

The popularity of Lost Lake has not destroyed it, however. The Forest Service has done an excellent job of dealing with the throngs that visit the lake each summer. The campground and most of the resort facilities have been kept away from the shore of the lake, so the view from the water is largely that of a wilderness lake. And the policy of not permitting motorized boats has helped keep the water clear.

To reach Lost Lake, drive east from Portland on Interstate 84 to Hood River. Take the West Hood River exit, exit 62, then turn right and drive toward the town, but turn south onto Thirteenth, which eventually becomes Hood River Highway. At the community of Dee, turn west and follow the signs to Lost Lake, about 90 miles from Portland. (An alternate route is to drive east on US Highway 26 from Portland to Zigzag, then turn north onto the Lolo Pass Road, but this route involves several miles of gravel road.)

The road into Lost Lake is generally open by Memorial Day. To avoid the crowds, visit the lake just before Memorial Day or after Labor Day. Depending on the year, a trip as late as November can be pleasant and peaceful. For current conditions at the lake, call the Mount Hood National Forest at the Hood River Ranger District (see the appendix at the back of this book).

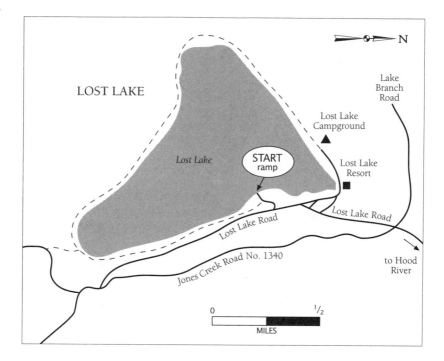

When you reach the lake, drive south past the turnoff to the campground and follow the signs to the boat ramp, which is located on the east side of the lake, about 0.25 mile south of the north end of the lake. Or rent a canoe at the Lost Lake Resort and launch from their dock.

Lost Lake is not large. With a surface area of just 231 acres, and a shoreline of only 2.8 miles, the entire lake can be circled in an hour or two. But take your time, and enjoy the experience. At the west end of the lake is a marshy area; watch for salamanders. You will also notice a well-maintained trail that follows the shoreline of the entire lake.

Of course, don't miss the view, especially the famous view from the northwest side of the lake looking southeast to Mount Hood. Few spots offer such a close-up view of the upper reaches of the peak. For those interested in geographic names, the ridge on Mount Hood running from the summit directly toward Lost Lake is Cathedral Ridge. Immediately to its right are the Sandy Glacier and the steep Sandy Headwall. On the horizon to the right is Illumination Rock. To the left of Cathedral Ridge is the North Face of Mount Hood, and the sharp rock just left of the summit is Cathedral Spire.

25 River Mill Lake

Location: Near Estacada
Distance: Up to 6 miles
Time: Up to 4 hours
Map: USGS Estacada 7.5"
Season: Year-round
Rating: A

Man-made reservoirs, built for purposes of power generation, irrigation, and flood control, usually make for poor paddling. Their banks are often lined with mud, stumps, or dead trees, their water levels fluctuate with flood-control needs, and their large size usually attracts water-skiers and loud powerboats. River Mill Lake (also known as Estacada Lake) is a notable exception, a unique lake that can offer secluded paddling in a beautiful gorge near Estacada.

Named for a sawmill that once stood nearby, River Mill Dam was built on the Clackamas River in 1911, forming a reservoir extending for 3 miles up a deep, narrow gorge. Because the dam is a small one, and because the canyon is so narrow, the lake has practically no storage capacity, but exists solely to provide pressure to operate hydroelectric generators installed at the dam. The lack of storage capacity is demonstrated by the fact that water that flows into

River Mill Lake

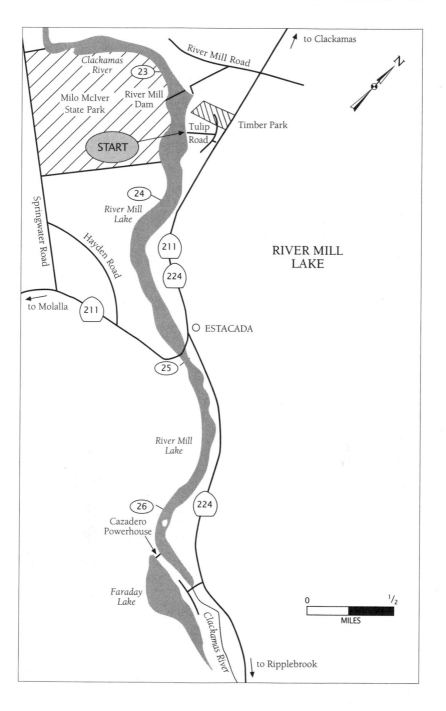

the reservoir from the Clackamas River usually remains in the reservoir for less than a week. Because it serves no storage function, its water level is relatively constant during most of the year. During the winter, the water level fluctuates only a few feet, not enough to hinder paddling.

Paddlers are prime beneficiaries of the building of the dam, although perhaps unintentionally so. The narrow walls of the gorge discourage water-skiers, and the high cliffs shield the lake from nearby civilization. The lake is popular with anglers, however, so the best time to visit the lake is before fishing season opens in late April or after it closes at the end of October. Although powerboats are permitted, the fishers who use them realize that the lake is small and narrow, and they are usually (but not always) courteous to smaller craft.

Access to the lake was once available at a boat ramp adjacent to Timber Park, but that ramp has been closed. At the time this book went to press, the only access was by a trail leading to a small dock in Estacada. However, a public boat ramp is planned to be built on the southwest side of the lake by early 2007, with access through Milo McIver State Park.

To reach the lake, drive southeast on Oregon Highway 224 toward Estacada. About a mile before reaching Estacada, turn right at milepost 22.3 at signs indicating Timber Park. Follow the signs toward the park, but turn left onto Tulip Road just before entering the park. From the foot of Tulip, carry your boat a few feet to the left (south) along a bike path, then turn right and follow a trail to the dock.

The narrow lake does not offer many route options. Follow the lake as it winds its way up the former riverbed. Although the *Atlas of Oregon Lakes* describes the lake as extending only 1.5 miles up to the Oregon Highway 211 bridge, the still waters of the lake do not actually give way to the strong current of the Clackamas River until the Cazadero Powerhouse is reached, 3 miles upstream from the dock.

The Cazadero Powerhouse stands next to the river, not in it, and generates power from man-made Faraday Lake, built on a bench south of the river. The lake is supplied with water from Cazadero Dam, 2 miles upstream.

The lake narrows as you paddle up it, and shallow spots are occasionally encountered. If the water level is down a few feet, a rocky area may be exposed near the upper end of the lake (some maps show it as an island) about 0.25 mile below the powerhouse. A strong current might also be encountered, depending on the water level and upstream discharges. If the water level is high, and the discharges low, the current is not noticeable until the powerhouse itself is reached.

The narrow walls of the canyon provide several small waterfalls, interesting cliffs, and even a few overhangs and small caves, but few areas of level ground. One or two level spots can be found near water level, but some paddlers will end up scrambling up onto the top of one of the rocky outcrops for lunch. Poison oak abounds, however, and lunch sites should be selected with care.

26 Fish Lake

Location: West of Santiam Pass
Distance: Up to 4 miles
Time: 3 hours
Map: USGS Echo Mountain 7.5"
Season: Late spring to early summer
Rating: A

Fish Lake (one of several Fish Lakes in Oregon) is an attractive mountain lake just west of the Cascade crest near Santiam Pass. Its only disadvantage is a short paddling season. The season gets a late start because of the winter snowfall at the lake, which lies at 3200 feet on the west slope of the Cascades. Then the paddling season ends prematurely when the lake dries up to a fraction of its previous size late each summer. So plan your trip early in the summer. For information on current conditions at the lake, call the McKenzie Ranger District of the Willamette National Forest (see the appendix at the back of this book).

The lake is located near the north end of the Clear Lake Cutoff (Oregon Highway 126) about 1.5 miles south of the junction with the South Santiam Highway (US Highway 20), or about 4.5 miles south of Santiam Junction,

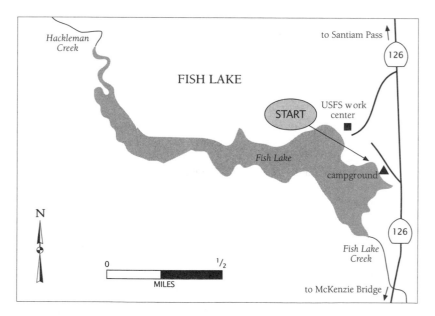

where US Highway 20 and Oregon Highway 22 meet. Launch your boat at the small campground just off Oregon Highway 126. (The buildings just northwest of the campground are a Forest Service work center.)

The lake is small, only about 1.5 miles long. Its shoreline is irregular, so the total length of the shoreline is probably less than 4 miles. As a result, the entire lake can be explored in a couple of hours.

The geologic history of the lake is not difficult to decipher. Fish Lake was formed when lava flows blocked the flow of Hackleman Creek, causing the creek's valley to become flooded. Similar forces created nearby Clear Lake (see Trip 27, Clear Lake). In the case of Fish Lake, however, the porous volcanic soils allow so much water to escape that the reduced summer water flow from Hackleman Creek is insufficient to maintain the water level in the lake, and the lake shrinks to a few small pools by late summer.

The deepest parts of the lake are along the south shore of the upper west end. By late summer, those parts still hold water, while the east end is simply a large meadow. For that reason, the fishing season at Fish Lake ends early (June 1) to give the fish a sporting chance of survival. Because powerboats are not allowed, you will see few other boats on the lake after June 1. But don't wait too long. Depending on snowfall and rainfall, the lake could be gone by late July or early August.

The upper end of the lake is the most interesting to explore. Early in the season, paddlers can venture a considerable distance up Hackleman Creek. Watch for sandpipers along the shore of the creek and along the upper end of the lake. In fact, you will probably hear their distinctive "peet-weet-weet" call long before you see the small birds. Also watch for deer and otters (or perhaps their tracks) along the stream.

27 Clear Lake

Location: West of Santiam Pass
Distance: Up to 3 miles
Time: 3 to 4 hours
Maps: USGS Clear Lake, Santiam Junction, and Echo Mountain 7.5"
Season: Late spring to fall
Rating: A

Clear Lake is aptly named. The headwaters of the McKenzie River, the lake is ultraoligotrophic, or crystal clear, permitting views deep into a subterranean world with an interesting geological and biological history. The lake was formed three thousand years ago during a volcanic eruption of nearby Sand Mountain. During the eruption, lava flows dammed the McKenzie River, forming a 148-acre lake 175 feet deep. Trees standing in the valley were killed by either the volcanic eruption, the flooding of the valley, or both. The trunks of the trees

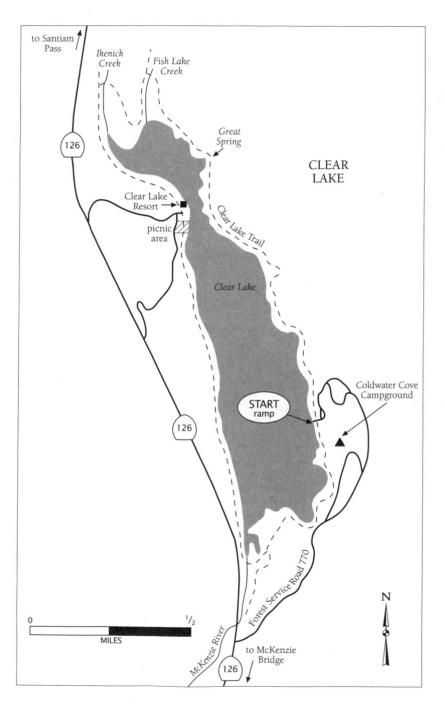

to Santiam Pass

Ikenick Creek

Fish Lake Creek

126

Great Spring

CLEAR LAKE

Clear Lake Resort

Clear Lake Trail

picnic area

Clear Lake

126

START ramp

Coldwater Cove Campground

126

Forest Service Road 770

McKenzie River

to McKenzie Bridge

126

0   ½
MILES

N

Clear Lake

still stand on the bottom of the lake, visible through the same clear water that has preserved them for three millennia. Some of the trunks reach to within a few inches of the lake's surface. Using carbon-14 dating, scientists have been able to estimate that the eruption took place in 1141 BC.

To reach Clear Lake, turn south onto Oregon Highway 126 about 3 miles west of Santiam Junction, or follow Oregon Highway 126 east and north from McKenzie Bridge. Then turn east onto Forest Service Road 770 at a prominent sign pointing to Coldwater Cove Campground. The campground, located on the east shore of the lake, has a boat ramp designed for canoes and other small craft. Small boats may also be launched from the picnic area near the resort on the west side of the lake, or (for a small fee) at the Clear Lake Resort just north of the picnic area. If you plan to camp at the lake, use the campground; there are no campsites elsewhere on the lake.

The lake is leased from the Forest Service by the Santiam Fish and Game Association, a nonprofit group formed to protect the lake and the quality of the fishing there. The group operates the resort on the west side of the lake, complete with a restaurant/store and cabins to rent. No motors are allowed on the lake.

The lake is a popular destination; on most weekends, expect to share the lake with dozens of anglers. But because motors are not allowed, their rowboats are just as unobtrusive as your canoe or kayak. Be considerate, however, and give them and their lines a wide berth.

In addition to the clear water and good fishing for trout, the lake has several interesting features and much wildlife to view. The lake is small enough that the entire 3.2-mile shoreline can be followed in a few short hours, so there is no need to rush. On the east side, the lava flows that formed the lake are still evident, both on shore and extending deep into the clear waters. Look closely, and you will see a trail that follows the shoreline a short distance above the water. In some places, the trail has been paved to facilitate crossing the broken lava. A trail also follows the west shore, completing a 5-mile loop around the lake. Also look for ospreys and their nests atop snags along the east shore.

The north end of the lake is separated from the main portion by a narrow passage, where the lodge of Clear Lake Resort stands on the west shore. The west side of the north end of the lake has several preserved trees just under its surface.

At the northeast corner of the north end, look for a stream entering the lake, then hike 100 yards or so along the stream to find Great Spring (named Big Spring on some maps), one of the major tributaries of the lake. The spring is also aptly named; it is a large pool of ice-cold water. Actually, it is a constant 38 degrees, just warm enough to keep the lake from freezing in the winter. Before visiting early in the season, however, call the McKenzie Ranger District of the Willamette National Forest to determine whether the lake is free of snow.

At the north end of the lake, Fish Lake Creek enters the lake inconspicuously, and at the northwest corner, Ikenick Creek contributes its flow in a pretty area of marshes and woods. (Boats are not allowed on any of the inlets or the lake's outlet.) Near the inlets, keep an eye open for kingfishers and American dippers. Out on the main lake, watch for mallard ducks, common goldeneye, and common mergansers. From the far north end of the lake, look for a long-distance view of the Three Sisters.

One other source of the lake's water cannot be seen from the surface. Deep on the bottom of the lake, underwater springs enter the lake from beneath the tongue of the lava flow.

In contrast to the lava flow that enters the lake on its east side, the western shore is heavily wooded, and offers a cool, shady paddle on a hot summer afternoon. At the southwest corner of the lake, the McKenzie River leaves the lake and passes under a footbridge. Don't venture near the bridge; signs warn that swift water lies ahead. If you would like to view the first few feet of the McKenzie, try landing well to one side of the small bay, then venture inland to find the trail.

28 Scott Lake

Location: West of McKenzie Pass
Distance: Up to 2 miles
Time: 2 to 3 hours
Map: USGS Linton Lake 7.5"
Season: Summer and fall
Rating: A (portages may be required)

The *Atlas of Oregon Lakes* describes the setting of Scott Lake as "one of the most beautiful in the Cascades." You don't need to be an expert on the subject of Oregon lakes to agree; just paddle a short distance on Scott Lake, then look south to take in a breathtakingly close view of 10,000-foot North Sister, Middle Sister, and South Sister. You will not have any powerboats to disturb the scene because motors are prohibited.

Scott Lake sits in a flat, wooded valley at 4800 feet, just off the McKenzie Pass Highway (Oregon Highway 242), about 6 miles southeast of the pass. Scott Lake is almost a miniature version of Sparks Lake (see Trip 30, Sparks Lake). Both are clear, shallow, high mountain lakes with beautiful views and circuitous shorelines that divide the lakes into three distinct pools. Scott Lake is best visited early in the summer, as soon as the snow is gone, for two reasons. First, the passages between the three pools are narrow and so shallow (especially the first passage) that they may require short portages after midsummer, depending on the year. Second, the combination of a shallow lake and a flat valley means large marshy areas, which mean a lot of bugs in July and August. Also keep in mind that the McKenzie Pass Highway is closed each winter, usually reopening in late June or early July, depending on the snowpack. For current conditions at the lake, call the McKenzie Ranger District of the Willamette National Forest (see the appendix at the back of this book).

To reach the lake, turn north from the highway onto Forest Service Road 260 and follow it about 1 mile to the lake. Either launch where the road first skirts the south end of the lake, or follow the road west for another 0.25 mile and launch from the USFS Scott Lake Campground at the west side of the southern end of the lake.

The shoreline of Scott Lake may be marshy, but the water is clear, exposing a bottom of white pumice sand, which in turn exposes thousands of polliwogs in summer, which in turn become frogs in autumn. Most of the time, you can see the bottom as you paddle. The only deep spots are on the east side of the south pool and the east side of the middle pool; those spots exceed 15 feet in depth, while the rest of the lake rarely exceeds 5 feet.

Despite its three pools, the lake is small; its 1.8-mile shoreline could easily be explored in an hour or two. But the lake and its setting are so beautiful

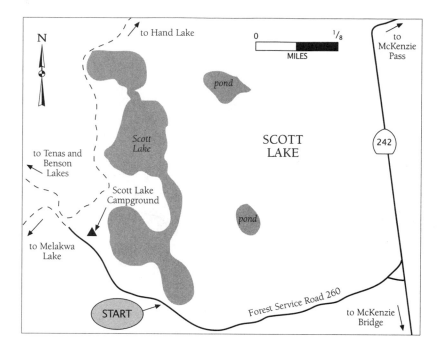

there is no point in hurrying. Consider spending the night at the small Scott Lake Campground, or paddle your gear to other boat-in (or hike-in) campsites (complete with picnic tables) on the southwest shore of the second pool. After exploring the lake, try hiking to nearby Hand Lake, Benson Lake, Melakwa Lake, or Tenas Lake. Or hike to the top of 6116-foot Scott Mountain, which rises to the north above the lake.

29 Three Creek Lake

Location: South of Sisters
Distance: Up to 2 miles
Time: 2 hours
Maps: USGS Broken Top and Tumalo Falls 7.5"
Season: Late spring to fall
Rating: A

Three Creek Lake is a small, clear lake in a dramatic alpine setting in the central Oregon Cascades south of the town of Sisters. The lake lies just below 9175-foot Broken Top and 7700-foot Tam McArthur Rim. If you are vacationing

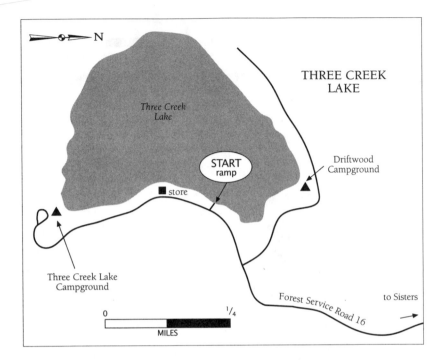

in the Sisters or Black Butte area, Three Creek Lake makes a fine day trip, or you may want to spend a night or two at one of the two Forest Service campgrounds on the lakeshore. At an elevation of 6550 feet, the lake is usually free of snow in June. Although the lake is a natural one, a dam constructed at its north end helps maintain the water level. For information on current conditions, contact the Sisters Ranger District of the Deschutes National Forest (see the appendix at the back of this book).

To reach Three Creek Lake from downtown Sisters, turn south onto Elm Street, which quickly becomes Forest Service Road 16. The paved road climbs gradually. After about 15 miles, the pavement ends. About 1 mile later, don't bear left onto Forest Service Road 370, but stay on Forest Service Road 16 for another mile to reach the lake. A boat ramp is located on this main road, on the east side of the lake just north of a small store that rents boats. Powerboats are not permitted on the lake.

The lake is only seventy-six acres in area, and only 1.5 miles in circumference, so only an hour or two are required to circle the lake and take in the sights. But there is no reason to hurry; the scenery is superb and wildlife is abundant. Watch for osprey overhead and Clark's nutcrackers in the trees and on the plentiful driftwood. At the south end, watch for spotted sandpipers on a sandy shoreline.

The southern skyline is dominated by Tam McArthur Rim, a 7700-foot glacier-carved cliff that blocks any view of Broken Top from the lake. The rim was named for Lewis A. McArthur, prominent Oregon historian and author of the definitive *Oregon Geographic Names.*

Three Creek Lake

30 Sparks Lake

Location: Cascades Lakes Highway
Distance: Up to 10 miles
Time: Up to 6 hours
Map: USGS Broken Top 7.5"
Season: Late spring to fall
Rating: A

Sparks Lake is simply one of the best paddling lakes in Oregon. Situated at the feet of South Sister, Broken Top, and Mount Bachelor, the scenic vistas are grand. The lake offers swampy marshes, open waters, and secluded nooks and crannies. Although the lake is just over 2 miles from end to end, its convoluted shoreline is more than 10 miles long.

To reach Sparks Lake, drive west from Bend on the Cascade Lakes Highway. A few miles after passing the Mount Bachelor ski area, watch for a sign on the left, then follow a gravel road (Forest Service Road 400) south to a fork. The right fork leads to a campground on Soda Creek, while the left fork leads about 2 miles to a boat ramp on the lake. Because this parking lot is also a trailhead, buy a Northwest Forest Pass before driving to the lake.

Sparks Lake and South Sister

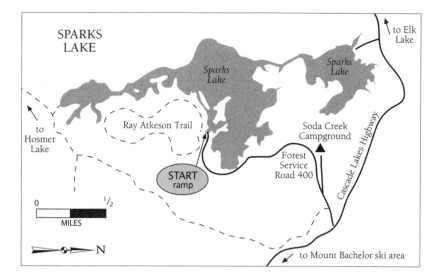

Motorboats are permitted on Sparks Lake, but few show up, partly because the speed limit is 10 miles per hour. Early in the season, call the Bend Ranger District of the Deschutes National Forest (see the appendix at the back of this book) to find out how much snow remains at the lake.

Sparks Lake is really three lakes in one. The boat ramp is located on the large central portion of the lake. Despite the size of the lake, the average depth in the central portion is only 2 feet. The shallow water has one distinct advantage: the lake quickly loses its winter chill, and the water temperature is tolerable for swimming, even early in the summer.

To the south is the best part of Sparks Lake, where the lake twists and meanders among volcanic outcroppings, creating a maze of opportunities to explore. This southern portion is also shallow, although one spot has been measured at the staggering depth of 7 feet. From the southeast corner of the lake, a trail leads to Hosmer Lake, 3 miles to the southwest (see Trip 31, Hosmer Lake).

The third portion of the lake lies to the north. It can be reached in one of two ways. Early in the season, the water level is usually deep enough to permit paddling up a channel from the northwest corner of the central lake to the northern lake. The second choice is to drive down a short primitive road from the Cascades Lakes Highway to a campsite and a hand launch at the northwest corner of the northern portion of the lake. The northern portion is similar to the central portion, but a bit marshier around its edges. In fact, the northern portion shrinks considerably late in the season.

Although the entire lake could be explored in a single day, the presence of several nice campsites and three different parts of the lake to explore makes Sparks Lake ideal for an overnight trip. Either car camp at the Soda Creek Campground (or one of the primitive sites along the road to the boat ramp), or

paddle to a campsite on the south part of the lake. Then spend two days exploring the lake, fishing, hiking to Hosmer Lake, watching wildlife, or enjoying the
three-mountain view. As always, practice minimum-impact camping, and leave
no evidence of your passing through one of the prettiest areas in the state.

And while you are there, hike the loop trail near the boat ramp. The
2.3-mile trail is dedicated to the memory of Ray Atkeson, the well-known
photographer of Oregon landscapes, who often photographed the beauty of
Sparks Lake.

31 Hosmer Lake

Location: Cascades Lakes Highway
Distance: Up to 5 miles
Time: Up to 5 hours
Map: USGS Elk Lake 7.5"
Season: Late spring to fall
Rating: A

Hosmer Lake is a special place. Lying at nearly 5000 feet near the Cascades Lake
Highway west of Bend, Hosmer Lake has it all: clear water, narrow channels, open
water, acres of lily pads and rushes, a contorted shape, outcrops of volcanic rock,
abundant wildlife, huge fish visible from your boat, and grand mountain views.

Fortunately, Hosmer Lake has been treated as the special place that it is. As
a high mountain lake, Hosmer originally had no fish in it. In the 1950s, a large
population of introduced carp and other "trash" fish was eliminated, and the
lake was stocked with Atlantic salmon and brook trout. Today, Hosmer is the

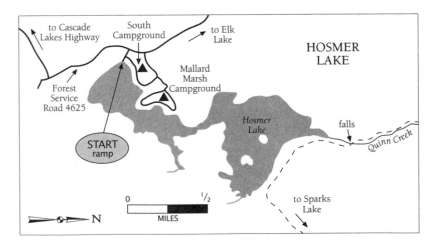

Hosmer Lake

only lake west of the Mississippi where Atlantic salmon have been successfully stocked, although the Oregon Department of Fish and Wildlife helps out each fall by removing eggs and sperm from several inhabitants of Hosmer Lake. The eggs are fertilized, then hatched and raised at Wizard Falls Fish Hatchery near Camp Sherman, to be returned a year and a half later, when they stand a lesser chance of being eaten by predators.

To protect the fish from humans, only fly-fishing with barbless hooks is permitted, and any salmon caught must be released to be caught again another day. (Brook trout may be kept, but check the current regulations to make sure.) In addition, no gasoline motors are allowed on the lake. Electric motors are allowed, but the speed limit is 10 miles per hour.

As a result, a paddler visiting Hosmer Lake encounters canoeists, kayakers, and a few small boats with silent electric motors, but no loud powerboats and their disturbing wakes. Most boats carry fly fishers, and many other fly fishers use flippers to paddle inner-tube-type devices.

The lake can generally be divided into two pools separated by extensive marshes. The southern pool is small, but it is the deepest part of the lake (12 feet at the deepest spot). The northern pool is shallow (3 feet or less in most places), but it is also large and exposed to the winds that tend to come up on summer afternoons. The lake is usually free of snow by mid-May each year; for information on current conditions at the lake, call the Bend Ranger District of the Deschutes National Forest (see the appendix at the back of this book). A Northwest Forest Pass is needed to park at Hosmer Lake.

To reach Hosmer Lake, drive west from Bend on the Cascade Lakes Highway. Hosmer Lake lies just east of Elk Lake. The easiest access is reached by turning east onto Forest Service Road 4625 south of Elk Lake, rather than turning east where Forest Service Road 4625 joins the main highway north of Elk Lake. Because of marshes that line the shore of the lake, only two access points are available for launching boats. The primary access is at a boat ramp on the west side of the southern pool of the lake. Just north of the ramp is South Campground, and a short distance farther north is Mallard Marsh Campground (the campgrounds do not offer any drinking water), where canoes can be launched by following a short trail between campsites 14 and 15. The trail leads to a small landing that provides access to a narrow channel through the marshes to the main channel between the two pools of the lake. (Don't confuse this trail with one leaving just past campsite 15, which is a loop trail to the north.)

As you paddle, watch the shallow bottom of the lake, and you will spot the reason for the lake's popularity with anglers. The fish you see drifting along the bottom can only be described as big and fat.

The fish are not all there is to look at. Bring your binoculars; birds are everywhere. Among the bulrushes, look for red-winged blackbirds, yellow-headed blackbirds, and Brewer's blackbirds. And those are just the blackbirds. Among the pondweed and water lily, look for American coots, pied-billed grebes, Barrow's goldeneye, ring-necked ducks, and northern shovelers. Along the shoreline, watch for sora and American bittern, both well camouflaged. And in the sky overhead, watch for soaring bald eagles and diving osprey.

Also watch for furry critters; both beavers and river otters can be found swimming in Hosmer Lake. Beavers are generally nocturnal, but they can be seen near dusk, and their lodges and the trees they have felled can be seen anytime. Otters are crepuscular (they are active from early morning until midmorning, and then again in the evening). In rock piles, look for pika, small gray rabbitlike animals with round ears, no tails, and a distinctive "eenk" call.

But also keep an eye on where you are going. The shoreline of the lake is circuitous, although much of the time you will have no idea where the shoreline is, because it is heavily concealed by marshes of bulrushes and sedges. The simplest technique is to work your way north from the boat ramp at the south end of the lake. You will find that the passages through the marshes are even more circuitous than the lake itself.

Although Hosmer Lake is only about 1.5 miles long, its contorted shape results in a 5-mile shoreline. A full day can easily be spent exploring every corner of this fascinating lake. From the northwest corner of the northern pool, follow a passage that leads to Quinn Creek at the northeast corner of the lake. In most years, you can paddle up the creek to within strolling distance of Quinn Creek Falls. Watch for a landing on the east bank giving access to a trail that follows the stream north to the falls and a footbridge. Or follow the trail south and then northeast to Sparks Lake (see Trip 30, Sparks Lake), 3 miles away by foot.

Or paddle up the narrow east arm, located about midway between the two main pools. That arm will seem familiar if you have paddled up similar inlets on nearby Sparks Lake. At the end of the arm, a small rock dam serves to maintain the water level of the lake. The stream that flows through the dam, however, disappears into the volcanic ground less than 100 yards later.

Campfires are not allowed anywhere around Hosmer Lake except in South Campground and Mallard Marsh Campground. The Forest Service also requests that parties not camp on either of the islands in the northern pool of the lake; the islands are tiny, damp, and fragile. The northern island in particular has been badly trampled due to overuse by insensitive visitors. Visit the islands for lunch if you must, but don't camp there.

32 Deschutes River—Wickiup to Wyeth

Location: Near La Pine, south of Bend
Distance: 9 miles
Time: 3 hours
Maps: Wickiup Dam and La Pine 7.5"
Season: Late spring through early fall
Rating: B (Warning: Do not paddle past Wyeth)

The Deschutes River begins at Little Lava Lake as a high mountain stream that follows the Cascade Lakes Highway. It eventually becomes a major whitewater river as it flows north to the Columbia. Along the way, it is interrupted by several dams. This trip begins at a dam near La Pine. Although the

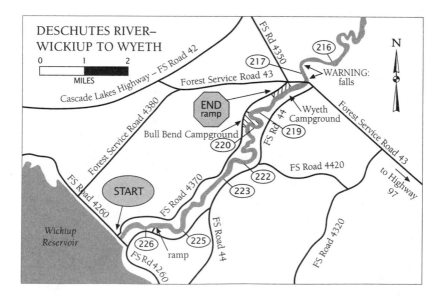

river cascades over several falls before reaching Bend, this 10-mile trip is flat, fast, and clear.

The water level of this section of the Deschutes is reasonably constant from late spring through early fall. At other times, the flow from Wickiup dam may decrease abruptly. Call the Bend office of the Oregon Department of Water Resources at (541) 388-6669 for current information.

Start this trip by leaving an extra car at Wyeth Campground. To reach the campground, drive south on Highway 97 from Bend about 26 miles to Wickiup Junction, about 2 miles north of La Pine. Turn west onto Burgess Road, which becomes Forest Service Road 43. Follow it about 8 miles to Wyeth Campground. Leave an extra car near the boat ramp, then continue west on Road 43 to gravel Forest Service Road 4380 and a sign pointing to Wickiup Dam. Turn left (south) and follow Road 4380 for 3.5 miles to the dam. Then turn left and drive along the dam for slightly more than a mile to a left turn just before the outlet of the reservoir. Turn left, drive about 100 yards, park near a gate, and carry your boat a few hundred yards down to the spillway. (To avoid the portage, continue east on the dam past the outlet, then turn left and drive about 0.7 miles to the Tenino Boat Launch, a USFS day-use area.)

Below the dam, the river flows swiftly through the Ponderosa pine forest. The water is cold and clear, but no rapids are encountered. Fishers will be abundant, usually in drift boats anchored in the river. A few other paddlers will be present, usually in canoes. Overhead, osprey will be abundant.

Deschutes River

Don't let the flat nature of the river fool you. A capsize in the cold, swift current is always possible. Wear your life jacket and watch carefully for strainers, which are common on this section of the river.

Most of the banks along this section are Forest Service land, and lunch spots are easy to find. Some of the land is private, particularly between rivermile 224 and 225, where a cluster of homes have been built.

Bull Bend Campground is reached at rivermile 220. The campground is located on an oxbow; the campground's boat ramp is passed about a half-mile later.

The Wyeth boat ramp is located on the left at rivermile 217.75. As you approach the campground, stay close to the left bank to land at the ramp. Do not under any circumstances paddle past Wyeth Campground; Pringle Falls, a class 4 rapids, lies just beyond the campground.

33 Little Deschutes River

Location: Near La Pine, south of Bend
Distance: 8.25 miles
Time: 4 hours
Map: USGS Anns Butte 7.5"
Season: Spring through fall
Rating: A (possible small logjams)

The Little Deschutes is a gentle, heavily meandered river that joins the main Deschutes River near Sunriver, south of Bend. Nearly 100 miles long, it begins far to the south in Klamath County.

The section described here begins and ends at points only 4.5 miles apart as the crow flies, but the river is 8.25 miles long between those points due to the countless meanders and oxbows. Even if you carry a compass, you will have a hard time determining where you are on the river. A GPS would work, but life is too short; sit back and enjoy the ride.

Start this trip by leaving an extra car or bicycle near the bridge on South Century Drive (Forest Serve Road 42). To reach the bridge from the main entrance to Sunriver, drive west on Spring River Road 0.7 miles, then turn south onto South Century Drive for 3 miles and turn right, following South Century Drive. Continue for another 0.3 miles to the bridge. Parking at the bridge is nearly nonexistent; leave your extra car at a pullout about 0.2 miles east of the bridge.

Then return to the intersection 0.3 miles east of the bridge and turn south onto Huntington Road. Follow it 4 miles to State Recreation Road and turn right. Continue for another 0.9 miles and turn left to an informal boat ramp just before a bridge. Launch here.

The river is shallow, but the water is clear and the current is gentle and steady. You might pass a few travelers in inner tubes or inflatable boats. You

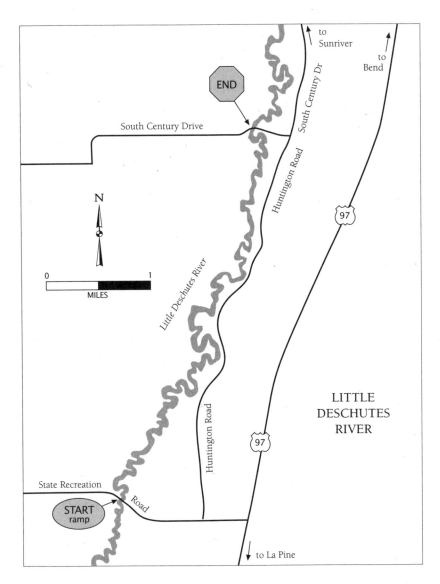

might even see a few kayaks and canoes. If you paddle steadily, you'll complete the trip in about three hours. Because the river is narrow, one or two small logjams might be encountered along the way.

The current is gentle enough that paddling upstream is not difficult. In fact, paddlers wishing to avoid using a car shuttle could launch at State Park Road or at South Century Drive and paddle upstream for as long as time permits, then paddle back downstream to their car.

34 Waldo Lake

Location: Near Willamette Pass, southeast of Eugene
Distance: 2 to 21 miles
Time: 2 hours to several days
Maps: USGS Waldo Lake and Waldo Mountain 7.5"
Season: Mid-June to early fall
Rating: A

In the study of lakes and reservoirs, hydrologists, limnologists, and biologists have developed a classification system, known as the trophic system, to describe the biological productivity of various bodies of water. Those waters that contain a high level of nutrients, and thus support a complex and productive food chain, are described as eutrophic, while relatively sterile waters are described as oligotrophic. A murky swamp, for example, would be classified as eutrophic, while a clear mountain lake would be oligotrophic, and a particularly pristine lake would be classified as ultraoligotrophic. Simply put, Waldo Lake is one of the most ultraoligotrophic lakes in the world. According to the *Atlas of Oregon Lakes*, it is "dramatically ultraoligotrophic." According to one limnologist studying the lake, its water is more chemically pure than distilled water.

It also may be the best paddling place in Oregon. A huge, high mountain lake in a near-wilderness setting, Waldo Lake is unique. One of the largest, highest, deepest, and clearest lakes in the Northwest, Waldo Lake has no significant inlet streams. Instead, it is fed by precipitation and by underground springs whose naturally filtered water results in a crystal-clear, nearly sterile lake. Due to the small volume of water that enters the lake each year, water is retained for an average of thirty-two years before it flows through the lake's outlet. Due to the lack of nutrients, the lake supports few fish, and only two species of plants (both mosses) can be found on the lake's floor.

Like most mountain lakes, Waldo Lake has no native fish population. The State of Oregon once regularly planted trout in the lake, but most of the fish perished due to lack of nutrients. Between 1938 and 1990, roughly 20 million fish were planted in Waldo Lake by the Oregon Department of Fish and Wildlife. The number that survived is indicated by surveys of anglers. In 1969, for example, a survey of thirty-two anglers recorded a total catch of three fish. In the mid-1960s, 600,000 freshwater shrimp were introduced in an attempt to provide a food supply for the planted fish. The shrimp didn't fare any better than the fish. In fact, the planted fish and shrimp have seriously damaged the zooplankton and amphibian populations of the lake. Although fish plantings ended in 1991, scientists are now wondering, after fifty years of failing to create a sustainable fish population, whether a lake as sterile as Waldo should ever have been the target of fish plantings and other

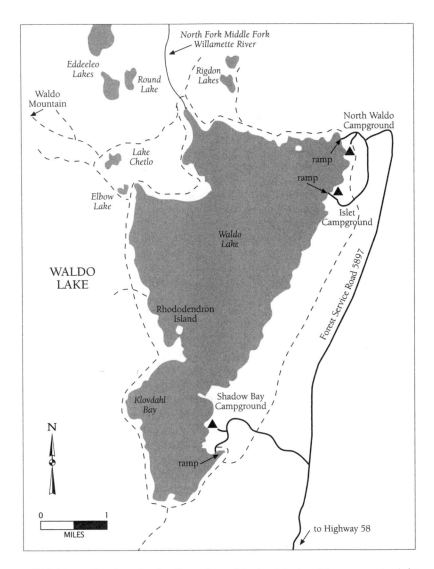

artificial introductions in the first place. Maybe Mother Nature got it right the first time.

In many ways, Waldo Lake is similar to its remarkable neighbor to the south, Crater Lake. Both are large, high mountain lakes that lack inlet streams, and both are extremely deep. Although Waldo Lake does not approach the depth of Crater Lake, no other lake in Oregon exceeds Waldo's 420-foot depth.

But even Crater Lake is not as ultraoligotrophic as Waldo Lake. In 1969, a Secchi disk, an 8-inch white metal disk used to measure water clarity, was lowered into Crater Lake. It was still visible from the surface at a depth of 144 feet, then a world record. The record stood until claimed by Waldo Lake, with a Secchi reading of 157 feet.

The clear, deep waters of Waldo Lake can produce unusual sights. On a sunny day, a boat's shadow can often be seen gliding along the floor of the lake, dozens of feet below. The same eerie effect has been reported on calm, moonlit nights.

Fortunately, the remote beauty of Waldo Lake has been carefully preserved. Although the U.S. Forest Service has built three large campgrounds and three modern boat ramps on the east side of the lake, they have been kept out of sight from the main body of the lake. The paucity of fish discourages anglers, and a 10-mile-per-hour speed limit prevents waterskiing. So with the exception of a few persistent fishers and a handful of small sailboats, paddlers generally have the lake to themselves.

And what a lake it is. Twenty-one miles of shoreline, a surface area of nearly ten square miles, dozens of miles of hiking trails leading to countless nearby peaks and lakes, and grand vistas of the central Cascades from the 5400-foot-high surface of Waldo Lake make paddling as pleasant as can be.

To reach Waldo Lake, drive southeast from Eugene on Oregon Highway 58. About 18 miles southeast of Oakridge, turn north and drive 12 miles on paved Forest Service Road 5897. Of the three campgrounds and boat ramps, one (Shadow Bay) is located near the south end of the lake, and two (Islet and North Waldo) are near the north end. A Northwest Forest Pass is required when parking at the boat ramps.

Although a day trip on Waldo Lake is certainly worthwhile, a longer trip is ideal. The lake is roughly 6 miles long and 2.5 miles wide, and much of it can be explored in a day. The irregular shoreline is 21 miles long, however, so two or three days could easily be devoted to its exploration. One of the camp-grounds could be used as a base of operations, but the best way to explore the lake is to plan an overnight tour; camping is permitted at several primitive sites along the shore. In order to protect portions of the shoreline that are in danger of overuse, however, camping is no longer permitted on the north shore or on any of the islands, including Rhododendron Island.

When camping on Waldo Lake, take care to protect this amazing lake from any sign of your passing. Camp only at previously used campsites. Put abso-lutely no food, soap, or other contaminants in the water. Instead, wash pots and pans 200 feet from the water's edge. Bury human waste at least 200 feet from all water sources, and pack all litter out. Leave your pets at home. And carry a small backpack stove rather than building a fire.

Although the water of Waldo Lake is very clean, it should be treated before drinking, just in case. Most paddlers carry their own drinking water.

The lake is generally calm, but a moderate-to-gentle southwest wind usually blows each afternoon. Plan to travel south in the mornings and north in the afternoons, and do not make any open crossings if strong winds are blowing. When the wind does blow, a kite or sail speeds downwind travel.

In July and early August, Waldo Lake is host to a sizable mosquito population. Carry mosquito repellent and a screened tent, and camp on breezy points rather than protected bays.

When touring the lake, several features are particularly interesting. At the northwest corner of the lake, a narrow bay feeds the headwaters of the North Fork of the Middle Fork of the Willamette River. On the west shore of the lake, just north of a prominent point, is an island covered by rhododendrons.

Just south of Rhododendron Island, on the west side of the lake, lies Klovdahl Bay, named for Simon Klovdahl, an engineer who, starting in 1905, dug a 500-foot tunnel west from the shore of Waldo Lake toward Nettie Creek and the canyon of Black Creek. The project, which was underwritten by the Waldo Lake Power and Irrigation Company, required the building of a road into the east side of the lake and the barging of heavy equipment across the lake to Klovdahl Bay. In 1915, the federal government revoked the company's permit to withdraw water when it became apparent that the amount to be withdrawn would exceed the amount supplied by the rainfall, snowmelt, and springs that feed the lake. Although the name of the company implies that the water would have been used for power generation and irrigation, the exact purpose of the project is no longer known. Nevertheless, the tunnel still exists, marked by a large concrete structure on Klovdahl Bay. The structure has a history of springing leaks and required major repairs in 1929, in the late 1940s, and in the late 1980s. The Forest Service hopes the latest repairs will permanently seal the tunnel, ending a long and curious chapter in the history of unusual Waldo Lake.

Exploring Klovdahl Bay at Waldo Lake

35 Dalton Point to Corbett Station

Location: Western Columbia Gorge
Distance: 7 miles
Time: 4 hours
Maps and chart: USGS Bridal Veil and Washougal 7.5"; NOAA chart 18531
Season: Year-round
Rating: B

Paddling in the Columbia Gorge is more like ocean kayaking than river paddling. The waters are open, windy, tidal, often rough, and often populated by large commercial craft, particularly tugs and barges. As a result, they are more suited to sea kayaking than paddling an open canoe. And they are more suited to experienced paddlers than novices.

The paddle from Dalton Point to Corbett Station offers an excellent sampling of the western gorge. Paddlers see extensive basalt cliffs (some at a distance and others up close), a rocky island, Rooster Rock, and Crown Point.

Begin this trip by checking the tides and the weather. If the weather is windy, or might otherwise turn bad, consider another trip. But if conditions are good, leave an extra car at the Corbett Station boat ramp, immediately northeast of the Corbett exit, exit 22, on Interstate 84, 22 miles east of Portland. This boat ramp was closed and gated in 1999 by the Oregon Department of Transportation, but paddlers may still land here. Park at the gate, which is a couple hundred yards from the water.

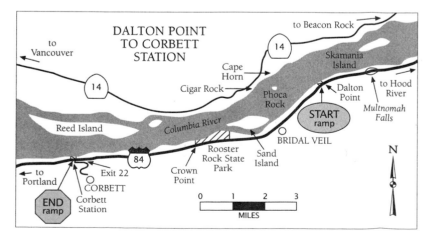

129

Cape Horn

Then proceed to the put-in at Dalton Point. Access to Dalton Point is from the westbound lanes only of Interstate 84; to reach Dalton Point from Corbett, drive east 9 miles to Multnomah Falls, then return 2 miles in the westbound lanes to Dalton Point at milepost 29, 7 miles east of Corbett. Launch your boat at the Dalton Point boat ramp.

The paddle down to Corbett offers a variety of interesting geologic features along the way. For example, paddlers might start the trip by crossing the Columbia to the Washington side to visit the basalt cliffs known as Cape Horn, along the way passing Phoca Rock, a tiny rock island in the middle of the river. The cliffs at Cape Horn rise directly out of the river, with occasional small caves at their base. Watch for aptly named Cigar Rock, famous from C. E. Watkins' photographs of the late 1800s.

A return to the Oregon shore takes you past Sand Island. In late summer, when water levels are low, the channel behind Sand Island is dry at its western end.

The route then passes Crown Point and Rooster Rock. Rooster Rock and Phoca Rock have one thing in common: each started life much higher on the cliffs and were deposited in or near the river by massive landslides thousands of years ago.

Wherever you paddle in this section of the Gorge, watch carefully for tugs, barges, and other commercial craft. As you paddle downstream to Corbett, the shipping lanes pass close to Cape Horn, then shift over to near the Oregon shore in the vicinity of Rooster Rock. Maintain a constant lookout because the tugs and barges can sneak up on an unwary paddler. Even if you are paddling among anchored fishermen, be wary: the anglers are adept at suddenly untying from their anchors and scurrying away when a barge approaches, leaving you alone in the middle of a shipping lane about to be used by a large barge.

And don't expect the tug captain to see your tiny kayak. Even if he did see you, it would be too late to maneuver his massive cargo. Get well out of the way as soon as you see a barge approaching.

36 Beacon Rock

Location: Western Columbia Gorge
Distance: Up to 6 miles
Time: 2 to 4 hours
Maps and chart: USGS Beacon Rock, Multnomah Falls, Tanner Butte, and Bonneville Dam 7.5"; NOAA chart 18531
Season: Year-round
Rating: B

The area around Beacon Rock in the Columbia Gorge offers spectacular scenery and interesting islands to circumnavigate. It also offers strong winds, strong currents, rough water, cold water, and commercial shipping traffic, particularly tugs and barges. As a result, this area is best suited to experienced paddlers in sea kayaks rather than novices in open canoes.

This trip begins and ends at the boat ramp at Beacon Rock State Park, on Washington Route 14 on the north shore of the Columbia, in the heart of the Columbia River Gorge National Scenic Area. To reach the state park, drive east from Vancouver, Washington, on Washington Route 14 to milepost 34.22, then turn south and follow Beacon Rock Moorage Road a short distance to a boat ramp and dock. (This section of the park is about 0.5 mile west of Beacon Rock itself.) Or drive east from Portland on Interstate 84, cross the Bridge of the Gods at Cascade Locks, then drive back west on Washington Route 14 about 8 miles to the turnoff at milepost 34.22. A fee is charged to launch boats at this state park.

The area around Beacon Rock offers several routes for paddlers. First, you could paddle west to Skamania Landing. Or you could paddle around two-hundred-acre Pierce Island, a Nature Conservancy preserve which lies just east of the Beacon Rock boat ramp. The island's inhabitants include great blue heron, Canada geese, osprey, and beaver. Although Pierce Island is open to the public during daylight hours from July 15 to February 15, it is not a park. Visits should be brief, and no pets, camping, or fires are permitted. Just east of Pierce Island lies Ives Island, most of which is owned by the U.S. Forest Service. The north shore of the river, just east of Beacon Rock, is the Pierce National Wildlife Refuge.

The gorge is a very windy place, and the current of the river can be strong, particularly in the winter and spring. Oftentimes, the wind blows upstream against the current, causing rough water. If your skills are not up to rough water, heavy winds, and strong currents, do not try this trip. But if your skills are up to such conditions, the Beacon Rock area can be both scenic and exciting. On windy days, try using a sail or a kite to take advantage of the wind. But be careful; the gorge is no place for throwing caution to the wind. Always maintain a lookout for commercial shipping traffic, and head for shore if the weather turns rough.

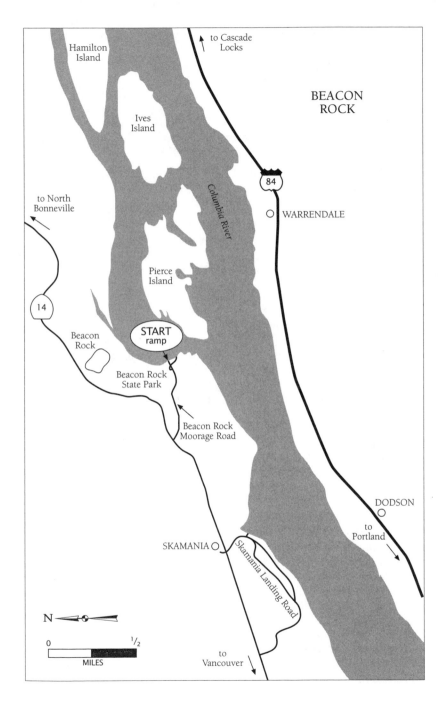

37 Lacamas Lake and Round Lake

Location: North of Camas, Washington
Distance: Up to 5 miles
Time: 4 hours
Maps: USGS Lacamas Creek and Camas 7.5"
Season: Winter and spring
Rating: B

Lacamas Creek is a pretty stream that drains much of the farmland east of Vancouver. About 1 mile north of Camas, Lacamas Lake and Round Lake were formed when two small dams were built, backing up the stream's water for about 3 miles. This is a particularly good trip to paddle in the off-season, when the creek is high enough to paddle, and powerboats will probably be absent from the lake. During the summer, expect a lot of water-skiers.

This trip can be approached in at least three ways, with three different launch points. The first is best in winter and spring when water levels are high, the third is best in the summer when water-skiers may be present, and the second is somewhat of a compromise between the two.

For most of the variations, begin the trip by leaving an extra car or bicycle at Camas Heritage Park, operated by the city of Camas. From Vancouver, the park can be reached by driving east on Washington Route 14 about 13 miles to the Camas exit. In downtown Camas, drive east on Third Street, then turn left onto Garfield Street (Washington Route 500). Follow Route 500; it eventually turns into Everett Street. About a mile north of town, turn left onto Lake Road and drive 0.3 mile to the park.

The first variation: In winter and spring, when the water level on Lacamas Creek is high, canoes and kayaks can be launched about a mile upstream from the lake at the Goodwin Road bridge, where the creek begins to lose its strong current. The launching point is reached by driving north on Lake Road, then turning right onto Northeast 202nd, as shown on the sketch map, following it to Goodwin Road, where you turn right and continue toward the bridge on Goodwin Road. Immediately before crossing the bridge, park on the right.

Lacamas Creek is swift and shallow as it passes under the bridge. Downstream and within sight from the bridge, the current slows considerably, becoming quite placid. After entering Lacamas Lake, the trip paddles the length of the lake to Lacamas Park near the dam.

The second variation: If Lacamas Creek is not navigable due to low water, or if you don't have a shuttle available, launch on Lacamas Lake itself, either at Camas Heritage Park, or at the Department of Fish and Wildlife public boat ramp on

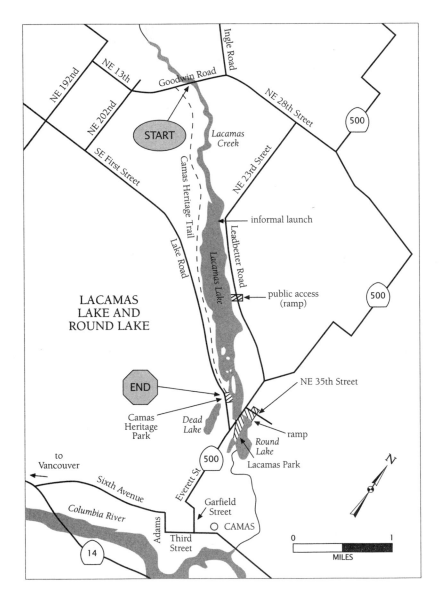

Leadbetter Road, which can be reached by driving north on Washington Route 500, then turning left onto Leadbetter Road. About halfway up Lacamas Lake, look for the public access area on the left. Parking is on the right. A Washington Vehicle Use Permit is necessary to use this ramp. (The sound of a nearby shooting range sometimes mars the tranquility of the lake.) An alternative informal launch is located about 1.3 miles north, where the road first curves away from the lake.

If you do launch on Lacamas Lake, be sure to paddle back up into the mouth of Lacamas Creek—the transition zone between the fast water of the stream and the still water of the lake is one of the prettiest parts of this trip. The narrow channel, which broadens as it approaches the lake, presents numerous opportunities to linger. The bird population is particularly diverse. Geese, ducks, hawks, kingfishers, herons, coots, and numerous songbirds can be expected to make appearances.

The third variation: If you would like to avoid the main portion of Lacamas Lake (when water-skiers are present in the summer, for example), launch at either Camas Heritage Park or at Lacamas Park, where Lacamas Lake joins Round Lake. From Lacamas Park, you may either launch in Round Lake, or carefully portage your boat across Washington Route 500 to launch in Lacamas Lake, or paddle under the very low bridge from one lake to the other. Depending on the water level, kayakers can pass under the bridge easily, while canoeists will need to hunker down considerably. Or launch at a canoe launch on the north side of Round Lake, which can be reached by continuing north on Route 500 across the bridge, then turning right onto Northeast 35th Street.

Lacamas Lake itself is long and open. Watch the southern horizon for glimpses of Mount Hood. In windy weather, try to stay close to the shore for both shelter and safety. The east side of the lake offers a bay filled with lily pads. The southern end of Lacamas Lake offers a half dozen islands for exploring, lunching, or napping and acres of lily pads for exploring, plus a lot of birdlife to watch. Even when the main part of Lacamas Lake is full of speedboats, the southern end can be quiet and relaxing.

The Lacamas Heritage Trail leads from Camas Heritage Park north to Goodwin Road. Along the way, it passes a private waterfront park, open only to residents of the nearby subdivision.

If you would also like to explore Round Lake and you did not launch from it, from Lacamas Lake either paddle under the very low bridge, or carefully portage across the highway. Round Lake is a pretty green lake in a wooded bowl, surrounded by parkland and a hiking path that circles the lake. No gasoline motors are permitted, so expect some peace and quiet. Although the USGS topographic map shows two narrow arms extending from the west side of Round Lake, both arms are blocked by dams used to regulate the height of the lake and supply water to a reservoir southwest of the lake. Round Lake is small, so only a short while is required to explore its thirty-three acres, but keep your eyes peeled for birds, such as the green heron.

Paddlers from Oregon will note that Washington's Lacamas Lake and Round Lake have a bit more litter than is common in Oregon. Anyone who believes that bottle deposit laws do not help the litter situation should try a few paddle trips in these two neighboring states. Much of the floating litter collects in eddies on Lacamas Creek or on the windward side of the two lakes. I was able to collect a large pack full of bottles and cans in about 20 minutes. If you are so inclined, bring a plastic garbage bag and spruce the place up a bit.

38 Vancouver Lake

Location: Northwest of Vancouver, Washington
Distance: Up to 8 miles
Time: 2 to 5 hours
Map: USGS Vancouver 7.5"
Season: Year-round (except during hunting season)
Rating: A

Vancouver Lake is a large tidal lake just northwest of downtown Vancouver. Its 2800-acre surface is unprotected from winds, and thus the lake is an excellent place to practice paddling on large, open bodies of water. Even on relatively calm days, a gentle wind is usually present. On windy days, the lake can quickly turn rough. Paddlers should consider staying close to shore if strong winds are a possibility, and novice paddlers should be even more careful. On the other hand, it's also a good place to use a kite for sailpower.

In the past, paddlers rarely visited Vancouver Lake. Even though it is quite close to Portland and Vancouver, access to the brush-choked shoreline was difficult. In recent years, the Clark County Park and Recreation Department has acquired 234 acres on the west shore, and a portion has been developed as Vancouver Lake Park, with large parking areas, expansive lawns, rest rooms, and a sandy beach.

In addition, not long ago the lake was little more than a large muddy lagoon. Starting in 1983, the lake underwent extensive dredging; the dredge spoils were used to construct a large island in the middle of the lake. An inlet near the south end of the lake was also created, permitting water to enter directly from the Columbia, thus flushing out the lake with relatively fresh water.

Vancouver Lake Park has become particularly popular with beginning windsurfers, who use the lawns to rig their gear. The gentle winds and lack of a strong current contrast sharply with the nearby Columbia River Gorge, where more experienced windsurfers are drawn.

To reach the park, exit Interstate 5 at Mill Plain Boulevard (exit 1C) or Fourth Plain Boulevard (exit 1D), then drive west. Less than 2 miles from the freeway, the two boulevards join as Mill Plain Boulevard, eventually becoming West 26th Street (Washington Route 501), and then New Lower River Road. When Lower River Road turns west (5.3 miles from the freeway), continue north, through a gate on New Lower River Road (Erwin Rieger Memorial Highway). The park is 5.8 miles from the freeway, 0.5 mile north of the gate. A small fee is charged to enter the park in summer months. Although the developed portion of the park has no boat ramp, boats can be carried across the lawn to the water. Two other less developed launching sites (with shorter walks to the water and no entrance fee) are located just north and south of the gate. The gate is locked each day at dusk.

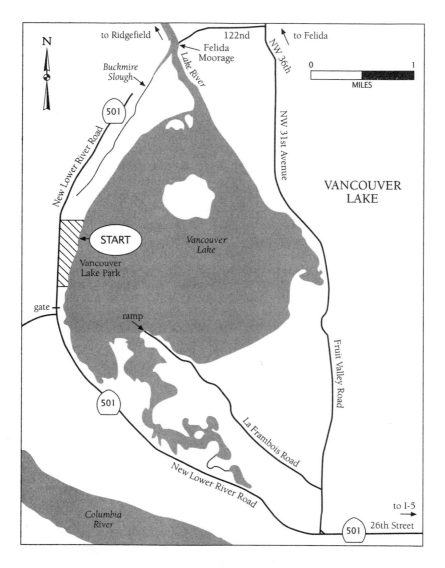

Other launching sites are located on the south and north shores of the lake. Those wishing to explore the southern part of the lake may wish to launch at a gravel boat ramp, part of the Vancouver Lake Wildlife Access Area managed by the Washington Department of Fish and Wildlife. Reach the ramp from West 26th Street by turning right onto Fruit Valley Road, then left onto La Frambois Road. The ramp is located at the north end of La Frambois Road. A Washington Vehicle Use Permit must be displayed on vehicles using this facility. Those wishing to explore the north part of the lake and Lake River might prefer to launch at Felida Moorage (for a small fee). Reach the moorage from West 26th Street by turning right onto Fruit Valley Road, which turns into Northwest 31st and then Northwest 36th Avenue. Turn left onto 122nd and follow it to its end at Lake River. Vancouver Lake is a short upstream paddle south from the moorage.

The large size of Vancouver Lake offers several options to paddlers. One is to simply follow the shoreline, looking for interesting bays and inlets to explore. Another option is to head north, where Lake River leads to the Felida Moorage, the mouth of Salmon Creek, and eventually Bachelor Island Slough. (See Trip 39, Salmon Creek, and Trip 40, Ridgefield National Wildlife Refuge.) If you choose to paddle down Lake River, make sure to check the tide table first, because the paddle back up the river to Vancouver Lake can be tiring if the tide is on its way out.

No matter where you paddle, keep an eye out for the abundant birdlife that inhabits the lake. Following the shoreline of the lake is a particularly rewarding way to watch for birds, particularly the large great blue herons that are common on the lake. Also look for cormorant and osprey.

Because the lake is quite shallow, the shoreline may be difficult to approach in many places. For the same reason, and also because of the dense underbrush,

Vancouver Lake

finding a place to land for lunch or a rest stop may be difficult. A small beach near the northeast corner of the lake is one option; the shoreline of Lake River is another.

Vancouver Lake is also popular with duck hunters. Stay away from early October to mid-January.

39 Salmon Creek

Location: North of Vancouver, Washington
Distance: 4 to 6 miles
Time: 2 to 3 hours
Map: USGS Vancouver 7.5"
Season: Late fall through spring
Rating: A

Sauvie Island is one of the most popular paddling locations in Oregon, but just across the Columbia from Sauvie Island, southwestern Washington offers dozens of paddling areas that Oregon paddlers rarely visit.

Salmon Creek is an excellent example. It offers secluded paddling, good scenery, and abundant wildlife, all within a few minutes drive north of Portland, yet few paddlers know of its existence. Salmon Creek is at its best for paddling in late fall, winter, or spring, when the water level is highest. Winter is also a good time to watch wildlife, especially birds, along Salmon Creek. Great blue heron are evident, along with Canada geese and tundra swans.

Because Salmon Creek flows into the Lake River, which drains Vancouver Lake, this trip can begin and end at several locations. The trip described here begins near the community of Felida, a suburb of Vancouver. It descends Salmon Creek to Lake River, then paddles up a short section of the Lake River to a private moorage at the outlet of Vancouver Lake. The trip could also be extended to paddle farther south, across Vancouver Lake to the public park on its west shore (see Trip 38, Vancouver Lake), or you could paddle north, down the Lake River to the town of Ridgefield (see Trip 40, Ridgefield National Wildlife Refuge).

The trip could also be paddled in reverse because the entire distance is on tidal waters. In fact, if the tide is coming in, the trip is much faster and easier if paddled upstream with the incoming tide. Consult a current tide table before deciding which direction to paddle, or you might end up paddling against a strong current.

To begin the trip, drive north on Interstate 5 from Vancouver, Washington, to exit 4. Turn left onto Northeast 78th Street and follow it 1.5 miles to a T intersection with Northwest Lake Shore Avenue. Turn north, following Lake Shore Avenue as it eventually becomes Northwest 31st Avenue and then Northwest 36th Avenue. In Felida, turn left onto Northwest 122nd Street and

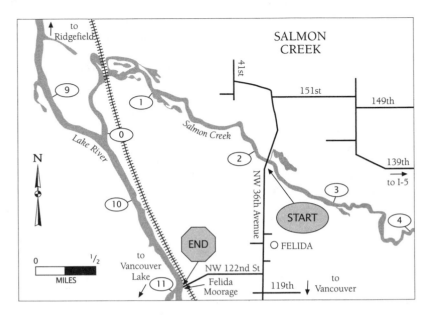

follow it to its foot at Felida Moorage. This private facility charges a nominal fee for parking cars and launching boats.

After leaving an extra car or bicycle at Felida Moorage, return on Northwest 122nd Street to Northwest 36th Avenue, and proceed north from Felida on Northwest 36th Avenue to a bridge over Salmon Creek, about 1 mile north of Felida. Park on the east side of the road at the south end of the bridge, where a trail leads down to the water. The trail is steep; if it is too steep for your liking, try launching on the west side of the road. Watch carefully for traffic on this busy road.

If time permits, start out by paddling up Salmon Creek as far as the water level or the current permits. Most of the land upstream from the Felida Bridge is part of the Salmon Creek Greenway, which includes Klineline Ponds near Interstate 5. However, much of the land downstream from Felida Bridge is privately owned, and should be treated as such.

When you have finished exploring upper Salmon Creek, turn around and head downstream toward the Lake River. A railroad bridge marks the approach to the mouth of Salmon Creek, where it joins the Lake River. A left turn takes you to Felida Moorage in 2 miles.

If time permits, a side trip out onto the open waters of Vancouver Lake (see Trip 38, Vancouver Lake) could be considered before returning to Felida Moorage for the takeout. Or a right turn could be made down Lake River, which leads paddlers downstream 7 miles to Ridgefield (see Trip 40, Ridgefield National Wildlife Refuge).

This entire area is popular with duck hunters; stay away during the hunting season, which usually runs from early October to mid-January.

40 Ridgefield National Wildlife Refuge

Location: North of Vancouver, Washington
Distance: 1 to 10 miles
Time: 1 to 5 hours
Maps and chart: USGS Ridgefield and St. Helens 7.5"; NOAA chart 18524
Season: Year-round (except during hunting season)
Rating: A

The Ridgefield National Wildlife Refuge lies just across the Columbia River from the north end of Sauvie Island. Like Sauvie Island, the refuge offers countless paddle trips on its various sloughs, creeks, rivers, and lakes. The geography of the area gives a hint of the possibilities: the refuge is bisected by the Lake River and Bachelor Island Slough, which flow into the Columbia near the mouth of the Lewis River and Gee Creek, while just across the Columbia, Multnomah Channel empties into the Columbia from behind Sauvie Island.

The refuge consists of three parts: the northernmost Carty Unit (where Gee Creek leads to a group of lakes), the southernmost River S Unit, and Bachelor Island. Canoeing is not allowed on the lakes and sloughs of the River S Unit, but boating is allowed on the Lake River, Bachelor Island Slough, and Gee Creek.

Several launching sites are available within striking distance of the refuge, but most boaters use one of two boat ramps in the town of Ridgefield, near the heart of the refuge. To get there, drive north from Vancouver on Interstate 5 to exit 14, then turn west and follow Washington Route 501 (Northwest 269th Street) about 3 miles, where it becomes Pioneer Street in Ridgefield. At the stoplight, turn right (north) onto Main Street. To use a boat ramp shared with powerboats, drive north two blocks, then turn left (west) onto Mill Street at a sign pointing to the Ridgefield City Marina. A public parking lot and boat ramp are located at the foot of Mill Street. Even better, to reach a ramp dedicated to nonmotorized craft, continue north on Main Street another two blocks, then turn left onto Division Street and follow it to a launching area at the foot of Division. (As of this writing, a $6 fee is charged to use either of the ramps; carry quarters or dollar bills to buy a ticket from the vending machine located at the marina. A $40 annual pass for the marina, a $20 annual pass for the nonmotorized ramp, and daily passes can be purchased at the Ridgefield Hardware Store or at the offices of the Port of Ridgefield.)

Both launching sites are located on the Lake River. From either one, a left turn onto the river eventually leads upstream past the mouth of Salmon Creek (see Trip 39, Salmon Creek) to Vancouver Lake, about 10 miles away (see Trip 38, Vancouver Lake). A right turn (downstream) leads to Bachelor Island

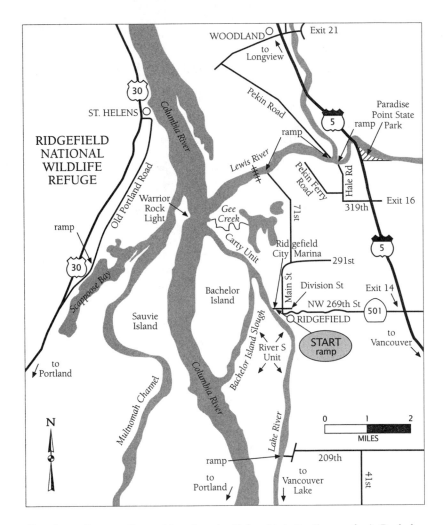

Slough, a mile away. From this point, the Columbia is 3 miles south via Bachelor Island Slough, or 1.5 miles north via the Lake River. Or a circumnavigation of Bachelor Island could be accomplished in about 9 miles of paddling.

A 1.5-mile paddle north to the mouth of the Lake River at the Columbia gives at least three more choices for short diversions. One choice is to paddle up the Lewis River toward Woodland (see Trip 43, Lewis River—Main Stem). Another choice is to cross the Columbia to the Warrior Rock Light near the north end of Sauvie Island. This light sits on a rocky headland that offers a splendid place to lunch and watch the boats go by. Just make sure to watch out for those boats (and large ships) during the half-mile crossing of the Columbia. A third choice is to paddle up tiny Gee Creek into the Carty Unit,

Gee Creek in winter

where paddlers will find an intricate system of lakes and lagoons filled with unusual rocky outcrops and islands.

Paddling up Gee Creek offers the only boating access to those lakes and lagoons; portaging boats from the east is not permitted. Gee Creek is not for the timid or the inexperienced, however. It is navigable only when water levels are high (perhaps 10 feet or more on the Columbia River gauge at Vancouver), but even then a trip up the narrow creek will involve paddling over, under, and around many downed trees. Consult a tide table to determine which way the current will be running. And carry topographic maps and a compass. The sketch map in this book doesn't do justice to the intricate lakes and sloughs, and finding your way back out again may be difficult. Finally, although the Carty Unit is generally closed to hunting, the area north of the creek is private property and usually populated by hunters during the waterfowl hunting season. During the season, which usually runs from early October to mid-January, don't paddle up Gee Creek, for your own safety and out of courtesy to the hunters.

Throughout the refuge, keep in mind that some of the riverbanks are in private hands, and even some parts of the refuge may be closed to public access from time to time. For a map of the refuge showing private property lines and current closures of public land, stop by the refuge headquarters at Third and Mill Streets in Ridgefield, or call them (see the appendix at the back of this book).

Refuge managers should also be consulted during hunting season. Before planning a trip in the fall or winter, check with them to find out when and where hunting is being permitted. Hunting on the Ridgefield refuge is closely regulated, with hunting usually permitted every other day during the hunting season, but only on parts of the refuge. Also keep in mind that hunting is permitted every day during the season on the private property adjacent to the refuge.

41 Lewis River—East Fork

Location: North of Vancouver, Washington
Distance: 9.5 miles
Time: 4 to 5 hours
Maps: USGS Battleground and Ridgefield 7.5"
Season: Winter to early spring
Rating: C

The East Fork of the Lewis River is misnamed: it is south, not east, of the main branch of the river, and it is large enough to warrant a separate name. Its upper stretches are clear and swift, whereas the last few miles are tidal. The portion described here covers the transition zone between mountain stream and coastal river. The first few miles are choppy and not for the inexperienced, while the lower miles, as the river passes through expansive pasturelands, require steady paddling on flatwater. Caution: by June each year, this section of the river can be very rocky and impassable.

Begin the trip by leaving your shuttle car at Paradise Point State Park, 25 miles north of Portland on Interstate 5. Take exit 16 and turn north onto Paradise Park Road. As you enter the park, keep to the left, away from the campground, to reach the ramp area. The boat ramp is directly under the freeway bridges. (For a slightly longer trip, leave your extra car at an informal boat ramp at the north end of Hale Road, west of the freeway.)

The launching point is reached by driving south and east to Daybreak Park. Follow Paradise Park Road south as it becomes Frontage Road, then turns left to become 299th Street. At the T intersection, turn right onto Eleventh Avenue and follow it to 264th Street. Turn left and continue to Tenth Avenue; turn right and then left onto 259th Street. Follow 259th Street east to 82nd Avenue and turn left to Daybreak Park. At the park, rather than turning into the east portion, turn west to the boat ramp. Although you could launch a canoe or kayak in the park's east section, launching at the boat ramp allows you to avoid the rapids under the bridge.

Before you launch, look closely at the river and the rapids under the bridge. If the rapids look difficult to you, you probably ought to find another trip to paddle because the 3 or 4 miles immediately below this bridge involve several similar rapids. (An alternate launching point is available at a primitive boat ramp near rivermile 3, near La Center, as shown on the sketch map. From Paradise Park Road, turn east onto La Center Road and then south onto Timmen Road, then turn left onto Pollock Road.)

None of the rapids are particularly difficult, but all require quick choices between channels and possibly a few quick turns. The river channel has undergone considerable change and will no doubt continue to do so; be careful, particularly in cold weather or when paddling down blind channels.

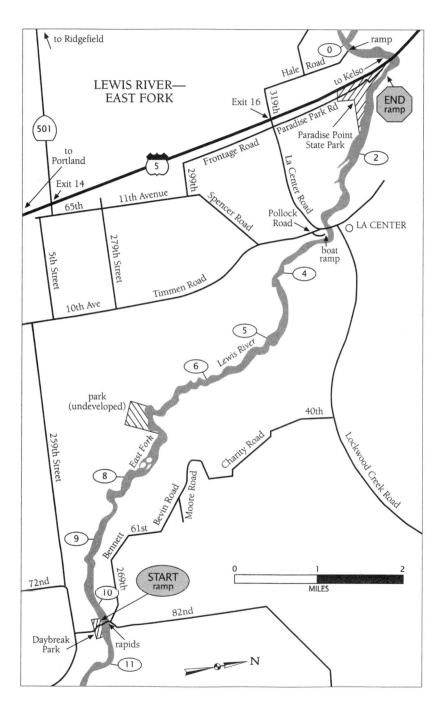

LEWIS RIVER—
EAST FORK

to Ridgefield

ramp

0

Hale Road

to Kelso

Exit 16

319th

END
ramp

501

Paradise Park Rd

to
Portland

5

Frontage Road

Paradise Point
State Park

2

299th

La Center Road

Exit 14

65th

11th Avenue

Spencer Road

Pollock
Road

LA CENTER

279th Street

5th Street

boat
ramp

4

10th Ave

Timmen Road

5

Lewis River

6

259th Street

park
(undeveloped)

40th

Lockwood Creek Road

East Fork

Charity Road

8

Moore Road

9

61st

Bevin Road

Bennett

269th

72nd

START
ramp

10

0   1   2
MILES

82nd

Daybreak
Park

rapids

11

N

East Fork Lewis River at La Center

The river valley widens considerably near rivermile 7. Dikes and broad pastures dominate the scene, particularly in the winter when both are occasionally under several feet of water.

The town of La Center, near rivermile 3, is marked by a distinctive arched bridge just past a primitive boat ramp on the left (the alternate put-in point). Paradise Point is about 2 miles downstream, but the time taken to paddle this last section depends partly on whether the tide is coming in or going out.

42 Lewis River—Northern Section

Location: Woodland, Washington
Distance: 9 miles
Time: 4 to 5 hours
Maps: USGS Ariel and Woodland 7.5"
Season: Winter and spring
Rating: C (with one portage)

The Lewis River is a southwestern Washington river that enters the Columbia near the Oregon town of St. Helens. The trip described here, however, ends a few miles up the river at the Washington town of Woodland.

To start this trip, drive north from Vancouver on Interstate 5 about 21 miles to the town of Woodland (exit 21). Just east of the freeway interchange, cross

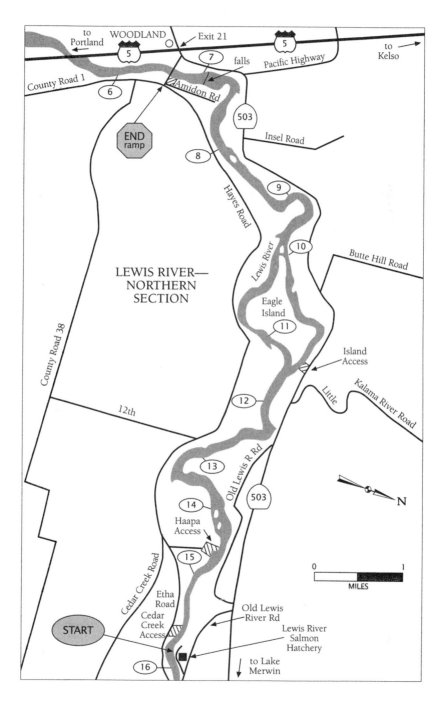

the river via a bridge, and leave your extra car or bicycle at the gravel boat ramp and parking area on the north side of the bridge. While you are there, look upstream about 0.5 mile to the small waterfall that blocks the river. The size of these falls fluctuates with the tide, but they often require a short portage.

Then cross back over the bridge and drive north and east on Washington Route 503, pausing near the corner of Cherry Blossom Lane and Route 503 to take a close look at the waterfall/rapids. Most paddlers bypass the rapids by staying to the left and following a channel around a small island, but some paddlers will want to stop at the head of the island and portage past the rapids. Do not try to paddle through the rapids.

Then keep following Washington Route 503 toward Lake Merwin, staying on the north side of the river. (Two alternate access points, Cedar Creek Access and Haapa Access, are located on the south side of the river.) About 7.7 miles from the Woodland Bridge, turn right at signs marking the Lewis River Salmon Hatchery. After stopping for a few minutes to watch the thousands of immature salmon, drive through the hatchery and turn right onto a small gravel road just past the last pond. Launch your boat from the large gravel area below the ponds.

Throughout this trip, watch carefully for rocks in shallow areas and for fallen trees and tree branches that might impede progress. The latter can be particularly dangerous because a boat can be swept under them. The upper half of the trip travels through steep wooded territory. The current is strong, but little rough water is encountered. Between rivermiles 15 and 14, several small islands require careful choices to avoid shallow water.

Past rivermile 12, the head of 258-acre Eagle Island appears. Although a public fishing and launching area (Island Access) is located a short distance down the right-hand channel, the main channel continues to the left and is the best course to follow past this 2-mile-long island. The channel past the access area is usually navigable, but it has a few more rapids than the left channel. Stay close to the right shore if you decide to stop at the access area.

Eagle Island was purchased by Clark County in 2000, along with nineteen acres along the north shore, to preserve salmon habitat. The character of the river begins to change slightly as it passes the island. Like a coastal river approaching the ocean, the banks become sandy in places and are populated by beach grasses and Scotch broom. On a warm day, find a sandbar for a lunch break or an afternoon nap.

As you approach the town of Woodland, the number of vacation houses and mobile homes increases, changing the wilderness quality of the river. Several houses along this part of the river were destroyed or damaged by the flood of 1996. As you enter the town, look and listen for the falls at rivermile 7. As mentioned above, these falls often require a portage, usually on the left bank, or they can usually be bypassed using a channel behind an island on the left. Occasionally, high tide or high water levels on the Columbia may make them navigable, but at least scout them from shore prior to attempting to paddle them. If in doubt, portage. The Woodland bridge and the end of this trip are about 0.5 mile downstream from the falls.

43 Lewis River—Main Stem

Location: Woodland, Washington
Distance: 10 miles
Time: 4 to 5 hours
Maps and chart: USGS Woodland, Ridgefield, and St. Helens 7.5";
NOAA chart 18524
Season: Year-round (except during hunting season)
Rating: A

Just a few miles north of Portland, near the town of Woodland, Washington, the Lewis River and the East Fork Lewis River join to form the main stem of the river. Although both forks began their journeys as mountain streams, they are flat tidal streams in the Woodland area. This trip paddles the last few miles of the Lewis River to its mouth on the Columbia, and then briefly travels through part of the Ridgefield National Wildlife Refuge.

Although the trip begins and ends in Washington, the section of this trip on the Columbia is just across the river from Oregon's Sauvie Island. In fact, Warrior Rock Light on Sauvie Island makes an excellent destination for a side trip, especially for those looking for a scenic lunch spot.

Because the trip passes through the Ridgefield National Wildlife Refuge, and because hunting is permitted on the refuge and adjacent private land during hunting season, check with the refuge headquarters during the season (generally early October to mid-January) to determine whether canoeing is advisable. During certain parts of the season, and often after the early morning hours, few game birds and few hunters are present, making paddling safe and enjoyable, but call the refuge to make sure (see the appendix at the back of this book).

Begin the trip by leaving an extra car at the Ridgefield City Marina, which can be reached from Interstate 5, exit 14, by turning west onto Washington Route 501. When Route 501 becomes Pioneer Street in Ridgefield, turn right onto Main Street and drive four blocks to Division Street, where a sign points to the city marina. Turn left to find the marina at the foot of Division Street. (At the time of this writing, a $2 fee is charged to use this boat ramp; carry quarters to buy a ticket from the coin-operated dispenser.)

Then return to Interstate 5 and drive north to exit 21 at Woodland. At the foot of the freeway off-ramp, turn right (east), then immediately turn right again and cross the Lewis River on a bridge. At the east end of the bridge, bear left, then immediately turn left to a primitive park and boat ramp just north of the bridge.

The river is wide and usually calm as it winds its lazy course toward the Columbia. As it leaves the town of Woodland, the river parallels the freeway. A glance at a map reveals that the straight course next to the freeway is not

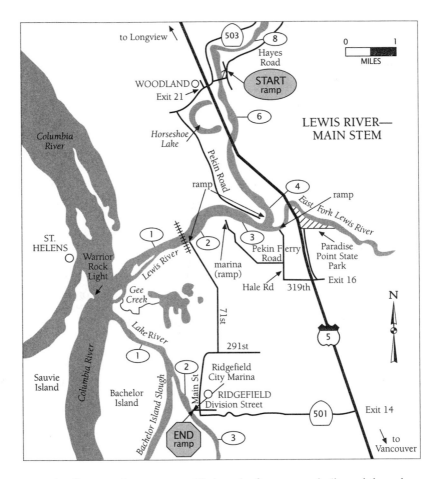

natural; a former oxbow was cut off when the freeway was built, and the oxbow now stands on the west side of the freeway with a new name, Horseshoe Lake.

Several alternate launching sites are available near rivermile 3 for those wishing to shorten the trip. At rivermile 3.5, the East Fork Lewis River joins the main stem. Less than a mile up the East Fork is Paradise Point State Park, the ending point for Trip 41, Lewis River—East Fork. Launching at Paradise Point shortens this trip by about 2 miles. Other possible launching sites are a ramp on the north side of the river near rivermile 3.5, and a private marina offers a boat ramp on the south side of the river at rivermile 3.

After passing under a railroad bridge (and a primitive boat ramp on the south shore) at rivermile 1.75, the river widens and then joins the Columbia 2 miles later. To the west, on the Oregon shore (Sauvie Island) stands the Warrior Rock Light. A side trip to the Oregon shore is worthwhile if time, weather, and tides permit. However, this trip turns south along the Washington shore for a few hundred yards, then turns up the Lake River into the Ridgefield National Wildlife Refuge. About 1.5 miles later, where Bachelor Island Slough is on the right, bear left onto Lake River. The Ridgefield City Marina is about a mile up Lake River.

This trip can be used to link up several other trips. Trips 42, Lewis River—Northern Section, and 41, Lewis River—East Fork, describe the sections of Lewis River immediately upstream from Woodland and Paradise Point. Trip 40, Ridgefield National Wildlife Refuge, describes the various paddles available within the Ridgefield National Wildlife Refuge, including Lake River, Bachelor Island Slough, and Gee Creek.

Warrior Rock Light

44 Silver Lake

Location: East of Castle Rock, Washington
Distance: Up to 7 miles
Time: Up to 4 hours
Map: USGS Silver Lake 7.5"
Season: Year-round
Rating: A

If you were a bass, you would want to live in Silver Lake. You would have three thousand acres of lake to roam in, millions of lily pads to hide under, several islands to swim around for exercise, and views of Mount St. Helens and Mount Rainier to gaze upon. You would just have to be wary of more than a few bass fishermen. All in all, it would be a good life.

Paddlers face much the same situation when they visit Silver Lake. The lake is huge, with a lot of nooks and crannies to visit and acres of lily pads to paddle through. And those views of Mounts St. Helens and Rainier. And islands to paddle around. Not to mention wary bass to fish for.

To reach Silver Lake, drive north on Interstate 5 about 60 miles north from Portland. Just north of Castle Rock, Washington, take exit 49, turn east onto Washington Route 504 (the Silver Lake Highway) and follow it 7.8 miles to Kerr Road. Along the way, you will pass the Mount St. Helens National Volcanic Monument Visitor Center and several small resorts on Silver Lake. You will

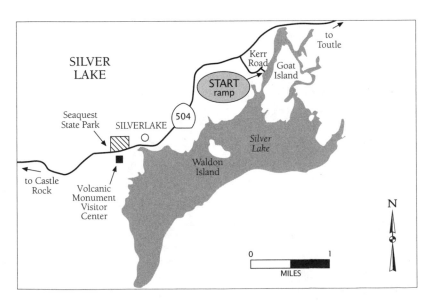

also pass Seaquest State Park near the northwest corner of the lake. (The park offers camping, but no boat launching facilities.) Nearby is the community of Silverlake. Turn right onto Kerr Road and follow it to a boat ramp maintained by the Washington Department of Fish and Wildlife. Users must display a Washington Vehicle Use Permit when using this facility.

From the boat ramp, you have a lot of choices. As you can see from the sketch map, the lake is large and convoluted; don't expect to cover the entire lake in one day. Despite its size, the lake is only about 10 feet at its deepest spot. As a result, much of the lake is marshy. If at all possible, buy the USGS Silver Lake 7.5-minute topographic map, which shows the lake in much more detail than the sketch map. In particular, the USGS map shows the marshy areas of the lake in excellent detail, including distinguishing between areas covered with lily pads and areas that are so dense with vegetation that they resemble dry land.

Powerboats are permitted on Silver Lake. The bass fishers, who usually use boats with small motors, are generally courteous to paddlers. During warm summer months, however, you will encounter a few high-powered boats, generally in the open areas south of Goat Island and Waldon Island.

During the winter, you may have the lake entirely to yourself. In the spring and fall, you will have a few other boaters for company, but you will also have abundant birdlife to watch. Even in the summer watch for coots, mallards, kingfishers, and osprey. In the water, watch for frogs, largemouth bass, crappie, carp, bullhead catfish, yellow perch, and rainbow trout.

To avoid the powerboats, and to maximize the amount of wildlife to be seen, stay in the marshy areas of the lake. Fortunately, the northern end of the lake near the boat ramp is very marshy. An interesting loop trip can be made by paddling northeast from the ramp, then following a narrow channel to the southeast. The channel eventually returns to the main part of the lake east of Goat Island.

45 Cowlitz River—Vader to Castle Rock

Location: Near Castle Rock, Washington
Distance: 13 miles
Time: 4 to 5 hours
Maps: USGS Castle Rock and Winlock 7.5"
Season: Late fall to early summer
Rating: B

When Mount St. Helens erupted in May 1980, countless tons of volcanic ash, logs, and other debris swept down the North Fork of the Toutle River into the Cowlitz River near Castle Rock. Although Castle Rock and the Cowlitz River were more than 40 miles west of the volcano, the damage done to the Cowlitz was extensive. Within hours after the eruption, the Cowlitz, once a clear stream, became choked with logs and ash, its normally cold temperature

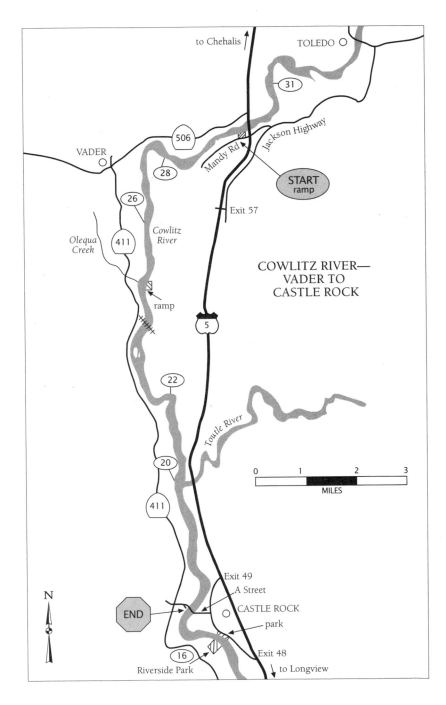

to Chehalis

TOLEDO

31

506

VADER

Jackson Highway

Mandy Rd

START
ramp

28

Exit 57

26

Olequa
Creek

411

Cowlitz
River

COWLITZ RIVER—
VADER TO
CASTLE ROCK

ramp

5

22

Toutle River

20

0   1   2   3

MILES

411

Exit 49

A Street

END

CASTLE ROCK

park

N

16

Exit 48

Riverside Park

to Longview

rising to that of bathwater. The turbid waters of the Toutle not only flowed down the Cowlitz after the Toutle joined the larger river, but flowed up the Cowlitz as well, reaching a point 2 miles upstream from the mouth of the Toutle. The once attractive riverbanks of the Cowlitz were buried beneath a thick layer of gray volcanic ash.

This canoe trip ends in Castle Rock, amid all of the destruction, but starts 13 miles upstream near the towns of Vader and Toledo, where the river has retained its natural charm. The trip follows the Cowlitz for 10 miles to the mouth of the Toutle, then continues amid the ash 3 miles to Castle Rock.

Start the trip by leaving an extra car in Castle Rock, leaving Interstate 5 at exit 48 or 49. From downtown Castle Rock, turn west onto A Street. Shortly after crossing the Cowlitz on a bridge, turn left and leave your car on the riverbank just south of the bridge.

Then return to Interstate 5 and drive north to exit 57, turn right, and follow Jackson Highway (old Highway 99) north for 2 miles. Turn left onto Mandy Road and follow it 0.7 mile to a public boat ramp just downstream from the two I-5 bridges. A Washington Vehicle Use Permit is necessary to use this facility.

The river is wide, strong, and clear. The first 4 or 5 miles can be paddled in less than an hour, but don't let the swift current keep you from slowing down to enjoy the scenery. Watch particularly for osprey diving for fish, or watch for

Cowlitz River

green heron and kingfishers. At rivermile 24.75, where two tall abutments of a former bridge stand by the river, a public boat ramp is on the left bank. Opposite, Olequa Creek enters through a picturesque ravine. A good-size stream, the Olequa can be explored by canoe for a short distance.

In several places on this trip, the Cowlitz splits around small islands, but the main channel is usually an obvious choice. Near rivermile 23 (shortly after passing under a railroad bridge), the left channel is the deepest as the river passes two islands. At rivermile 22, after flowing through two sharp curves, the river passes through its first ash deposits, and then widens and slows considerably. When the mouth of the Toutle is reached at rivermile 20, however, the Cowlitz regains its former speed. Watch carefully for turbulence when the two rivers meet.

The last few miles of the river are lined with dikes and huge mountains of ash, silent reminders of the destructive forces that swept down the Toutle that day in May 1980. The takeout, and your car, are on the right bank immediately downstream of the Castle Rock bridge.

46 Cowlitz River—Castle Rock to Longview

Location: Near Castle Rock, Washington
Distance: 16 miles
Time: 4 to 5 hours
Maps: USGS Castle Rock, Kelso, and Rainier 7.5"
Season: Late fall to midsummer
Rating: B

This trip follows the Cowlitz River on the last leg of its journey to the Columbia. The trip starts in the town of Castle Rock and ends near the mouth of the Cowlitz in Longview. The entire trip is downstream from where the Toutle River joins the Cowlitz. As a result, this stretch of the Cowlitz is lined with volcanic ash and sand from the effects of the eruption of Mount St. Helens in 1980.

Start the trip by leaving an extra car at Gerhart Gardens, a large public park in Longview. To reach the park from Interstate 5, take exit 36, drive west on Washington Route 432, then turn right onto Dike Road shortly after crossing the Cowlitz. Gerhart Gardens consists of two parking areas and two boat ramps. Powerboaters and jet skis tend to use the northernmost parking area and ramp, so leave your car in the southern of the two parking lots.

Then return to Interstate 5 and drive north to Castle Rock, using exit 48 from I-5. From downtown Castle Rock, turn west onto A Street. After crossing the Cowlitz on a bridge, take the first left and launch your boat from the riverbank just south of the bridge, near the entrance to the fairgrounds.

The Cowlitz and its strong current circle around the west and south sides of the town of Castle Rock. As the river leaves the town, the rock for which the town was named stands sentinel on the east bank of the river. Just south of the rock, Lions Pride Park is on the same side of the river, and Riverside Park is on the opposite bank.

Throughout this trip, keep your eyes open for gravel bars, small islands, and small rapids, particularly in midsummer or later. The river is still trying to find its way after the eruption of 1980 and the flood of 1996. A few shallow spots may be encountered in the first half of the trip. Plan to have lunch somewhere along the northern half of this trip because the southern half becomes much less rural in character.

Although there were once two public boat ramps on this section of the river, they were destroyed by the flood of 1996. As a result, the only boat ramp available to you is the one where you left your car in Longview.

By the time you reach the railroad bridge near rivermile 6.5, the current slows considerably, and progress requires much more effort, particularly if the wind is blowing. At rivermile 5, paddle under two highway bridges between Kelso and Longview. If you arrive at Gerhart Gardens on a warm summer day, the boat ramps will be frequented by loud jet skis. Keep close to shore and out of their way.

If you have extra time and energy, explore the calm waters of the Coweeman River (also spelled Coweman on some maps), which enters the Cowlitz under a railroad bridge directly across the Cowlitz from Gerhart Gardens.

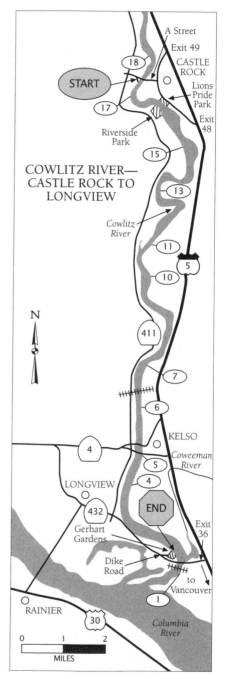

COWLITZ RIVER—
CASTLE ROCK TO
LONGVIEW

47 Coldwater Lake

Location: Near Mount St. Helens
Distance: Up to 6 miles
Time: 2 to 6 hours
Maps: USGS Elk Rock and Spirit Lake West 7.5"
Season: Spring to fall
Rating: B

When Mount St. Helens erupted in 1980, countless tons of ash and rock were sent rushing down the Toutle River. Most of the destruction occurred in the valley of the North Fork of the Toutle River, where the landscape was dramatically altered. About 8 miles northwest of the volcano, where Coldwater Creek joined the North Fork of the Toutle, the eruption left the Coldwater Creek valley dammed with rock and ash, and Coldwater Lake was formed.

Shortly after the eruption, the U.S. Forest Service and the state of Washington began plans to construct facilities for the many visitors that would come to the new Mount St. Helens National Volcanic Monument. Today, a drive up Spirit Lake Memorial Highway shows the results of those efforts: five visitor centers line a beautiful new highway built to replace the highway that was destroyed by the eruption. Near the end of that new highway lie Coldwater Lake and a new visitor center standing on a bluff above the lake, affording a dramatic view across the lake to the crater of Mount St. Helens. For current information on Coldwater Lake, call the Mount St. Helens National Volcanic Monument headquarters or the Coldwater Ridge Visitor Center (see the appendix at the back of this book).

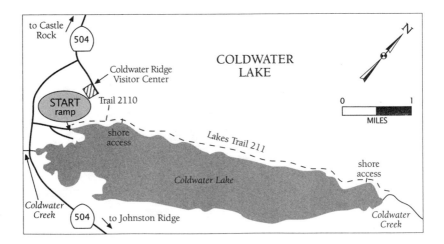

Coldwater Lake

To reach Coldwater Lake from Interstate 5, take the Castle Rock exit, exit 49, then turn east onto Washington Route 504 and follow it for 43 miles. Along the way, you will pass four visitor centers. The main Mount St. Helens Visitor Center is near Silver Lake, about 5 miles east of Interstate 5. The Hoffstadt Bluffs Visitor Center is about 27 miles east of the freeway, and the Mount St. Helens Forest Learning Center is located at North Fork Ridge about 6 miles farther east. At milepost 43, just before reaching the Coldwater Ridge Visitor Center, turn at the signs pointing to Coldwater Lake and Johnston Ridge, and follow the new highway 2 miles down the hill. Just before crossing a bridge over Coldwater Creek, turn left to the boat ramp at the lake. The fifth visitor center is about 7 miles past the lake, on 4300-foot-high Johnston Ridge.

The lake is about 2.7 miles long. Fishing and boating are allowed, but no gasoline motors are permitted. In addition, to preserve the fragile environment, boaters are not allowed access to the shoreline except at the boat ramp and at two points along the north shore. The first access point is about 1 mile northeast of the boat ramp, and the second is at the extreme northern end of the lake. Both points offer access to Lakes Trail 211, which follows the north shore. The first access point also offers public rest rooms. Both points are marked by signs visible from the water. A sign at the boat ramp shows both access points on a map, or a copy of the map is available at the Coldwater Ridge Visitor Center. Boaters are not allowed to land at any other points.

The setting of Coldwater Lake is dramatic. It lies in a narrow canyon that winds its way northeast to twin-pointed Minnie Peak. Although much of the Coldwater Creek valley was logged before the eruption, evidence of the destruction of the volcanic eruption is everywhere. Very few trees were left standing. A few snags can be seen here and there, looking like lonely bristles on a boar's back. At the head of the lake, the face of Minnie Peak rises dramatically, covered with downed logs evidencing the force of the blast.

Coldwater Lake has two significant drawbacks. The first is the wind. The high mountain landscape offers little protection from the wind, which can come up unexpectedly, particularly in the afternoon. On some days, the lake may be calm and serene, but on many days it is rough and blustery. On windy days, the lake is no place for open canoes, nor is it a good place to paddle with small children. A sea kayak piloted by an experienced paddler would be much better.

The second drawback is the user fee. Visitors to Coldwater Lake are required to purchase a Monument Pass, which presently costs $8 per person over the age of 15. The same pass is required at the main visitor center and the visitor centers at Coldwater Ridge and Johnston Ridge. A Northwest Forest Pass is also acceptable.

48 Upper Columbia Slough

Location: Northeast Portland and Gresham
Distance: Up to 6 miles
Time: Up to 4 hours
Map: USGS Camas and Mount Tabor 7.5"
Season: Year-round
Rating: A

The Columbia Slough is a narrow backwater channel that runs parallel to the Columbia River in its historic floodplain north of Portland and Gresham. About 19 miles long, the slough begins at Fairview Lake and empties into the Willamette River near Kelley Point. A few hardy souls have paddled the entire length of the slough in a single day, including three portages and paddling through two culverts. The rest of us, however, divide the slough into three sections and paddle one section at a time. The upper slough flows from the Gresham area to Northeast 143rd Avenue, the middle section flows from Northeast 143rd to Northeast 18th avenues, and the lower slough flows from Northeast 17th Avenue to the Willamette River at Kelley Point Park. Each of those segments of the slough is separated from the other sections by a large dike. This trip tours the upper section of the slough in Gresham

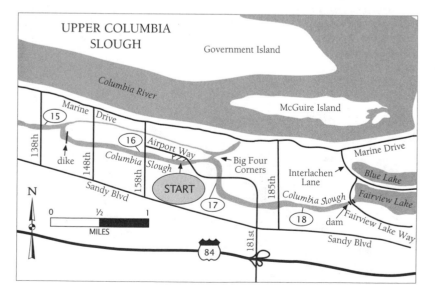

UPPER COLUMBIA SLOUGH

Government Island

Columbia River

McGuire Island

Marine Drive

15

Marine Drive

138th

16

Airport Way

Big Four Corners

Interlachen Lane

Blue Lake

dike

148th

Columbia Slough

158th

START

185th

Columbia Slough

Fairview Lake

Sandy Blvd

17

18

dam

Fairview Lake Way

N

0   ½   1

MILES

84

181st

Sandy Blvd

and northeast Portland. To paddle the middle and lower sections of the slough, see Trip 49, Middle Columbia Slough, and Trip 50, Lower Columbia Slough.

Begin this trip at the public canoe launch at 16550 NE Airport Way in northeast Portland. From Interstate 84, take the Northeast 181st Avenue exit, then turn north onto Northeast 181st Avenue and follow it as it turns west and becomes Airport Way. Along the way, you'll cross the slough on three bridges. The parking lot for the launch is located on the left just past the third bridge, before a large Portland Water Bureau tank.

Launch your boat from the floating dock near the bridge, or from the rocks under the bridge. You may then paddle either west or east. If you paddle west, the slough will lead you under bridges at Northeast 158th and 148th Avenues, eventually reaching a dike at Northeast 143rd Avenue, about 1 mile west of the dock. Although the dike can be portaged, it is quite large, and most paddlers simply return to the dock, for a round trip of about an hour.

For a longer and more interesting trip, paddle east from the dock to an area known as Big Four Corners, named for the I-shaped intersection of the Columbia Slough and the North Slough. This area is heavily wooded with cottonwood and willow; it has the most wildlife and is the most scenic of any portion of the slough. Expect to see a lot of blackberries and nightshade. The latter is poisonous.

The bottom of the I is located less than a quarter mile east of the launch. Turning left (north) at this intersection leads to a T intersection with the North Slough. The west fork of the North Slough (marked by a wood pedestrian bridge on the left bank) is not navigable, but the east fork leads about a quarter

Upper Columbia Slough

mile to Pump Station 4 on Marine Drive. This pump station, and another at Northeast 17th Avenue, are used to prevent flooding by pumping water from the upper slough into the Columbia River and into the lower slough. Keep a safe distance from the pump station. The pumps operate throughout the year, not just during periods of high water, to remove stagnant water so it will be replaced with clean groundwater.

Turning east from the bottom of the I leads south and then east toward Fairview Lake. This section of the slough passes under several bridges (Airport Way, 181st, and 185th) and around a few islands west of 181st Avenue. Progress is halted at the mouth of Fairview Lake when the slough passes under a bridge and is blocked by a small dam. Retrace your route back to the launch. (Note that the bridge at Fairview Lake is an alternate launch site.)

Unlike the lower Columbia Slough, the water level in the upper slough is somewhat constant. The lower slough is connected to the Willamette River, and thus the water level in the lower slough fluctuates with the river level and the tide. The upper slough is separated from the lower slough and from the Columbia by dikes, floodgates, and the two pump stations. In most years, the water level in the upper slough varies little, from about 8 feet in late summer to about 10.5 feet in winter. Gauges (posts with river levels marked on them like a ruler) can be viewed from most of the bridges along this route. The current is usually gentle or nonexistent. A few shallow spots may be encountered late in the summer.

Although this trip may be enjoyed year-round, the slough accumulates considerable amounts of algae during periods of low water in late summer; the best paddling is when water levels are higher.

At any time of year, the Columbia slough is a rich wildlife resource. Watch for ducks, green heron, snipe, red-tailed hawks, osprey, turkey vultures, killdeer, otters, nutria, muskrat, beaver, and freshwater clams. Don't eat the clams or any fish caught in the slough. The slough is getting cleaner every year, but it's still not in the best of shape.

49 Middle Columbia Slough

Location: Northeast Portland
Distance: Up to 8 miles
Time: Up to 6 hours
Map: USGS Portland and Mount Tabor 7.5"
Season: Year-round
Rating: A (Note: This trip passes through a culvert)

This section of the Columbia Slough stretches from Northeast 143rd to Northeast 18th Avenues, a total of 125 blocks, or about 8 miles. Although this trip is in the midst of a major urban area, watch for otters, nutria, green herons, and owls. This trip may be enjoyed year-round, but the slough accumulates

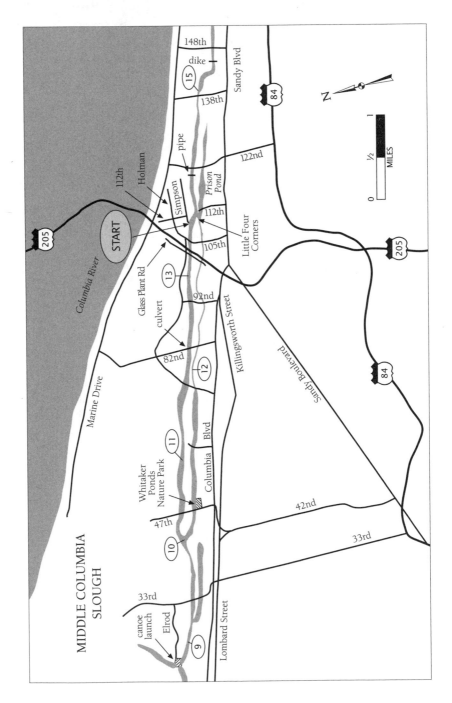

considerable amounts of algae during periods of low water in summer; the best paddling is when water levels are higher.

Before starting on this trip, read the entire trip description and decide whether you would like to paddle from Northeast 112th Avenue to Northeast 47th Avenue (including a passage through a culvert), or from Northeast 112th to Northeast 18th Avenue, or whether you would prefer to explore the area around the put-in at Northeast 112th, and then return to the put-in. To do the paddle to Northeast 47th Avenue, leave your extra car or bicycle at Whitaker Ponds Nature Park at 7040 Northeast 47th, north of Columbia Boulevard. Park near the locked gate next to the unlocked pedestrian gate. (Do not park inside the fence, at the risk of being locked in.) To do the paddle to Northeast 18th, leave your extra car or bicycle at 1880 Northeast Elrod Drive. (From Columbia Boulevard, turn north onto Northeast 33rd Avenue, then turn west onto Northeast Elrod and drive west to its end at a parking lot marked "Canoe Trail Parking." Note that the slough along Northeast Elrod is not the Columbia Slough.)

The put-in is located at 11198 Northeast Simpson Street, on the north shore of the slough, just south of the Airport Way interchange (exit 24) on Interstate 205. From Airport Way just east of the interchange, drive west on Northeast Holman, turn south onto Northeast 112th Avenue, then turn west onto Northeast Simpson. A canoe launch has been constructed here on the grounds of Portland Water Bureau well site 29. Limited parking is available; do not block the driveway to the well. Carry your boat across the lawn to the left of the well, where a walkway leads to a floating dock specially designed to accommodate canoes and kayaks.

From the dock, you have two options: paddle upstream to the east or downstream to the west. A short paddle upstream leads to an I-shaped intersection known as Little Four Corners. You will be entering the intersection by way of the northwest branch. If you continue east, the northeast fork leads six blocks to a low pipe at Northwest 118th Avenue. During periods of low water, you may be able to paddle under the pipe, or you may be able to slide your boat under the pipe while you walk (perhaps with some difficulty) around the pipe on the north shore. If the water is high, you may need to carry your boat around the pipe (again, with some difficulty), or you may prefer to turn around and return to Little Four Corners. (To paddle the part of the slough beyond the low pipe, launch on the North Slough at Northeast 122nd Avenue or at the bridge at 138th Avenue. The slough is navigable from the low pipe east to a dike at 143rd Avenue. The culvert under 122nd is usually navigable, depending on water levels.)

If you turn south at Little Four Corners, you will immediately notice that the quality of the water suddenly improves. At the south end of the intersection, the southwest fork is on the right, but it is narrow and often clogged with logs and other debris. Instead, turn left onto the southeast branch and paddle to a small wooden bridge at Northeast 112th Avenue. Suddenly, the water becomes even clearer. The slough under the bridge is not passable, but resourceful paddlers will be able to portage around the bridge on the south side into a portion of the slough known as Prison Pond. (Don't try paddling under the bridge; the bridge is very low and the current can be strong. Don't portage on the north bank; it is part of the Inverness Jail, and entry is not permitted). Although Prison Pond is only five blocks long, it is wide and very interesting due to springs on the bottom of the pond where clear water enters. Look for bare patches of sand on the floor of the slough; the water can be seen flowing up through the sand. Prison Pond ends at two small culverts at Northeast 118th Avenue, east of which the south slough is not navigable.

After exploring the Little Four Corners area, if you'd like to complete the paddle to Northeast 47th Avenue (or beyond to Northeast 18th), then head downstream, past the put-in. The slough continues west for about twenty blocks without encountering any obstructions. At Northeast 82nd Avenue, the slough flows through a large culvert under a major highway. If the water level permits, stow your paddle in your boat and float through the culvert. For propulsion, either use the gentle current (if present) or use your hands on the sides of the culvert to push your boat through. (Gloves would come in handy here.) Watch for spider webs! After you reach daylight at the other end, the slough continues west unobstructed another 65 blocks to Northeast 18th Avenue.

If you paddle west past the 82nd Avenue culvert, and your only car is at Northeast 112th, the big problem will be getting back to your car. Paddling up the slough against the gentle current is usually not difficult, but the culvert is too narrow to permit paddling. Depending on the current, you might (or might not) be able to use your hands on the walls of the culvert to push your boat back through.

A culvert on the Middle Columbia Slough

Below 82nd Avenue, the slough passes two possible left turns. The first possible left turn is located five blocks west of the Northeast 47th Avenue bridge, where Whitaker Slough, a southern arm of the Columbia Slough) leads back to the east to a bridge at Northeast 47th. Just east of this bridge, landing at a floating dock on the south bank will enable you to carry your boat to your car at Whitaker Ponds Nature Park, about 100 yards to the south. To reach your car, use the unlocked pedestrian gate next to the locked auto gate. (If you'd like, you could continue paddling on the southern arm as far east as Northeast 63rd Avenue, where an impassible culvert prevents farther progress. If you portage over Northeast 63rd, you could paddle another dozen blocks east to Northeast Alderwood Road.)

For an even longer trip, continue paddling west on the main channel to the next possible left turn west of Northeast 33rd Avenue, where another southern arm, known as Buffalo Slough, leads east for about five blocks to a dead end at Northeast 33rd. Or continue west on the main channel, which dead-ends at a dike at Northeast 18th Avenue. If you left your car here, turn north to a canoe launch located at the back of a small bay. A 100-yard portage trail will lead you to your car. From the parking lot, another 100-yard portage west, over the dike, will lead to the lower Columbia Slough, described in Trip 50.

50 Lower Columbia Slough

Location: North Portland
Distance: Up to 7 miles
Time: Up to 4 hours
Maps and charts: USGS Sauvie Island, Linnton, and Portland 7.5";
NOAA chart 18526 or 18524
Season: Year-round
Rating: A

This section of the Columbia Slough offers three public canoe launches, one at each end and one in the middle. This section can be paddled in either direction. The trip described here begins at the east end and paddles downstream to the west end at Kelley Point Park, near the Willamette River. (To avoid the use of a car shuttle, begin and end your trip at any of the three public boat launches. Simply paddle up or down the slough as far as time and energy permit, then paddle back to your car.)

When planning your trip, however, consult a tide table to determine the direction of the gentle tidal current. Unlike the other sections of the slough, this section is connected to the Willamette River and is influenced by the tide. Also take a glance at a current weather forecast. Kelley Point Park is a favorite of kite fliers, with good reason. Plan ahead, and don't end up paddling back to your car while fighting both the tide and the wind.

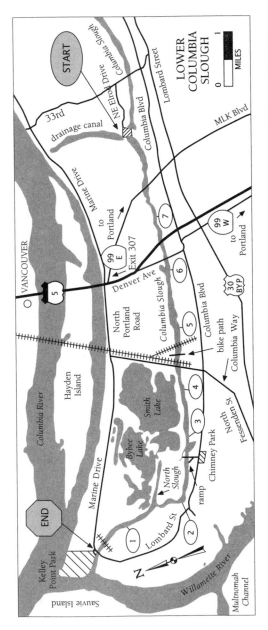

Begin this trip by leaving an extra car at the launch at Kelley Point Park, reached from Interstate 5, exit 307, by driving west on Marine Drive. The canoe launch is just inside the entrance to the park; turn left onto the second dirt road after entering the park.

Then drive to the easternmost ramp, at 1880 Northeast Elrod Drive, to launch your boat. From Columbia Boulevard, turn north onto Northeast 33rd Avenue, then turn west onto Northeast Elrod and drive west to its end at a parking lot marked "Canoe Trail Parking." Two trails lead from this parking lot to two canoe launches. The trail at the east end of the parking lot leads to the middle section of the slough (see Trip 49, Middle Columbia Slough), while the trail at the west end of the parking lot leads over the dike to this lower section.

For a shorter trip, begin or end your paddle at the canoe launch in the middle of this section, at rivermile 2.7 near Chimney Park and the old St. Johns Landfill (now closed). From the 9300 block of Columbia Boulevard, turn north onto an inconspicuous road almost exactly across Columbia Boulevard from the entrance to Chimney Park and the Stanley Park Archives and Records Center. (Addresses here are somewhat misleading; look for the park entrance.) Follow this road about a quarter mile north toward a bridge.

SMITH AND BYBEE LAKES 169

Don't cross the bridge, but instead turn left to find a boat ramp and parking area just west of the bridge.

Several optional side trips are available in this section of the slough. One side trip would be to explore the arm known as the North Slough, at rivermile 1.5. Another would be to portage into Smith and Bybee lakes, just north of the slough. The best place to portage is at the east end of the North Slough, at a water control structure. (See Trip 51, Smith and Bybee Lakes, for details.) A third side trip at the east end of this section would be to portage into the Peninsula Drainage Canal, which leads north about 2 miles, nearly reaching the Columbia River.

You will encounter a four-way intersection on the main slough near rivermile 3, plus some islands near rivermile 5. Carry a map to make sure you take the correct route, although the slough will quickly dead-end if you don't. Also near rivermile 5 is a new pedestrian bridge, part of the Forty Mile Loop Trail.

Wildlife activity along the slough is at a peak in the spring and fall. Take your bird book and a pair of binoculars, and watch for herons, hawks, and other species. In the fall, shorebirds migrate through the area. Some paddlers prefer visiting the slough in the spring. The slough has little current during the summer, and it becomes quite stagnant, but the high water of winter and spring tends to flush it out.

51 Smith and Bybee Lakes

Location: North Portland
Distance: 2 to 12 miles
Time: 2 to 6 hours
Maps and charts: USGS Portland, Sauvie Island, Linnton, and Vancouver 7.5"; NOAA chart 18526 or 18524
Season: January through June
Rating: A

Smith and Bybee Lakes are two large bodies of water in north Portland, but most Portland residents have never seen them or even heard of them. Bybee Lake is 250 acres in area with a 5.9-mile shoreline; Smith Lake is even larger, at about 600 acres with a 6.9-mile shoreline. The two lakes represent a huge natural area in the middle of a major industrial zone. No motorboats are allowed, except electric motors; the only noise disturbing the scene will probably be planes approaching or departing from Portland International Airport to the east, the sound of a distant train, or perhaps race cars at nearby Portland International Raceway.

The best access point to Smith and Bybee Lakes is located on Marine Drive on the north side of Smith Lake. From Interstate 5, exit 307, follow Marine Drive westbound. About 2 miles after leaving Interstate 5, Marine Drive climbs over a large overpass with railroad tracks beneath. (The top of this overpass offers one of the few views of Smith and Bybee Lakes, and allows you to judge the water level in the lakes.) Shortly after leaving the overpass, turn left into a small public parking lot on the south side of the road marked by a Smith and Bybee Lakes Wildlife Area sign at 4949 Marine Drive (oddly enough, it is across the street from 5337 Marine Drive). Proceed east through the parking lot and follow the road/bike path past restrooms and a second parking area to a third parking area 0.5 miles from Marine Drive. Carry your boat down a 300-foot gravel path to Smith Lake. During periods of low water, a mudflat may need to be crossed to reach the water.

An alternative access point requires launching on the Columbia Slough, either at Kelley Point Park or at the ramp near Chimney Park. (See Trip 50, Lower Columbia Slough, for directions to these two points.) From either of these points, paddle to the junction between the main Columbia Slough and the North Slough, then paddle 0.75 mile to the east end of the North Slough, where boats can be portaged near the water control structure at the west end of the southernmost passage between Smith and Bybee Lakes, into the south end of Bybee Lake.

The water level in the two lakes is controlled by the water control structure, built in 2003 to replace a dam originally built in 1982. The 1982 dam was intended to help control outbreaks of avian botulism, but the elimination of tidal influences had unintended negative impact on the ecology of the lakes. As a result, in 2003 it was replaced by a water control structure that allowed the tidal influence to return. Native trees are also being replanted around the lakes.

The control structure is located at the east end of the North Slough. Each winter, when steady rains arrive, the control structure is closed and the water level in the lakes is permitted to rise, partly to control invasive reed canary grass, and partly to provide salmon habitat. Paddling is best during this period because the extensive mudflats around the lakes are flooded. In mid-June, the control structure is slowly opened and the water level is reduced by several vertical feet. During this drawdown period, paddling near the water control structure may be dangerous due to the steep outfall. By mid-August, the water level in the lakes reaches the level of the Columbia Slough, and the drawdown is complete. For the rest of the year, the lakes fluctuate with the tidal influence from the Columbia Slough. Extensive mudflats result, which benefit migrating shorebirds, but also make for poor paddling. After the drawdown is complete, paddlers may be able to paddle from the North Slough through the control structure into Smith and Bybee Lakes, depending on the level of the tide. The lakes will be very shallow, however, and mudflats will likely prevent farther progress into the lakes. Be very careful to not get stranded on the mud by a falling tide.

As a result of the seasonal fluctuations, the best time to paddle on the lakes is usually from January to June. Ideally, wait for a calm day; the area can be very windy.

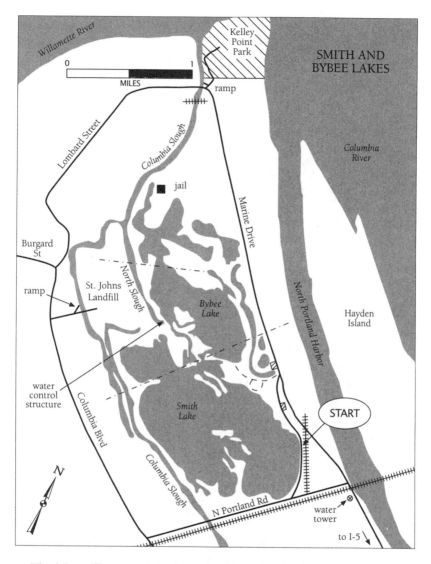

The lakes offer a myriad of sloughs, islands, and inlets to explore. When water levels are low and the water control structure is open, consult a tide table before launching and watch the tide carefully to make certain your route can be retraced to your launching point. If the water control structure is closed, the tide does not influence the level of the lakes.

The two lakes are connected by two sloughs. The southernmost of the sloughs is not difficult to locate where it connects the southeast corner of Bybee Lake to the northwest corner of Smith Lake. The other slough is farther north; it is shorter, narrower, and more difficult to find. Keep track of familiar landmarks, and carry a compass and a detailed map at all times. During periods of low water, the two sloughs might not be navigable. When paddling back to the Marine Drive launch from the southern slough, the water tower in the distance is a good landmark to aim toward.

When water levels are extremely high, the lakes will be greatly enlarged and boats can be paddled from the Columbia Slough without any need to portage. As a general rule, the water control structure and several portions of the berm between the lakes and the slough will be under water when the Columbia and the Willamette Rivers are at about 15 feet or higher on the Portland or the Vancouver gauges. Check your daily newspaper for gauge levels, or see the appendix at the back of this book for other sources.

South of Bybee Lake, across the North Slough, is the St. Johns Landfill, now closed and resurfaced with dirt and grass. Some of the dump fees were placed in a trust fund and are now used to maintain Smith and Bybee Lakes; tax dollars are not used.

At the east end of Smith Lake, North Portland Road lies along a dike that played an important role in the history of Portland. On May 30, 1948, when the Columbia River was 5 feet above flood stage and Smith Lake was swollen with flood waters, this dike broke, flooding the town of Vanport, a "temporary" World War II town built to house shipbuilders and their families. Fifteen people were killed and 18,500 were left homeless in the flood.

Today, Smith and Bybee Lakes are popular with local fishers who angle for crappie, bluegill, bullhead catfish, and largemouth bass. If you don't bring a fishing pole, at least bring your binoculars: the lakes attract extensive wildlife. Waterfowl, shorebirds, and birds of prey abound, as do several earth-bound species. Two are of particular note.

The beaver population of the lakes has become so extensive (about fifty beavers in the two lakes) that authorities have decided to trap some of them and transport them out of the area to reduce the damage being done to the vegetation. It is hard to not notice the hundreds of trees that have been felled by these industrious rodents, particularly in the northwest area of Smith Lake near the two channels to Bybee Lake. In the winter of 2005–06, the beavers built a lodge that blocked the main channel between the two lakes; the lodge may still be present when you visit. Don't expect to see any beavers in broad daylight, however; they are nocturnal, appearing shortly after sundown. Instead, wait for a full moon and paddle quietly late in the evening.

The other notable residents are about 250 western painted turtles, a species that has been declared "sensitive" by the state of Oregon. On warm days after March or April (when the turtles emerge from hibernation), look closely at muddy banks and floating logs, where these cold-blooded reptiles like to sun themselves. Most of the turtles have shells about 2 or 3 inches long; some are as large as 9 inches. The colors of their shells vary, but many of the smaller turtles resemble brown leaves drying in the sun.

52 Sauvie Island

Location: North of Portland
Distance: 1 to 12 miles
Time: 1 to 6 hours
Maps and chart: USGS Sauvie Island and St. Helens 7.5"; NOAA chart 18524
Season: Late April to late September
Rating: A

Sauvie (not Sauvies) Island is one of the largest freshwater islands in the country. Much of it is covered by myriad lakes and sloughs, offering endless opportunities for flatwater paddling. Imagine an island so large it has its own rivers, lakes, islands, and sloughs.

The island has a long history, from early Indian settlements to settlements by Europeans in the 1830s. It was named for a French-Canadian employee of the Hudson's Bay Company dairy that once operated on the island. Today, the southern part of the island is farmland while the northern part is maintained by the Oregon Department of Fish and Wildlife as the Sauvie Island Wildlife Area.

Sauvie Island is noted for its bird populations. Great blue herons are common, watch for sandhill cranes in the winter, and in the spring a dozen or more bald eagles might be seen in a single day. Underfoot, you will see (and smell) field mint, the only mint native to the Northwest. In the shallow waters, watch for carp swimming near the surface.

Nearly all of the wetlands on the island are closed to the non-hunting public during the waterfowl hunting season. Although the hunting season usually runs from early October to mid-January, the closure usually begins October 1 and ends April 16. Call the wildlife area manager for current information (see the appendix at the back of this book). The wildlife area is open to the public all summer, but the water levels are best for paddling in spring and early summer.

To get to Sauvie Island from Portland, drive north on US Highway 30 about 12 miles to the Sauvie Island Bridge. Cross the bridge and drive north past the store on Sauvie Island Road. (See the sketch map for Trip 53, Multnomah Channel and Scappoose Bay, for an overview of the island and this access route.) But also remember to stop at the store and buy a daily permit for parking in the Sauvie Island Wildlife Area. If you plan to return, buy an annual permit.

The sketch map shown here hardly does justice to the many sloughs, lakes, and islands of Sauvie Island. For the safest journey, carry a compass and the USGS topographic maps to help you find your way through the intricate landscape. You may be surprised by the number of paddlers you encounter who don't have detailed maps and are in various degrees of lost. Even if you carry

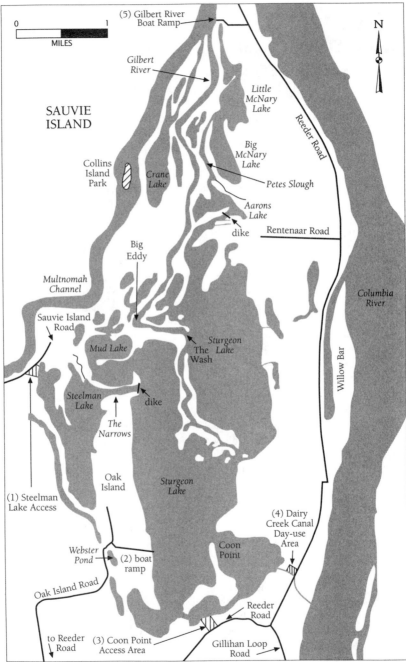

0 ___ 1
MILES

(5) Gilbert River
Boat Ramp

Gilbert
River

Little
McNary
Lake

SAUVIE
ISLAND

Big
McNary
Lake

Collins
Island
Park

Crane
Lake

Petes Slough

Aarons
Lake

dike

Rentenaar Road

N

Reeder Road

Big
Eddy

Multnomah
Channel

Columbia
River

Sauvie Island
Road

Mud Lake

Sturgeon
The Lake
Wash

Willow Bar

Steelman
Lake

dike

The
Narrows

Oak
Island

Sturgeon
Lake

(1) Steelman
Lake Access

(4) Dairy
Creek Canal
Day-use
Area

Webster
Pond

(2) boat
ramp

Coon
Point

Oak Island Road

Reeder
Road

to Reeder
Road

(3) Coon Point
Access Area

Gillihan Loop
Road

the USGS maps, however, don't expect them to be perfect. The landscape changes from year to year and season to season, due to fluctuations in the water level, changes caused by other natural forces, and even a few man-made changes.

The launching point for your boat depends on the season, the tide, and the portions of the island you want to explore. Five possibilities are described here, with Sauvie Island Road the starting point for all of them.

1. Steelman Lake Access: Steelman Lake can be explored as well as used to reach Sturgeon Lake. The two lakes are connected by a passage at the north end of Oak Island known as the Narrows. A small dike blocks the east end of the Narrows. The dike is generally under water when the Portland or the Vancouver River gauges read 13 feet or higher. Below that level, a short portage will be required, and Steelman Lake will be free of tidal influences. To reach the Steelman Lake Access from the Sauvie Island Bridge, drive north on Sauvie Island Road for 9 miles. Just north of where the pavement ends, the access area is on the right, on the west shore of Steelman Lake.

2. Oak Island Boat Ramp: For quick access to the main part of Sturgeon Lake, Oak Island (actually a peninsula) can be reached from Sauvie Island Road by turning northeast onto Reeder Road, and then turning left onto Oak Island Road. Drive north for 3.8 miles to a right turn just past Webster Pond, then drive east 0.5 mile to the boat ramp.

3. Coon Point Access Area: The main part of Sturgeon Lake can also be reached by boat from Coon Point Access Area, except in late summer or early fall when the Coon Point area is dry. To reach the access area from Sauvie Island Road, turn onto Reeder Road, drive northeast on Reeder Road past the turnoff to Oak Island Road and continue to a small roadside parking area on the left, then carry your boat over the dike. The portage is about 100 yards. Paddle northeast, then northwest to get around Coon Point to the main portion of Sturgeon Lake, or during high water a passage can be found to the west at the base of the Coon Point peninsula.

4. Dairy Creek Canal Day-use Area: In recent years, a canal was constructed between Dairy Creek and the Columbia, allowing water to circulate more freely into and out of Sturgeon Lake. The canal can be used by paddlers to reach Sturgeon Lake from Reeder Road. Unfortunately, launching here has two disadvantages. First, the banks of the canal are steep, and launching is not as easy as it is at one of the boat ramps. Second, the section of Sturgeon Lake west of Diary Creek Canal is shallow and may turn into mudflats at low tide, particularly late in the summer. To reach the day-use area from Sauvie Island Road, turn onto Reeder Road and drive northeast past Oak Island Road and Coon Point Access Area. At the intersection with Gillihan Loop Road, continue 0.4 mile north on Reeder Road to Dairy Creek Canal. Park at the day-use area and carry your boat down to the canal. Once in the canal, paddle west onto Sturgeon Lake. (Don't use the canal to paddle east to the Columbia, because it crosses private property.) When you reach Sturgeon Lake, carefully note how to find your way back to Dairy Creek; it may be hard to find.

5. Gilbert River Boat Ramp: This boat ramp is on Multnomah Channel, but it provides access to the Gilbert River, the mouth of which is only a few yards south of the ramp. In addition, Little McNary Lake, one of the numerous lakes north of Sturgeon Lake, can also be reached from near the Gilbert River boat ramp. (This road is occasionally closed due to high water; if the river gauge is above 11 feet, call the refuge manager to check on the status of the road.) To reach the ramp from Sauvie Island Road, turn onto Reeder Road and follow it past the Oak Island, Coon Point, and Dairy Creek Canal access areas. After Reeder Road turns to gravel, follow it for another mile to a left turn, which leads to the ramp. To paddle in the lakes, launch on the south side of the road a few yards before the parking lot for the boat ramp, then paddle south as far as time and water levels permit through Little McNary Lake, Big McNary Lake, Aarons Lake, and Sturgeon Lake. The slough connecting these lakes is known as Petes Slough. Short portages may be required in spots, depending on water levels.

If you paddle south as far as Aarons Lake, the return trip to your car can be made via the Gilbert River, which will lead you to the boat ramp at its mouth. For paddlers traveling south through the McNary Lakes and Aarons Lake, the Gilbert River can be reached at three points, enabling paddlers to complete three different loop trips. The shortest route (about 4 miles round trip) portages into the Gilbert River from the southwest corner of Aarons Lake. The longest route (about 10 miles) enters the Gilbert River near the east shore of Sturgeon Lake. An intermediate choice (about 8 miles) enters the Gilbert River at the Wash. The two longer loops almost always require a short portage at the back of a small bay on the southern shore of Aarons Lake. If the tide is going out, paddle these trips clockwise. If the tide is coming in, paddle counterclockwise.

An even longer loop trip would involve paddling south through the McNary Lakes and Aarons Lake, into Sturgeon Lake, through the Narrows, and across Steelman Lake, followed by a portage into the Multnomah Channel, which leads back to the Gilbert River boat ramp. See Trip 53, Multnomah Channel and Scappoose Bay, for a description of the access to the Multnomah Channel just south of the Steelman Lake access area.

The type of trip you will experience on Sauvie Island depends on water levels. Check river gauge levels and tide tables when planning your trip. When the Columbia River gauge at Vancouver reads 10 feet, navigating is easy, and at 12 feet the two portages described above are under water. Once the water levels drop below those portages, Aarons Lake and the McNary Lakes are no longer subject to any tidal influence. Later in the year, when the gauge is around 5 feet, most of the banks are steep and muddy, particularly on the Gilbert River.

Wherever you launch, beware of the wind and the tide. On Sauvie Island, a low tide can do more than make you paddle against a tidal current. It can strand you and your boat in the middle of huge mudflats with no chance of escape until the next high tide twelve hours later, particularly on Sturgeon Lake. If you encounter shallow water and the tide is going out, head for dry

Gilbert River dock on Sauvie Island

land pronto. Even better, don't paddle into a shallow body of water unless the tide is going in with you. If your boat becomes stranded in the mud, do not attempt to walk on the mud: it will not support your body weight. The mud is 4 feet deep in Sturgeon Lake, and some stranded boaters who have attempted to walk on the mud have required helicopter rescue. Again, study the tide tables carefully when planning your trip, particularly late in the year when water levels are low.

53 Multnomah Channel and Scappoose Bay

Location: North of Portland
Distance: 1 to 10 miles
Time: 1 to 5 hours
Maps and chart: USGS Linnton, Sauvie Island, and St. Helens 7.5";
NOAA chart 18524
Season: Year-round
Rating: A

Multnomah Channel forms the western shore of Sauvie Island, which sits in the mouth of the Willamette where it joins the Columbia. The 21-mile channel runs from the Willamette River at the south end of Sauvie Island to the Columbia River, near Scappoose Bay and the town of St. Helens. The channel is quite close to Portland, yet offers a rural atmosphere. While powerboat traffic occasionally disrupts the tranquility of the channel, the size and frequency of the traffic is limited when compared to the main stem of the Willamette or the Columbia. The channel's 21 miles offer considerable opportunities for exploring, as well as several boat ramps and commercial marinas for easy access, although some of the commercial operators may charge a small launching fee. The lack of a current (other than the tide) means that two-way trips are easily accomplished, eliminating any car shuttle logistics.

Multnomah Channel also offers access to several smaller sloughs leading to the interior of the north end of Sauvie Island. When planning a trip into Sauvie Island, remember that the Sauvie Island Wildlife Area, which consists of most of the north end of the island, is generally closed to non-hunters from October 1 to April 16 each year.

The sketch map shows three public boat ramps, one on the mainland and two on the island side of the channel. Either paddle from one ramp to another, or start and end at the same ramp. (Several commercial marinas can also be found on the channel; they generally charge a modest fee to use their boat ramps.) In addition to the three public boat ramps, an informal access to Multnomah Channel can be found on Sauvie Island Road. Some of these access points require a parking permit, available at the store on Sauvie Island; see

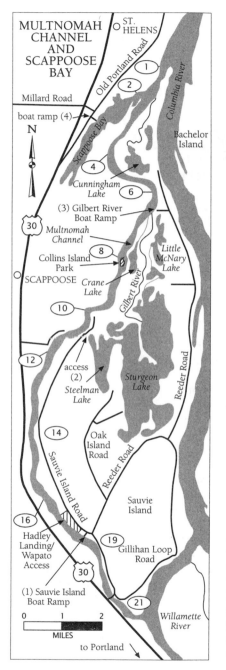

Trip 52, Sauvie Island, for details. The access points are listed below, from south to north.

1. Sauvie Island Boat Ramp (about rivermile 18): To get to Sauvie Island from Portland, drive north on US Highway 30 about 12 miles to the Sauvie Island Bridge. Cross the bridge and drive north to just past the turnoff to Reeder Road. The boat ramp is on the left.

2. Sauvie Island Road Access Area (about rivermile 11): Drive north on Sauvie Island Road past Sauvie Island Boat Ramp. Nine miles from the bridge, just north of where the pavement ends, an informal public access area to Multnomah Channel is on the left.

3. Gilbert River Boat Ramp (about rivermile 7.5): From the Sauvie Island Bridge, drive north on Sauvie Island Road to Reeder Road. Turn onto Reeder Road and follow it past Oak Island Road and Gillihan Loop Road, continuing north. After Reeder Road turns to gravel, follow it for another mile to a left turn, which leads to the Gilbert River boat ramp. A parking permit is required.

4. Scappoose Bay Boat Ramp (about a mile up Scappoose Bay from rivermile 2 of Multnomah Channel): From Portland, drive north on US Highway 30 past the town of Scappoose to Bennett Road at milepost 25.8. Turn right, and then turn left onto Old Portland Road and drive 0.4 miles to the boat ramp and marina. A fee is charged to park at this boat ramp. Three docks are available, but one is reserved for canoes and kayaks. Scappoose Bay

Houseboats along Multnomah Channel

Kayaking offers kayak sales, rentals, and guided tours from its location at this marina; phone (503) 397-2161.

At rivermile 17.5, a public floating dock (Hadley Landing) has been constructed adjacent to a public access area known as Wapato Access. Hiking trails lead to Sauvie Island Road, but the distance is much too long to portage a boat.

When planning your trip, be conservative in estimating how many miles you will want to paddle. It is unlikely that you will want to paddle much more than 10 or 12 miles, especially if the wind or tide is working against you. If you would like to cover much more than that, consider an overnight visit to Collins Island Park (shown on some maps as Coon Island) at rivermile 8, one of the few areas on the channel where camping is permitted.

If you get tired of paddling up and down the channel, several adjacent areas are worth exploring. Scappoose Bay is large and intricate, but also extremely shallow at low tide. Sauvie Island offers three sloughs that can be entered from Multnomah Channel. (Two of the three are closed to the non-hunting public during the fall and winter bird-hunting season; see Trip 52, Sauvie Island.) At the north end of the island, near rivermile 2 across from Scappoose Bay, Cunningham Slough leads to Cunningham Lake. Although this section of the wildlife area is open to the public year-round, paddlers should nevertheless avoid the area during hunting season. Near the narrow portion of the island, just upstream from the Gilbert River boat ramp at about rivermile 6.5, two sloughs enter Sauvie Island. The southernmost leads to Crane Lake, and the northern of the two (the Gilbert River) travels about 5 miles into the interior of the island to Sturgeon Lake. (See Trip 52, Sauvie Island, for a more detailed map of the Crane Lake/Sturgeon Lake area.)

54 Lower Columbia River Water Trail

Location: Lower Columbia River
Distance: 146 miles or less
Time: 1 week or less
Charts: NOAA charts 18531, 18524, 18523, and 18521
Season: Year-round
Rating: B

The Lower Columbia River Water Trail (also known as the Lewis and Clark Columbia River Water Trail) was established in 2004, the first year of the Lewis and Clark Bicentennial, by a committee formed under the Lower Columbia River Estuary Partnership. The LCRWT roughly follows the route of the Corps of Discovery from Hamilton Island (just below Bonneville Dam) to the mouth of the Columbia. The trail consists of a series of access points and campsites; the access points existed prior to the establishment of the trail, but the designation of campsites is an ongoing process. Some of the campsites were previously designated in conjunction with the Columbia River Heritage Canoe Trail (see Trip 55, Columbia River Heritage Canoe Trail), while others were subsequently designated. (The water trail upstream of Bonneville Dam is known as the Northwest Discovery Water Trail.)

The LCRWT is an ongoing project as additional campsites are established. Several campsites have been formally designated, but numerous other informal campsites can be found along the river, particularly on various small islands.

Paddling the length of the LCRWT is a serious undertaking, involving winds, tides, river currents, inclement weather, commercial shipping traffic, ocean waters, and other hazards. Paddlers should carefully consult tide tables and weather forecasts, paying particular attention to the winds that often blow each afternoon. The entire 146-mile trail has been paddled in as few as three days, but most paddlers will want to spend as long as a week, or they may wish to paddle several short sections of the trail over a longer period of time.

Unlike the Columbia River Heritage Canoe Trail, the LCRWT does not follow any particular route on the river; paddlers are free to select their own routes among the dozens of islands that dot the lower Columbia. For that reason, no map is shown here. Carry the NOAA nautical charts, and consult the Lower Columbia River Estuary Partnership website for the latest list of designated landings and campsites. The website is *www.lcrep.org* or *www.columbia watertrail.org*, and the phone number is (503) 226-1565. Several portions of the LCRWT are described in detail in this book as Trips 55 through 64. Also see *The Lewis and Clark Columbia River Water Trail* by Keith Hay, published in 2004 by Timber Press.

Nearly all paddlers choose to paddle downstream to take advantage of the river current. When paddling sections of the trail on the lower portions of the river, however, winds and tides may allow paddlers to paddle upstream on some days. In fact upstream travel may be preferable at times.

Although the trail officially ends at Ilwaco, Washington, many paddlers will prefer to avoid the open ocean waters at the mouth of the Columbia. Those paddlers might prefer to end the trip near Fort Clatsop, south of Astoria, where Lewis and Clark spent the winter. Although boats may not be landed at the historic canoe landing at Fort Clatsop, a canoe landing and parking lot have been built at Netul Landing, about 1 mile south of Fort Clatsop on the west bank of the Lewis and Clark River. (See Trip 64, Lewis and Clark River.)

55 Columbia River Heritage Canoe Trail

Location: Lower Columbia River
Distance: 45 miles or less
Time: 3 days
Maps and charts: USGS Clatskanie, Oak Point, Marshland, Nassa Point, Cathlamet, Skamokawa, Grays River, Knappa, and Cathlamet Bay 7.5"; NOAA charts 18521 and 18523
Season: Year-round
Rating: B

In 1991, the Oregon Historical Society created the Columbia River Heritage Canoe Trail, a 45-mile route that winds its way among dozens of islands on the lower Columbia River, from the town of Clatskanie to the mouth of the John Day River, just east of Astoria. Along the way, it passes through the Julia Butler Hansen National Wildlife Refuge for the Columbian White-tail Deer, on the Washington shore west of Cathlamet, and the Lewis and Clark National Wildlife Refuge on the Oregon side of the river. The sketch map shown here does not do justice to this intricate route, so either buy the USGS topographic maps or get the NOAA charts. (The USGS maps are preferable; the NOAA charts use some incorrect nomenclature, particularly on the sloughs near the Clatskanie River.) You should also contact the wildlife refuges (see the appendix at the back of this book), and ask for copies of their refuge maps.

This 45-mile trip is not for the inexperienced. The winds and open waters mean that this trip is best suited to a sea kayak; the use of a canoe is not recommended, despite the name of the trail. It is a substantial undertaking, requiring routefinding skills (be sure to carry a compass and detailed maps or charts) and two crossings of the main channel of the Columbia, with its open waters and commercial boat traffic. Throughout the trip, strong winds, rains, and tidal currents are often present. The route was once marked with signs to help point the way, but many of those signs are now missing, thanks

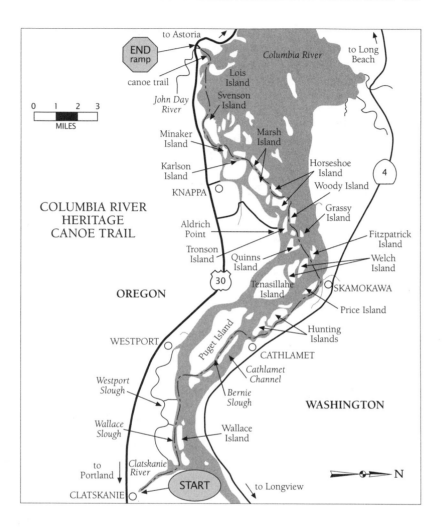

to vandalism. Before attempting this trip, carefully read Trips 56 through 62, which detail many parts of this route. Pay particular attention to the descriptions of windy weather, tides, and large ships. Also read the discussion of wakes under "Safety Techniques" in the Introduction. If you're looking for company, watch for announcements of guided trips led by local paddle clubs and other organizations.

The trip is designed to be completed in three days, requiring two overnight camps, but campsites are few and not evenly spaced over the route. Depending on the wind and the tide, it can be paddled from east to west, or vice versa. Both the wind and the tide can be strong; check the tide table when planning your trip, and remember that strong afternoon upstream winds are common.

If possible, get most of your paddling done each morning. Most paddlers follow the convention of boating downstream by starting at the east end of the trail (Clatskanie), but prevailing westerly winds may make the opposite the best choice. And to avoid getting stranded, don't paddle in shallow areas when the tide is going out.

To reach the put-in, follow US Highway 30 west from Portland to Clatskanie. At the northwest edge of Clatskanie, launch from Beaver Landing at milepost 61.8 on US 30.

Paddle down the Clatskanie River 3 miles to the Columbia, then turn west and follow Wallace Slough along the south side of Wallace Island and the south shore of the Columbia toward Westport. (An alternate route portages or paddles through a culvert from the west end of Anunde Island at the mouth of the Clatskanie River into Westport Slough, which leads to Westport.)

From the west end of Wallace Island (or from Westport), cross the Columbia to the southeast end of Puget Island (watch for large ships). An unimproved sandy campsite located on the southeast end of Puget Island about 9 miles from Clatskanie could be the first night's stopping point, or you can continue on to Cathlamet (another 7 miles, approximately). Follow the narrow passages at the east end of Puget Island to the east end of Bernie Slough on the northeast side of Puget Island, and then follow Bernie Slough to its west end. (The passages and sloughs at the east end of Puget Island, described in more detail in Trip 56, Puget Island, are not navigable at low tide.) Then cross the Cathlamet Channel to the town of Cathlamet and its boat harbor. The boater's campground at the mooring basin on the west side of Cathlamet is another possible stopping point for the first night.

The route next follows the Washington shore to Skamokawa (in essence, the route described in Trip 59, Skamokawa to Cathlamet, but in reverse), although you have a choice between paddling north of the Hunting Islands and Price Island for a sheltered route or south of them for an open-water route. The canoe trail route takes the sheltered route. The second night can be spent at Vista Park in Skamokawa, about 6 miles from Cathlamet.

From Skamokawa carefully cross the Columbia to the southwest, again watching for large ships, and pass between the following pairs of islands: Welch Island and Fitzpatrick Island (see the map for Trip 57, Tenasillahe Island); Grassy Island and Quinns Island; and Woody Island and Tronson Island (see the map for Trip 61, Aldrich Point). Paddle north of Horseshoe Island, then follow the passages that cut through Horseshoe, Marsh, and Karlson Islands (again, see the map for Trip 61, Aldrich Point). Pass on the west side of Minaker Island and the south side of Svenson Island to the South Channel of the Columbia, which can be followed to the mouth of the John Day River and its boat ramp (see the map for Trip 62, Cathlamet Bay).

No established campsites can be found along the 23 miles from Skamokawa to the John Day River, which makes for a very long third day. Camping is not permitted in either of the wildlife refuges, although efforts are under way to establish a paddlers campsite somewhere along the third leg of the trail. If such

A winter's morning on the river

a campsite is established, the third day could be split into two days, making a four-day paddle out of the entire trail, or the second day could be ended at the new campsite rather than at Skamokawa. In the meantime, most paddlers end the trip at Knappa (see Trip 61, Aldrich Point).

Also keep in mind that the trip can be shortened by ending at other points besides the John Day River or Knappa, such as Aldrich Point (Trip 61, Aldrich Point). Or portions of the trip can be paddled one day at a time, eliminating the camping element of the adventure. Other variations can be worked out using one or more of the various launch sites described in Trips 56 through 62, to follow.

If this trip appeals to you, there's more. A 100-mile Lower Columbia River Water Trail, extending from Portland to Astoria, was established in time for the bicentennial of the 1804–06 Lewis and Clark Expedition. See Trip 54, Lower Columbia River Water Trail, or *www.columbiawatertrail.org*.

56 Puget Island

Location: Near Cathlamet, Washington
Distance: 12 miles
Time: 6 hours
Maps and chart: USGS Cathlamet and Nassa Point 7.5"; NOAA chart
18523
Season: Year-round
Rating: A

Puget Island has it all: grand vistas, open waters, sandy beaches, backwater sloughs, an interesting history, and a 12-mile loop trip that does not require a car shuttle.

Puget Island is a 6-mile-long island (actually a group of islands) in the lower Columbia River between Cathlamet, Washington, and Westport, Oregon. Settled by Norwegian dairy farmers and fishermen at the turn of the century, it still boasts a Lutheran church and a Norse Hall. Although much of the island is below the high tide water level, dikes built in the early 1900s keep the island dry.

One important caution: The southwest side of Puget Island is the main channel of the Columbia, and thus carries the main shipping lanes. It is frequented by tugs, barges, and huge cargo ships. See the discussion of wakes under "Safety Techniques" in the Introduction. At all times, keep a constant watch in both directions for these commercial craft, which are very dangerous and have the right of way. The tugs and barges produce moderate wakes that demand respect.

The cargo ships are even worse. Their wakes are simply huge and dangerous, particularly in the narrow channel on the west end of the island. When cargo ships pass by, most paddlers should simply leave the water and haul their boats onto the beach. Better safe than sorry. But above all, do not let any commercial craft sneak up on you. Keep a careful eye both upriver and downriver at all times. The cargo ships probably cannot see you, so you must make certain that you see them and take appropriate action well in advance. With that warning, Puget Island offers delightful paddling.

Puget Island is connected to the Washington shore by a large bridge, and to the Oregon shore by a small (twelve-car) ferry. The toll ferry leaves Westport every hour at a quarter after, and leaves the island every hour on the hour. The ferry is quaint and the ride is scenic, but the most convenient way of reaching the island is via the Cathlamet Bridge. Reach Cathlamet by driving 25 miles west of Longview on Washington Route 4. From the bridge, drive south across the island on Washington Route 409 to the ferry landing, then turn east and go 0.6 mile on Sunny Sands Road to Puget Island Access, a public access area with a large gravel parking area. Carry your boat a few feet to a launching on a sandy beach. A Washington Vehicle Use Permit must be displayed to use this facility.

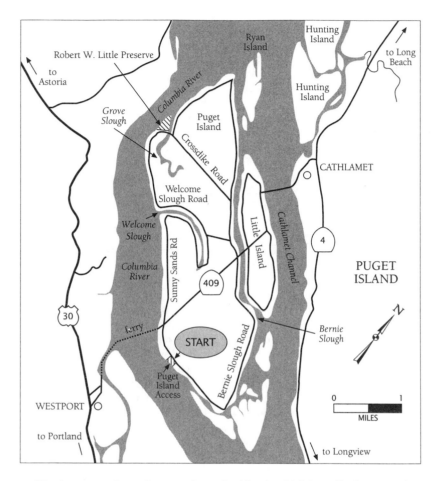

The best route is to circumnavigate the island, which is easily done in a day, assuming the wind and tide are on your side. Check the tide table and the weather forecast when planning your trip. If at all possible, try to be at the downstream end of the island at low tide, or at the upstream end at high tide. The latter is particularly important if you plan to explore the narrow sloughs at the upstream (east) end of the island, because they are not navigable at low tide.

For example, when launching at the public access area in the morning, if high tide occurs in the middle or late afternoon, paddle clockwise around the island, but if high tide occurs in the morning or midday, paddle counterclockwise.

Afternoon winds are common. If possible, get an early start. Or figure out which way the winds will be blowing (usually upstream) and bring a sail or a kite. If the wind is working against you, either plan on a long day or wait for better conditions.

If a circumnavigation of the island seems a bit ambitious, several shorter options may be more to your liking. Welcome Slough, a crescent-shaped channel on the southwest side of the island, offers sheltered paddling.

If the tide is in, the sloughs at the east end of the island offer considerable contrast to the open waters of the south side main channel. Reminiscent of southern bayous, the network of sloughs is much more complex and changeable than shown on the USGS maps, the NOAA chart, or the sketch map shown here. Carry a compass, and watch carefully for narrow, obscure passageways that lead out of the maze. The sloughs are not navigable at low tide (when the water level is less than 6 to 7 feet). Those sloughs are part of the Columbia River Heritage Canoe Trail, a 45-mile canoe route that runs from the town of Clatskanie west to the John Day River (see Trip 55, Columbia River Heritage Canoe Trail). The trail was established by the Columbia River Heritage Program of the Oregon Historical Society. Although the route is supposed to be marked by signs (look for purple arrows), few if any signs are evident. Rely on your own navigational skills.

On the north side of the island, paddlers may choose between the quiet water of Bernie Slough (also part of the Columbia River Heritage Canoe Trail) and the relatively open waters of the Cathlamet Channel. Watch for waterfalls on the cliffs east of the bridge to Cathlamet.

Throughout the island, watch for Columbian white-tail deer, the small subspecies protected by the nearby Julia Butler Hansen National Wildlife Refuge (see Trip 57, Tenasillahe Island, and Trip 59, Skamokawa to Cathlamet). On the west side of the island, the wooded area just south of the entrance to Grove Slough is the Robert W. Little Preserve, a thirty-acre Nature Conservancy preserve intended to help protect the deer. In the sloughs, watch for kingfishers, and everywhere watch for great blue heron and turkey vultures. Also watch for sea lions, which have entered the Columbia only in recent years, attracted by tasty sturgeon. In the winter, watch for bald eagles.

And always watch for cargo ships.

57 Tenasillahe Island

Location: Near Cathlamet, Washington
Distance: 2 to 5 miles
Time: 3 to 6 hours
Maps and chart: USGS Cathlamet and Skamokawa 7.5"; NOAA chart 18523
Season: Year-round
Rating: A

In the Columbia River, about 20 miles east of Astoria, several islands and part of the Washington mainland have been set aside as a refuge for a rare subspecies of deer. Tenasillahe Island is the largest of the islands that make up this

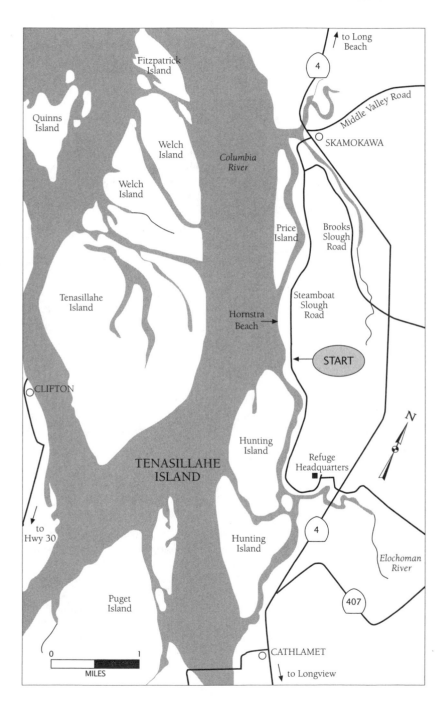

to Long Beach

4

Middle Valley Road

Fitzpatrick Island

SKAMOKAWA

Quinns Island

Welch Island

Columbia River

Welch Island

Price Island

Brooks Slough Road

Tenasillahe Island

Hornstra Beach

Steamboat Slough Road

START

CLIFTON

N

Hunting Island

Refuge Headquarters

TENASILLAHE ISLAND

to Hwy 30

Hunting Island

4

Elochoman River

Puget Island

407

0   1
MILES

CATHLAMET

to Longview

Julia Butler Hansen National Wildlife Refuge for the Columbian White-tail Deer. In addition to wildlife watching, the refuge offers pleasant canoeing on both quiet backwater sloughs and the open waters of the main channel of the Columbia.

The best launching spot is at Hornstra Beach on the Washington shore, on Steamboat Slough Road between Cathlamet and Skamokawa, Washington. The quickest way to get there is to drive Interstate 5 to exit 39 at Kelso, then drive west on Washington Route 4 about 27 miles to Cathlamet.

A more leisurely and scenic route from Portland utilizes the Wahkiakum County Ferry to Puget Island. From Portland, drive north on US Highway 30 (St. Helens Road) to Westport, where the ferry departs for Puget Island hourly at a quarter after (see the map for Trip 56, Puget Island). The ferry carries only twelve cars, but the ride is definitely worth the small toll and delivers you to within 3 miles of Cathlamet.

From Cathlamet, drive about 2 miles west and north on Washington Route 4. Just after crossing the Elochoman River bridge, turn left onto Steamboat Slough Road. Drive 2.6 miles to unmarked Hornstra Beach on the Columbia near navigational marker 37.

Launching from the Washington shore has one drawback: Tenasillahe Island is across the main Columbia River shipping lane. The island is less than a mile away, but the cautious paddler would be wise to not start the crossing in foggy weather or if any ships are visible in either direction. An alternate launching spot is at Aldrich Point (Trip 61, Aldrich Point), but it involves a longer paddle to the slough between Tenasillahe Island and Welch Island.

A dike has been built around the perimeter of most of Tenasillahe Island to keep it from being inundated at high water. Floodgates at the back of a small bay at the northwest corner of the island allow the water to flow out of the island's internal sloughs, but prevent it from entering the island during periods of high water. Tenasillahe Island is closed to foot traffic, except on the perimeter dike, which is an excellent hiking path.

Tenasillahe Island and nearby Welch Island offer excellent bird-watching. Watch for several species of herons, gulls, ducks, and hawks. In winter, be on the lookout for bald eagles. Also watch for sea lions dining on salmon, sturgeon, and other fish. Also keep an eye on the direction of the tide, so you will know whether your trip back to your car will be with or against it, and don't paddle in shallow areas when the tide is going out, or you will become stranded.

Although hunting is not currently allowed on Tenasillahe Island, the refuge does permit hunting along portions of the Washington shore during fall duck hunting season. If you plan on exploring the islands and sloughs on the Washington side of the river in the fall or early winter, visit or call the refuge headquarters (see the appendix at the back of this book) to determine when and where hunting is allowed.

58 Cathlamet to County Line Park

Location: Cathlamet, Washington
Distance: 12 miles
Time: 6 hours
Maps and chart: USGS Cathlamet, Nassa Point, and Oak Point 7.5";
NOAA chart 18523
Season: Year-round
Rating: A

The lower Columbia passes through a variety of landscapes. Much of the area is wooded foothills, and much is flat bottomland. In a few areas, however, the banks of the lower Columbia resemble the steep escarpments of the Columbia River Gorge a few miles upstream.

The Washington shore in tiny Wahkiakum County is such a place. Steep basalt cliffs line the channel, and numerous waterfalls cascade into the river. Unlike the well-known falls of the famous Gorge, these falls are rarely seen because no highway passes at their feet. Many of the falls along this stretch of the river are seasonal, although they are equal in size to many of the falls in the

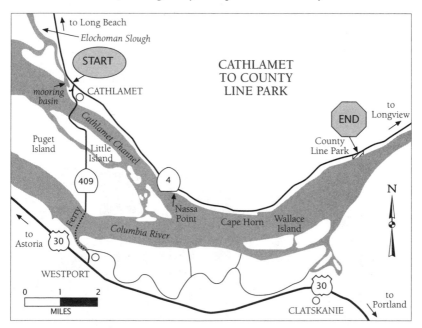

Gorge. The 12-mile paddle from Cathlamet east to the Wahkiakum County line includes the best stretch of cliffs and waterfalls.

Although the water is generally calm, it is not a trip suited to all. The entire length is exposed to long fetches, and the cliffs often make landings difficult or impossible. This trip is most suited to experienced paddlers in sea kayaks, due to the winds, rough water, and distances between landings. Novices in open canoes should look elsewhere.

Begin the trip by checking the tide tables and a weather forecast. The 12 miles of the trip are easily paddled with a favorable wind and an assisting tidal current, but can be unbearably long if either is working against the paddlers. Keep in mind that the wind usually picks up after noon, and usually blows upstream. If the wind and tide are cooperating, an upstream-bound trip can be as feasible as a downstream one. An upstream trip is described here.

Start the trip by leaving an extra car at County Line Park, located at mile-post 45.4 on Washington Route 4 just west of the Wahkiakum County line, about 15 miles west of Longview.

The launching point in Cathlamet is reached by continuing west on Washington Route 4 about 12 miles. At the foot of Third Street on the northwest edge of Cathlamet, find the Wahkiakum County Mooring Basin. When paddling out of the mooring basin, bear left onto Elochoman Slough, then continue east on the Columbia.

This section of the Columbia is known as the Cathlamet Channel; the main channel is 2 miles to the south, on the other side of Puget Island. After the small waterfront of Cathlamet is passed, the landscape quickly turns to cliffs, and the Cathlamet–Puget Island Bridge appears overhead. The bridge leads to Puget Island, a diked farming community of Scandinavian ancestry. A small toll ferry runs from the south side of Puget Island to Westport on the Oregon shore. (See Trip 56, Puget Island.)

Cliffs line the route for the next few miles. Waterfalls are seen every so often (in season), and boat traffic is usually light. Off to the south, Puget Island

Cape Horn, east of Cathlamet

seems to sit at the foot of the Oregon Coast Range. Red-tailed hawks and bald eagles can be seen, as well as a variety of waterfowl, particularly in winter.

The first section of the trip has few beaches suitable for lunching. One possibility is a small sandy beach just west of Nassa Point. Other beaches farther along the route appear to be private property. The second section of the trip is close to the highway, and the shore is lined with riprap.

For the last section, the highway turns inland and the cliffs return. Progress can be judged by the two main islands along the way, first Puget Island and then Wallace Island, but navigational markers along the way give a much more accurate measurement. Watch for these green markers, then compare their painted numbers with the numbers shown on the NOAA chart. Nassa Point, for example, is marked by marker 7, while County Line Park is located east of marker 77 and west of marker 79.

After the southeastern end of Puget Island is passed, be particularly watchful for other traffic because the shipping channel shifts over to the Washington shore near Cape Horn. River pilots and tug crews are not accustomed to looking out for craft as small as canoes and kayaks, so you will have to look out for them. Be particularly careful of their wakes. The wakes of tugs and barges are relatively manageable, but the wakes produced by cargo ships are large and dangerous. See the discussion of wakes under "Safety Techniques" in the Introduction, and consider beaching your craft if a cargo ship appears.

59 Skamokawa to Cathlamet

Location: Cathlamet, Washington
Distance: 6 to 7 miles
Time: 5 hours
Maps and chart: USGS Skamokawa and Cathlamet 7.5"; NOAA chart 18523
Season: Year-round (except during hunting season)
Rating: A

The lower Columbia River valley is full of history, much of which is reflected in the names of the communities along the banks of the river. Many names are derived from Native American languages. For instance, Skamokawa is a Chinook word meaning "smoke over the water," a reference to the foggy climate, while Cathlamet is named for a tribe of Chinook Indians. Both towns are located in tiny Wahkiakum County, named for an Indian village that was once located near the present site of Cathlamet.

In addition to cultural history, natural history is also abundant. Most of this trip passes through the Julia Butler Hansen National Wildlife Refuge for the Columbian White-tail Deer, an area set aside for the preservation of an endangered subspecies of deer. When paddling in the area, keep your eyes open for

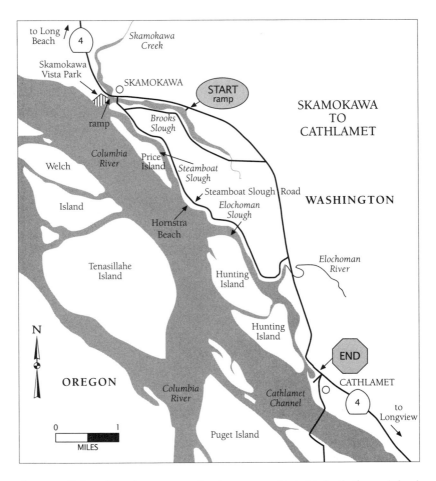

these small deer. The deer are good swimmers, and inhabit both the mainland and the nearby islands. Also watch for abundant birdlife.

Two parallel routes are offered, one on the open water of the Columbia and one on sloughs protected from the open water by three islands. Depending on the weather and the preference of the paddlers, the trip might be a rough open-water paddle for experienced kayakers, or a leisurely family canoe paddle on backwater sloughs.

The lower Columbia receives considerable influence from the tide. Because the tidal currents can be strong, try to take advantage of them rather than fighting against them. The prevailing winds are also important because the entire area, including the backwater sloughs, can be exposed to strong winds. Depending on the winds and the tidal currents, this trip can be paddled in either direction, although the route described here is west to east, from Skamokawa to Cathlamet, because upstream winds are most common, particularly in summer.

Begin the trip by driving to Cathlamet; from Interstate 5, exit 39, at Kelso, take Washington Route 4 west about 27 miles to Cathlamet. At the northwest end of Cathlamet, find the Wahkiakum County Mooring Basin at the foot of Third Street, and leave an extra car there.

To reach the launch site, drive about 5.5 miles west of Cathlamet along Washington Route 4 to milepost 30, where Brooks Slough Access, a public boat ramp, lies between the highway and Brooks Slough. (To shorten the paddle by about a mile, continue driving west on Route 4 to Skamokawa. Just after crossing the Skamokawa Creek bridge, turn left onto Pleasant Hill Road to a boat ramp, just downstream from the bridge. If the boat ramp is clogged with anglers and their powerboats, or if you would rather not pay the modest launch fee, launch on a sandy beach at the south end of the park).

From the boat ramp on Brooks Slough, paddle west down the slough toward Skamokawa. Many aging docks, warehouses, and other structures bring to mind Skamokawa's past as a bustling fishing, farming, and logging port. As evidence of the former economic vitality of the town, watch for a huge abandoned waterfront store building at the west end of Steamboat Slough. Today, the pace of the waterfront has slowed considerably, although some fishing still goes on.

Brooks Slough joins Skamokawa Creek at Skamokawa Vista Park. For a side trip, you might paddle up Skamokawa Creek and its tributary, West Valley Creek, for up to 2 miles if the tide is in. (See Trip 60, Brooks Slough and Skamokawa Creek). Otherwise, bear left to the Columbia, then turn left again to proceed up the Columbia. At this point, paddlers can choose between quiet Steamboat Slough behind Price Island or the open water of the Columbia. If

On the Columbia between Skamokawa and Cathlamet

the weather looks threatening, the slough is the safest bet. In addition, the shipping lanes of the Columbia are close to the Washington shore at this point; paddlers choosing the Columbia should be careful of the shipping traffic and the large wakes they produce. Maintain a constant lookout for commercial traffic. See the discussion of wakes under "Safety Techniques" in the Introduction, and consider leaving the water when large cargo ships approach.

For an open-water trip, simply follow the Columbia 6 miles upstream to the southeast end of the Hunting Islands, then turn north to the Cathlamet Mooring Basin. For a backwater paddle, stay between the islands (Price Island and Hunting Islands) and the mainland, following Steamboat Slough and Elochoman Slough to Cathlamet. By doing so, the only stretch of open water encountered is the 1-mile section between Price Island and Hunting Islands. Stay close to shore in this area to avoid the shipping lanes. The stretch between the two islands offers an excellent place to lunch. Near navigational marker 37, watch for a sandy beach (Hornstra Beach) where paddlers can lounge and watch the boats go by.

Several detours are available near the Hunting Islands. The islands themselves are crossed by several sloughs that make for interesting exploration, particularly at high tide. The Elochoman River, which empties into Elochoman Slough behind the Hunting Islands, can be explored for at least a mile or two, if not more.

When paddling in fall or winter, be mindful of hunters in the area. (National wildlife refuges are usually open for bird hunting in season.) Waterfowl hunting generally begins in early October and runs through mid-January. Although many paddlers stay away during the entire season, such precautions are not entirely necessary. For example, ducks and hunters are usually not present early in the season. The staff at the refuge can offer the best advice as to whether hunters are likely to be present (see the appendix at the back of this book). If you stop by the refuge headquarters on Steamboat Slough Road (see the map for Trip 57, Tenasillahe Island), ask for a copy of their refuge map.

60 Brooks Slough and Skamokawa Creek

Location: Skamokawa, Washington
Distance: 9 miles
Time: 6 hours
Maps and chart: USGS Skamokawa 7.5"; NOAA chart 18523
Season: Year-round (except during hunting season)
Rating: A

The Skamokawa area is well known to sea kayakers, particularly to those who enjoy paddling on the open waters of the Columbia. But the Skamokawa area also offers backwater sloughs for those who prefer to paddle on protected waters. This trip visits two sloughs, Brooks Slough and Skamokawa Creek, that meet at the Skamokawa waterfront.

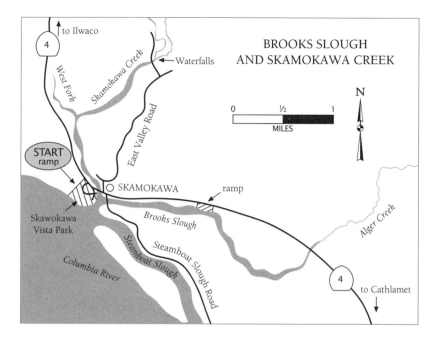

Although these two sloughs are protected compared to the Columbia River, tides and winds are still a significant factor. Consult a tide table and a weather forecast when planning this trip.

Begin the trip by driving to Skamokawa; from Interstate 5, exit 36, at Longview, drive west through Longview to Washington Route 4, then continue west about 30 miles to Skamokawa. Or take exit 39 in Kelso, and follow Route 4 west to Skamokawa. Just after crossing Skamokawa Creek on Route 4 in Skamokawa, turn left onto Pleasant Point Road and drive about a block to a primitive boat ramp, part of Skamokawa Vista Park. Campsites are available at the park, and canoes and kayaks can be rented a short distance away at the Skamokawa Center on the Skamokawa Waterfront.

Skamokawa Creek leads north from Skamokawa, and Brooks Slough leads east. Be careful not to mistake Steamboat Slough for Brooks Slough; Brooks Slough is the one with the bridge over it.

Depending on the tide and the season, Skamokawa Creek can be paddled for nearly 2 miles (4 miles round trip), while Brooks Slough is navigable for about 2.5 miles (5 miles round trip). The route is simple: paddle up one slough as far as time, energy, and water levels permit, then return to Skamokawa, and then paddle up the other. When deciding which to paddle first, keep in mind that the tidal current on Brooks Slough is generally more pronounced than on Skamokawa Creek.

Skamokawa Creek forks about a mile north of town. The left fork is the West Fork of Skamokawa Creek. It is navigable, but only for a short distance. The right fork is longer, eventually ending at two small waterfalls near a bridge.

Skamokawa waterfront

In contrast, Brooks Slough starts out much wider. About a mile east of Skamokawa, Brooks Slough Access, a public boat ramp, is on the left bank. About a mile later, the slough narrows and turns north, joining Alger Creek. The creek passes under a private steel bridge and then under a low cement bridge at Washington Route 4. Soon the creek becomes too narrow and shallow to permit farther progress.

Neither slough offers many opportunities to get out of your boat because the banks are generally steep or muddy. In addition, the property they pass through is private, except for the south bank of Brooks Slough, which is part of the Julia Butler Hansen National Wildlife Refuge for the Columbian White-tail Deer. For a lunch break, try the public boat ramp on Brooks Slough.

In both Skamokawa Creek and Brooks Slough, be careful that the outgoing tide does not leave you and your boat stranded in the mud.

61 Aldrich Point

Location: East of Astoria
Distance: 1 to 10 miles
Time: 1 to 5 hours
Map and chart: USGS Knappa 7.5"; NOAA chart 18523
Season: Year-round
Rating: A

Lewis and Clark National Wildlife Refuge includes dozens of islands in the Columbia River between Astoria and Aldrich Point, 15 miles to the east of Astoria. The refuge offers both open waters and narrow backwater sloughs. An excellent access point for visiting the eastern end of the refuge is Aldrich Point.

The main shipping channel on this part of the Columbia is close to the Washington shore. In contrast, the islands close to the Oregon side offer relatively undisturbed paddling. These islands all but disappear at high tide and are laced with mazes of passages and sloughs. Large grassy islands at low tide become mere marshes a few hours later, while narrow channels appear everywhere.

To reach the access point from Portland, drive north and west on US Highway 30. Eighteen miles past Clatskanie, look for a turnoff marked Brownsmead at milepost 79.4. Turn right, and follow the signs 6 miles to the boat ramp at Aldrich Point.

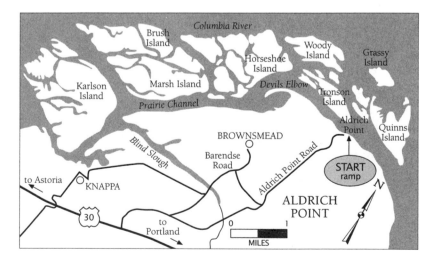

The USGS map listed in the information block covers the areas west and southwest of Aldrich Point. If you plan on paddling north or east from Aldrich Point, buy the adjacent maps. Otherwise, paddle west from the boat ramp, following Prairie Channel between the mainland and Tronson, Horseshoe, and Marsh Islands.

In the event of westerly winds (which are common, particularly in the afternoon), cross Prairie Channel immediately and work your way west along Devils Elbow in the lee of Tronson and Horseshoe Islands. The sloughs on these two islands alone provide at least a full day's exploration. Carry a compass to help find your way out of their mazes, especially if fog threatens.

Remember, the tide can produce strong currents, even in the small channels, so don't paddle a long distance with the tide unless you are sure you have the time and strength to paddle back against the tide. Combined with the unpredictable wind, the tidal currents can make a short trip into a long one. And to keep from getting stranded, don't paddle in shallow sloughs when the tide is going out.

Many of the islands become flooded at high tide. If you stop on an island for a lunch break, keep a close eye on your boat. The north side of Woody Island offers a beach for lunching.

Contrary to popular belief, national wildlife refuges are not exactly safe havens for birds. Only a small portion of the refuge is closed to hunters during the bird season. In the fall or early winter, call the refuge (see the appendix at the back of this book) to determine whether hunters will be present. And at all times of the year, take your binoculars and bird book along. Spring and fall migrations provide opportunities to see dozens of species. In winter, two of the largest residents are the bald eagle and the whistling swan.

62 Cathlamet Bay

Location: East of Astoria
Distance: 1 to 10 miles
Time: 2 to 6 hours
Maps and chart: USGS Astoria and Cathlamet Bay 7.5"; NOAA chart 18521
Season: Year-round
Rating: A

If you want miles of open water with a marine atmosphere, but don't want to venture into the Pacific, try Cathlamet Bay in the Columbia River near Astoria. Wait for a day with good weather, then drive north and west from Portland on

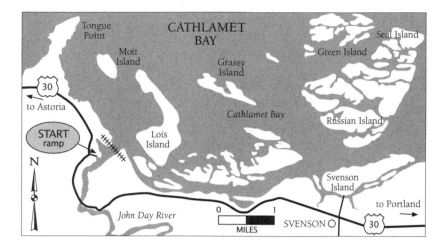

US Highway 30. After crossing the John Day River on a bridge, watch for a right turn to a public boat ramp. The ramp is situated on the John Day River, 0.25 mile from the bay. From Astoria, the ramp is 1.7 miles east of the Tongue Point turnoff.

From the ramp, turn left onto the river and paddle north under the railroad drawbridge. This bridge is manned 24 hours a day by a bridge tender who lives in the house at the east end of the bridge.

The bay is large, and so are the islands. At high tide portions of these islands are flooded, and finding solid ground is not easy. Mott Island and Lois Island might have dry areas, but Grassy Island is rather ethereal, being nonexistent at high tide. Depending on water levels, you might be able to find a sandy beach for lunch on Mott or Lois Islands, but secure your boat well above the high tide line. Camping is not permitted on either island because both are located within the Lewis and Clark National Wildlife Refuge. Watch for deer.

If the weather is at all questionable, stay close to shore, or at least don't venture out beyond the protection of the islands and Tongue Point, which was named for its obvious shape by Captain George Vancouver. Meriwether Lewis and William Clark tried to name it Point William, but the older, more descriptive name stuck. The point is now used as a Job Corps center and Coast Guard station.

Strong upstream winds are common in the afternoon. If the wind picks up or fog threatens, head for shore. Open water near the mouth of the Columbia is no place to be in bad weather. A foul-weather option is to paddle up the John Day River, although it is only navigable for about 3.5 miles upstream from the boat ramp. The current on the river is mainly tidal.

63 Youngs River

Location: South of Astoria
Distance: 7 miles
Time: 4 hours
Maps and chart: USGS Olney and Astoria 7.5"; NOAA chart 18521
Season: Winter to spring
Rating: A

The Youngs River is a small but pretty stream that begins in the northern Coast Range and flows into the Columbia at Astoria. Described here is a 7-mile paddle from near the town of Olney to Astoria. The first part of the trip involves paddling on the Klaskanine River, which soon joins the Youngs River. The trip ends on the open waters of Youngs Bay. As a result, it is more suitable for a sea kayak than an open canoe, and paddlers should be able to deal with wind and waves.

This entire stretch of the river is influenced by the tide. If at all possible (especially in late summer and fall), plan your trip so that launching can be made at high tide, so that you will not have to paddle against the tide.

Start the trip by leaving an extra car at the public boat ramp located at the Astoria Yacht Club. To reach the club from downtown Astoria, drive south on US Highway 101 to Youngs Bay. Turn east onto US Highway 101 Business (West Maritime Drive) and follow it toward the north end of the Youngs Bay Bridge. About two blocks before the north end of the bridge, turn left and follow signs to the yacht club. (See also the map for Trip 64, Lewis and Clark River.)

Then go to the put-in point by driving south on Washington Route 202 (Olney Avenue). After passing through the community of Olney, turn right onto Youngs River Loop Road and drive about 0.7 miles to launch at a public boat ramp next to a bridge over the Klaskanine River.

After only a mile and a half, the Klaskanine River joins the Youngs River. Turn north and follow the Youngs River as it gets wider and wider, eventually wide enough to hold several islands, particularly near rivermile 8. With little protection from the wind, this is a slow paddle on a blustery day.

The final section of the river as it enters Youngs Bay is particularly susceptible to bad weather coming in from the Pacific Ocean, and it is open to the wind, which often picks up each afternoon. Play it safe, and stay close to shore.

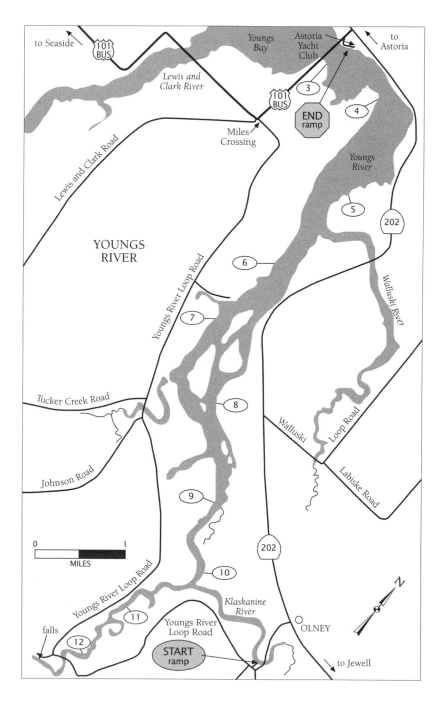

Youngs River Falls

64 Lewis and Clark River

Location: South of Astoria
Distance: 9 miles (or 6 miles)
Time: 4 to 5 hours
Maps: USGS Olney and Astoria 7.5"
Season: Year-round
Rating: A

In the winter of 1805 to 1806, Lewis and Clark constructed a small fort on the west bank of a stream near the mouth of the Columbia River. They spent the winter in this fort among the Clatsop Indians, who called the stream the Netul River. Today, the river is named after its most famous visitors. A replica of the fort was built in the 1950s, but it was destroyed by fire in October 2005, just two months before the bicentennial of the construction of the original. A new replica was built in 2006.

The lower 10 miles of the river are described here. The trip ends on the open waters of Youngs Bay, where a sea kayak is much safer than a canoe. Because this entire trip is tidal and the river is quite small, it is best to launch at high tide. If you disregard this advice, the upper part of the river may not be navigable, particularly late in the year. In addition, a low-tide launch means several hours of paddling against the tide. In fact, if a low-tide launch is planned, the paddler will be better off making the trip in the opposite direction of that described here (or the trip can be started at the bridge near rivermile 7).

For a high-tide launch, leave your extra car or bicycle at the Astoria Yacht Club near the north end of the Youngs Bay Bridge (US Highway 101 Business, not to be confused with the US 101 bridge to the west). From downtown Astoria, the boat ramp is reached by driving south on US 101. Before US 101 crosses Youngs Bay, turn east onto US 101 Business/Oregon Highway 202, and follow it about 1.25 miles to the Youngs Bay Bridge. About two blocks before the north end of the bridge, turn left and follow signs to the Astoria Yacht Club, where you will find a public park and boat ramp.

The launching point is reached by driving south on US 101 Business across Youngs Bay, then west across the mouth of the Lewis and Clark River. About a mile after crossing the river, turn left at a sign pointing to Fort Clatsop. Follow the main road, staying on the west side of the river, about 6 miles to Logan Road. Turn left and park just past the bridge. The launching at this bridge is only fair; try launching on the downstream side of the north end of the bridge.

If you would prefer a better launching site, or a shorter trip, several other put-in or takeout options are shown on the map. A boat ramp can be found on the west side of the river immediately upstream from the bridge near rivermile 7;

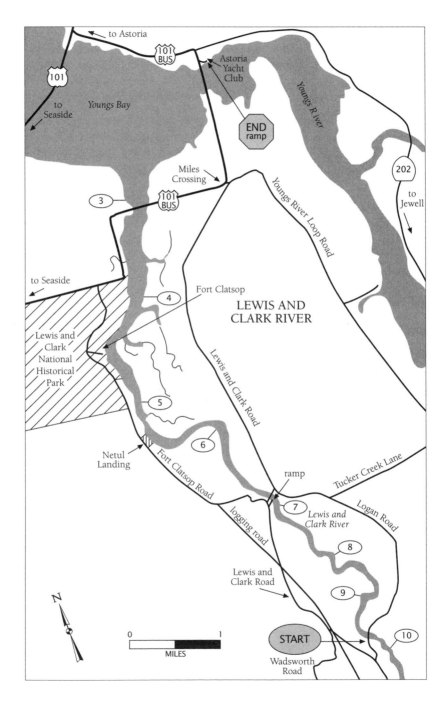

try launching here about two hours before high tide, then paddle upstream until the tide changes, then paddle back down. A canoe landing has also been built at rivermile 5.5, at Netul Landing, discussed below.

The first few miles of the river are relatively wooded, and an occasional log obstruction may be encountered, but by rivermile 7 the scenery becomes predominantly pastoral. On a windy day, the pastures offer little protection.

At rivermile 5.5, the National Park Service has built a new parking lot for the Fort Clatsop unit of the Lewis and Clark National Historical Park. The facility, known as Netul Landing, includes a picnic area and a canoe/kayak landing located 1.25 miles south of the entrance to Fort Clatsop. This new parking lot is used (along with a shuttle bus) during busy summer months, when the parking lot at the Fort is closed to the public. A 1.5-mile trail follows the river from Netul Landing to Fort Clatsop.

At a broad bend in the river at rivermile 4.5, watch closely for an opening in the brush on the west bank, marking the canoe landing used by Lewis and Clark and their Corps of Discovery while wintering at Fort Clatsop. The historic canoe landing is now maintained by the National Park Service as part

Fort Clatsop

of the Fort Clatsop unit of the Lewis and Clark National Historical Park, but out of a concern for maintaining the historic qualities of the site, boats are not allowed to land here. If you'd like to visit this historic landing, follow a short trail from the visitor's center at Fort Clatsop.

At rivermile 4, the river widens considerably as it begins to merge with Youngs Bay. Follow the south shore of the bay and paddle under the US 101 Business bridge, then cross this narrow part of the bay to the boat ramp at Astoria Yacht Club, just east of the bridge. Be wary of wind and waves when crossing the open waters of the bay. Westerly winds are common in the afternoon.

65 Long Island

Location: Near Long Beach, Washington
Distance: 2 to 15 miles
Time: 4 hours to overnight
Map and chart: USGS Long Island 7.5"; NOAA chart 18504
Season: Year-round
Rating: A

Willapa Bay is one of the largest estuaries on the southern Washington coast. Its most prominent geographic features are the narrow Long Beach Peninsula, which forms the bay's western shore, and five-thousand-acre Long Island, which lies on the east side of the bay.

The bay and its shores are teeming with wildlife. Three sections of the estuary, including the southern end of the bay, Long Island, and the tip of the peninsula, are part of the Willapa National Wildlife Refuge. Of the three areas, the island offers the best paddling, but most of the waters surrounding the island are open and can be rough in windy weather. A sea kayak is a better choice than a canoe for paddling near the island, or anywhere else in the bay.

Willapa Bay has a unique history stretching back to Chinook Indian days. White settlers were first attracted by the logging opportunities. Sawlog Slough on the east side of the island was once home to a row of floating cabins built by the loggers. Meanwhile, oystermen had built a shantytown at Diamond Point on the north end of the island. Today, oysters are still being harvested on Long Island, but logging ended in 1993.

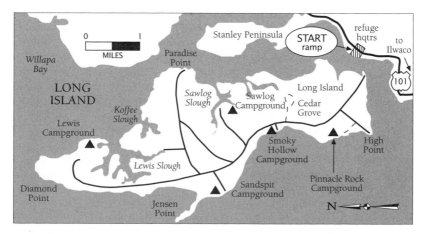

The best launch site to explore the island is at the refuge headquarters, on US 101 about a dozen miles north of Ilwaco, Washington, near the southeast corner of Long Island. A public boat ramp is located just across the highway from the headquarters. (Don't use the dock or the nearby ferry landing, and don't block either the ferry landing on the mainland or the one across the slough on the island.) Across the highway, at the refuge headquarters, is the Willapa Salmon Art Trail, which leads to a salmon-viewing pond. It is open only during business hours.

Although much can be seen in a few hours, the size of the island and the activities available make a weekend trip more desirable. Camping is permitted at five campgrounds on the island (Lewis, Sandspit, Sawlog, Smoky Hollow, and Pinnacle Rock Campgrounds), but drinking water must be carried from the mainland. Try to avoid holiday weekends during the summer, when visitor use of the island is at its highest. Arrivals at, and departures from, the campgrounds must be timed to coincide with high tides because extensive mudflats are present at low tide; all of the campgrounds require a 5- or 6-foot high tide for access, unless you enjoy carrying your boat through deep mud. Also remember to stow your boat well above the high tide line when stopping on the island. And don't paddle in shallow water when the tide is going out, or you may become stranded. For current information about camping on the island, call the refuge headquarters (see the appendix at the back of this book). Also ask for their excellent map of the island. Be sure to take a tide table and a copy of the current NOAA chart with you. Because the tide can be strong, time your travel to move with, not against it, and use the chart to find navigable water during low tide.

A reminder: Willapa Bay can be rough in bad weather or when the tide is running. If the weather is at all questionable, stay close to shore, or, if necessary, wait on shore for storms to pass. And remember that wind is very common on the bay, particularly in the afternoon, when a westerly wind often develops.

Shellfishing is probably the most popular activity. Clamming and crabbing are excellent, but the current oyster population has been planted and is considered private property. Clamming requires a Washington clam license, and is subject to limits. Also, most of the tidelands are privately owned and are closed to clamming. As of this writing, the public tidelands are located immediately east of High Point and from High Point north to within 0.25 mile of Sandspit Campground. Before digging for clams, however, check for current information by calling the refuge headquarters or the Washington State Shellfish Laboratory at Nahcotta (see the appendix at the back of this book). The map of the island published by the refuge usually shows the current status of public tidelands.

The interior of the island can be explored by hiking the gravel roads shown on the sketch map. Near the south end of the island is an old-growth cedar grove. The oldest trees in the grove, towering to 175 feet, are about one thousand years old, while the grove itself is three times that age. A hiking trail is shown on the sketch map. Elsewhere on the island, daffodils cover parts of an old farm on High Point, and Diamond Point is now maintained as a natural area. Throughout the island, watch for black-tailed deer, Roosevelt elk, black bear, and countless bird species. A pair of northern spotted owls once inhabited the cedar grove, but a pair of barred owls appears to have displaced them.

66 Nehalem River—Vernonia to Big Eddy

Location: North of Vernonia
Distance: 10 miles
Time: 4 to 5 hours
Maps: USGS Vernonia and Pittsburg 7.5"
Season: Winter to early spring
Rating: C

The upper portions of the Nehalem River offer pleasant canoeing through a beautiful corner of the state. Deep forests, winding roads, and quaint small towns characterize the Columbia County region drained by this pretty river.

Once the site of an annual canoe race, the 10-mile stretch from Vernonia to Big Eddy County Park is a justifiably popular trip. Unlike most of the small flatwater streams in Oregon, the Nehalem has a strong, clear current that drops quickly through mountainous country. Don't paddle this trip unless you are experienced at maneuvering your boat; the current is strong, and sharp turns are abundant.

The Nehalem is a shallow river, partly due to the geologic history of the area. If you glance at the banks of the river (particularly the west bank), you will notice that the river has cut its channel through shale, a sedimentary rock that tends to fracture horizontally, resulting in a relatively flat and broad riverbed. Due to the shallow channel, this trip should be done only in winter or early spring. After about April, your boat will suffer from a journey on this section of the Nehalem.

To do the trip, drive west from Portland on US Highway 26 about 30 miles to Buxton, then drive north on Oregon Highway 47 to Vernonia. From Vernonia, drive 8.5 miles north toward Mist to Big Eddy County Park. After entering the park, drive straight ahead to the boat ramp at the far side of the

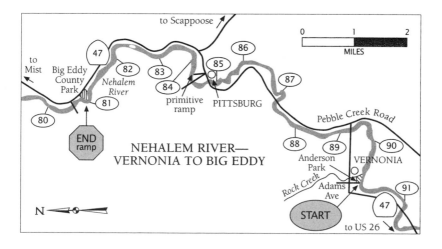

park, between campsites 6 and 7. Leave an extra car or bicycle here. A day use fee is charged at this park.

This trip is particularly well suited for using a bicycle as the transportation to fetch your car at the end of the trip. The pedal from Big Eddy County Park back to Vernonia on Oregon Highway 47 is short, flat, and scenic. As you drive or pedal through Vernonia, turn south at the locomotive on the corner of Adams Avenue and Bridge Street. The launching point is Anderson Park at the foot of Adams Avenue in Vernonia. (The park north of the locomotive is the wrong park, since it is on Rock Creek.) In Anderson Park, the best launching site is at the far side of the park, just downstream from the private bridge, built in 1996 to replace a bridge destroyed by the flood earlier that year. A day use fee is charged at this park.

Don't dismiss Vernonia as just another logging town. It is a quiet, slow-paced community far enough from the major highways to have retained its character. Stop long enough to visit the Columbia County Historical Society Museum and to admire the beautiful brick elementary school (particularly in contrast to the modern high school).

This trip is marked by several bridges. The first one, about a mile after launching, has a sharp drop beneath it. Be careful. Also watch for strainers and small logjams. After this bridge, Oregon Highway 47 to Mist parallels the river. The road is often quite close, but the traffic is light and rarely spoils the journey. A primitive boat ramp can be found just downstream of the fourth bridge, near the village of Pittsburg. Depending on the water level, a small island divides the river at rivermile 82.5.

The boat ramp at Big Eddy appears suddenly on the right as you make a sharp right turn. Keep an eye open for it, unless you plan on visiting Mist, 9 miles downstream. One way to tell you missed the takeout: the river passes under a private bridge about 0.2 mile after Big Eddy.

67 Nehalem River—Roy Creek to Nehalem

Location: Nehalem
Distance: 6.5 miles
Time: 3 to 4 hours
Maps: USGS Foley Peak and Nehalem 7.5"
Season: Year-round
Rating: A

The Nehalem River valley carves a huge crescent across the northwest corner of Oregon. From its source in northwestern Washington County, it flows north through Columbia County, then west through Clatsop County to the river's mouth in Tillamook County, a total distance of more than 100 miles.

The short paddle described here covers 6.5 miles of the river from Roy Creek Park, where the river first becomes tidal, to the town of Nehalem. Check the tide tables before you launch, if you do not want to be paddling against the tide or if you want to be sure of sufficiently deep water late in the year (try to start paddling close to high tide, or shortly thereafter).

Begin the trip by leaving an extra car or bicycle at either of the two public docks on US Highway 101 in Nehalem. One of the docks is located at the main intersection in Nehalem; the other is a block south.

Then drive south on US Highway 101 and cross the river to the junction with Oregon Highway 53, where you turn left. A mile later, just after another

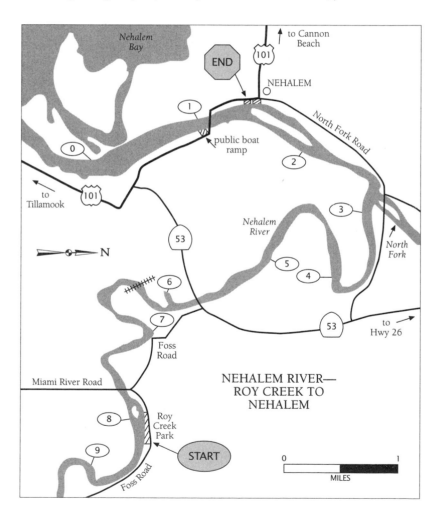

NEHALEM RIVER—
ROY CREEK TO
NEHALEM

bridge over the Nehalem, turn right onto Foss Road and drive 0.5 mile to Roy Creek Park and its gravel, but sometimes muddy, boat ramp.

Although the park is many miles upstream from the Pacific, the water level is affected by the tide. At low tide, particularly in late summer or fall, be careful of shallow spots. At rivermile 7, a shallow area among several islands is best passed on the extreme right.

Despite possible shallow water, a fall trip on this river is particularly pleasant. Fall colors line the route, along with dozens of fishers. Once some companions and I spent several minutes watching a fisherman play a huge steelhead until being told that he had been at it for more than two hours. Farther downstream, a red-tailed hawk sat on the top of a Douglas fir, perhaps hoping for a similar opportunity. These miles of the Nehalem are hardly pristine wilderness, but the fishermen, the dairy farms, and the small cottages along the banks create a serene, pastoral atmosphere.

The last 0.5 mile takes paddlers behind a large island that lies just off the town of Nehalem. A nice gravel beach can be found at the upstream end of the island. The takeout is at either of two public docks in downtown Nehalem, on the right channel opposite the lower end of the island.

68 Tillamook Bay

Location: Near Tillamook
Distance: 1 to 10 miles
Time: Up to 5 hours
Maps and chart: USGS Garibaldi and Netarts 7.5"; NOAA chart 18558
Season: Year-round
Rating: A

Tillamook Bay is one of the largest on the Oregon coast. The Tillamook, the Trask, the Wilson, the Kilchis, and the Miami Rivers all empty into this 6-mile-by-3-mile bay, which is the home of several small towns. The bay is also noted for its large and diverse bird population. The bay is large and it can be windy; a kayak is usually a better choice than a canoe.

The most interesting feature of the bay is the huge spit that forms its western side. Shortly after the turn of the century, a large resort community named Bayocean was developed on this spit, which was then an island. A ferry from Garibaldi was used to reach the community of 1600 lots centered around a hotel and natatorium. A causeway eventually connected the island to Pitcher Point. Erosion problems plagued the community until a 1948 storm broke through the island in several places. The town was eventually abandoned. Unfortunately, modern developers have yet to learn Bayocean's lesson.

Tillamook Bay is located due west of Portland at the west end of Oregon Highway 6. Several launching sites are available. To explore the west side of the

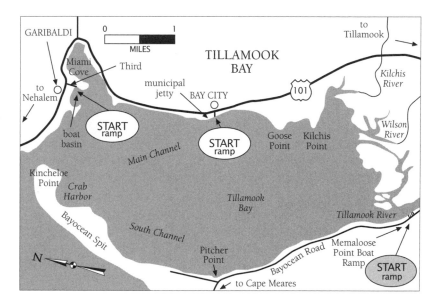

bay, take Bayocean Road to the road leading part of the way out the Bayocean causeway. From downtown Tillamook, drive west on Netarts Highway, following signs to Cape Meares. Due to large mudflats, however, launching from the causeway requires a careful eye on the tide and a close scrutiny of a current nautical chart to locate water deep enough to float a boat. Also, parking along the road is limited.

Several more reliable launching sites are available. To explore the south end of the bay, launch at Memaloose Point Boat Ramp on Bayocean Road, near where the Trask and the Tillamook Rivers enter the bay.

To explore the central or eastern part of the bay, launch at the Bay City waterfront municipal jetty, located on US Highway 101 at Bay City. The ramp is immediately north of the foot of the jetty.

To explore the north part of the bay, launch at the Garibaldi boat basin. To reach the public parking lot, from US Highway 101 in Garibaldi turn south onto Third Avenue. Launch your boat at the northeast corner of the boat basin, near the intersection of American Avenue and Jerry Creasy Drive.

Be cautious of the effects of wind and tidal currents throughout this bay. Use them to your advantage, but be aware of the possibility of rough water, particularly when the currents cross shallow areas or the wind picks up. Avoid the mouth of the bay at all times.

The Bayocean spit makes an excellent lunch spot, especially at Crab Harbor where landing is relatively easy. Hike across the spit for views of the ocean; also watch for deer.

No matter what time of year you visit Tillamook Bay, take your binoculars and bird book along. Fall and winter bird-watching ensures outstanding

Looking for deep water in Tillamook Bay

sightings, including hawks, owls, falcons, loons, bald eagles, and egrets, plus numerous species of gulls and ducks. Throughout the year the most obvious birds include great blue herons and cormorants. In the summer, brown pelicans can be seen diving for fish.

69 Nestucca River

Location: Pacific City
Distance: 9 miles
Time: 4 hours
Maps: USGS Nestucca Bay and Hebo 7.5"
Season: Late fall to spring
Rating: B

The Nestucca River is a beautiful clear stream that drains the Coast Range south of Tillamook. It is a small river; only the lowest portion is navigable most of the year. The trip described here passes through several picturesque coastal towns; it starts near Hebo, paddles past Cloverdale and Woods, and ends in Pacific City.

Start the trip by turning off US Highway 101 onto either Brooten-Pacific City Road or Pacific City Road (it is a loop road) and driving the short couple of

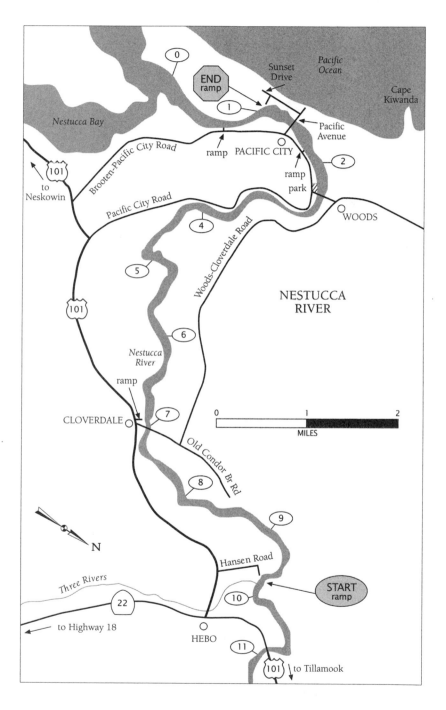

Nestucca Bay
Pacific Ocean
Sunset Drive
Cape Kiwanda
END ramp
0
1
ramp
Brooten-Pacific City Road
PACIFIC CITY
Pacific Avenue
2
to Neskowin
101
ramp
park
Pacific City Road
4
WOODS
Woods-Cloverdale Road
5
101
NESTUCCA RIVER
6
Nestucca River
ramp
CLOVERDALE
7
Old Condor Br Rd
8
9
N
Hansen Road
Three Rivers
START ramp
22
10
to Highway 18
HEBO
11
101
to Tillamook

0   1   2
MILES

miles to Pacific City. From the center of town, the public boat ramp is reached by driving west on Pacific Avenue. After crossing the bridge over the river, turn south onto Sunset Drive and 1 mile later watch for a left turn marked by a boat ramp sign. Leave your extra car or bicycle at the ramp. (For a slightly longer or shorter trip, two other public boat ramps are shown on the sketch map. The park near Woods has very poor river access.)

To reach the launching point from Pacific City, drive north and east on Pacific City Road to US Highway 101, and follow it 4.4 miles east to a left turn onto Hansen Road marked by a boat ramp sign. Follow this road to its end at the Three Rivers public access, west of the town of Hebo. (For a shorter trip, launch at the public boat ramp in downtown Cloverdale, behind the Tillamook County public works building, at the foot of Parkway Drive, just downstream from the Cloverdale bridge. To find the ramp, drive between the public works building and the hardware store.)

Most of this section of the Nestucca River is tidal, so a launch at high tide is preferable, but not essential. The first mile or two of the river drops rapidly and has a strong current to it, but the river quickly reaches tidewater and winds its leisurely way to the sea. The channel makes a few quick turns in this first section, but any pair of paddlers who have learned the basic canoe strokes should get through unscathed.

After paddling a few miles, you will not need this guidebook to tell you that the lower Nestucca Valley is dairy country. Something in the air will let you know. The valley is broad and flat, although occasionally the river channel nudges up against the steep hills that define it. Because the valley is close to the ocean and quite wide, it is subject to moderately strong winds. Although the trip is a short one, you might check the weather forecast before launching. Paddling into a headwind has only one reward: if you are using a bicycle to return to your car, the return trip will be relatively effortless.

70 Siletz River—Siletz to Morgan Park

Location: Northeast of Newport
Distance: 12 miles
Time: 3 to 4 hours
Maps: USGS Toledo North and Mowrey Landing 7.5"
Season: Spring or early summer
Rating: C

If you are looking for a river with more excitement than the usual flatwater trip, this could be the one for you. Although this 12-mile section of the Siletz River is not known for tight corners or difficult maneuvering, when the water

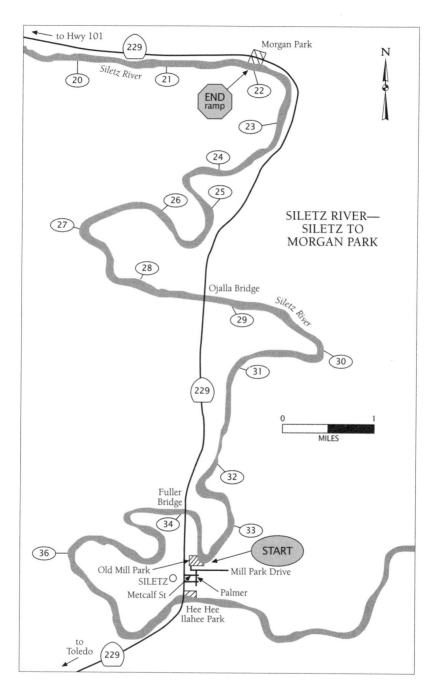

levels are high it can offer rougher water than any of the other trips described in this book.

Paddling this trip may whet your appetite to venture into more difficult whitewater situations; or then again, it may get you just plain wet. Because the hardest parts of this trip are in the first half, you might consider launching midway, at Ojalla Bridge, if you are not sure you are ready for the rough water upstream. Even so, the lower half of the route has plenty of swift water to deal with.

On the other hand, when the water levels drop in early summer, some of the rapids may disappear and parts of the river may become shallow and slow moving. At any time of year, watch carefully for strainers or small logjams.

Start the trip by driving south from Lincoln City, or north from Depoe Bay, on US Highway 101 to the Siletz River bridge, then turning east onto Oregon Highway 229 and driving 18 miles to Morgan Park. The park can be reached from the south from Newport on US 101 by driving east on US Highway 20 to Toledo, then turning north onto Highway 229. Drive past Siletz and across the Ojalla Bridge to Morgan Park. Leave an extra car or bicycle here.

While at Morgan Park, take a good look at the surroundings because the park may be difficult to recognize from the river until after the ramp has been passed. Note the parking lot/clearing and the small island just off the boat ramp. Also determine whether you will try to land at the boat ramp or a few feet upstream.

The launching point for the complete trip is Old Mill Park in Siletz. From Morgan Park, drive 6 miles south on Oregon Highway 229 to Siletz. In Siletz, drive one block east on Metcalf Street, then one block north on Palmer; one block later turn left onto Mill Park Drive. Launch at the boat ramp in the park. Don't leave any valuables in your car.

For those wanting a bit less excitement, the alternative put-in is a primitive boat landing at Ojalla Bridge, halfway between Morgan Park and Siletz, 3 miles south of Morgan Park. The landing is on the east side of the bridge's north end.

When the water is high, this is a fast trip due to the strong current. The portion above Ojalla Bridge takes only an hour when the water is high, and the lower part can sometimes be paddled in an hour and a half. When the water is low, however, the current is almost nonexistent.

The roughest rapids are a short distance downstream from Old Mill Park. After turning the first bend, the rapids begin on both sides of a small island. Landing at the head of the island to scout the rapids may be a good idea, but be careful of the strong current. Small rapids occur throughout the trip, although they steadily diminish in size and frequency. Below Ojalla Bridge near rivermile 29, the river offers few if any rapids.

Morgan Park may be difficult to spot from the river. Keep your eyes open for the parking lot, which appears as a clearing in the trees.

71 Siletz River—Morgan Park to Strome Park

Location: South of Lincoln City
Distance: 8 miles
Time: 4 hours
Maps: USGS Mowrey Landing and Depoe Bay 7.5"
Season: Winter to early summer
Rating: B

The Siletz River is a long, undulating coastal stream that drains much of northern Lincoln County. Unusual for its aimless course, the river is constantly twisting and turning in every possible direction.

The section described here involves such a twist. The river travels west for 5 miles, then makes a lazy U-turn and returns in an easterly direction for 2 miles. Paddling this section has a distinct advantage for those who use a bicycle as a shuttle vehicle: the distance by road is only 4 miles.

To start this trip, drive on US Highway 101 to Siletz Bay. Just north of the bridge over the Siletz River, turn east onto Oregon Highway 229 and follow it up the river. Almost 14 miles after leaving US 101, turn right into Strome Park (shown on some maps as Mowrey Landing). Leave your extra car or bicycle at this park. Note the surroundings, so you will be able to recognize the park from the water.

Then continue driving east on Highway 229. About 4 miles east of Strome Park, watch for signs designating Morgan Park on the right. Launch your boat from the boat ramp. At times, launching from this ramp can be a little tricky due to the moderately strong current.

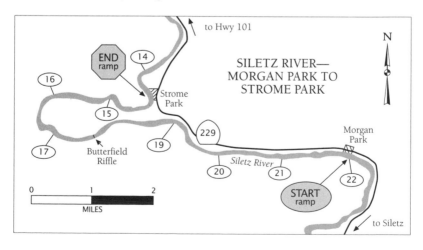

This section of the Siletz is particularly pleasant on a hot day, as it offers many shady portions and placid pools of cool water. A few gravelly sections, however, may become quite shallow by midsummer.

At rivermile 18, the "Butterfield Riffle" is shown on most maps. The riffle apparently only exists at low water. Because this portion of the river is influenced by the tide, you may or may not encounter these small rapids.

Landmarks are rare in this area of the river. A compass should be used to determine your approximate location from time to time, particularly near Strome Park, which is easy to miss. Stay close to the right bank, and watch carefully for the boat ramp.

72 Siletz River—Strome Park to Pikes Camp

Location: South of Lincoln City
Distance: 12 miles
Time: 7 hours
Maps: USGS Mowrey Landing and Devils Lake 7.5"
Season: Year-round
Rating: B

In this 12-mile section, the Siletz River changes from a small mountain stream to a broad tidal river. The upper portion of the trip involves paddling on a shady stream with a strong current, whereas the lower portion is wide and slow, with the only current generated by the tide.

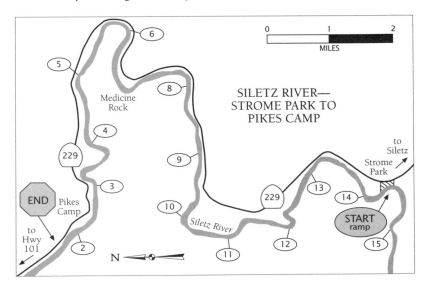

The Siletz River near Pikes Camp

This is a long trip for a single day of paddling, especially if the wind and tide are both moving in from the ocean. Plan the outing for a day when the tide is on its way out during much of your trip. Another option is to paddle only a portion of the section described here. Although no public boat ramps are located between Strome Park and Pikes Camp, several commercial marinas along the route permit boat launching for a small fee. The marinas are all located along Oregon Highway 229; you can pick one the day of your trip, or plan ahead by getting a copy of the "Oregon Boating Facilities Guide" from the Oregon State Marine Board (see the appendix at the back of this book) or viewing the guide online at *www.boatoregon.com*.

Drive north from Depoe Bay, or south from Lincoln City, on US Highway 101 to the intersection with Oregon Highway 229, just north of the Siletz River bridge. Turn east onto Highway 229 and follow it 0.9 miles to a small pullout on the right, an area known as Pikes Camp. Access to the river here is somewhat meager, and public access is difficult to find. This pullout is one of the few access points in this section of the river. Leave your extra car on the shoulder, then continue about 13 miles east on Highway 229 to Strome Park and its boat ramp.

If the tide is out, the first part of the trip involves a moderately strong current. Late in the year, you may encounter a few shallow spots, another reason for launching at high tide.

At rivermile 7, watch for a large rock slab exposed on the hillside a few feet from the left riverbank. This is Medicine Rock, believed in Siletz Indian lore to be the home of an evil medicine man. It was the Indians' custom to leave offerings at the base of the rock to appease the evil spirit.

The last half of this trip involves steady paddling on a long stretch of flatwater. The Pikes Camp area is best recognized by the house on the left bank, which was used in the filming of the movie version of the Ken Kesey novel *Sometimes a Great Notion*. Soon you will spot your car where you left it on the right bank.

73 Yaquina River

Location: East of Newport
Distance: 10.5 miles
Time: 5 to 6 hours
Maps: USGS Elk City, Toledo South, and Toledo North 7.5"
Season: Year-round
Rating: A

The Yaquina River flows into the Pacific Ocean just south of Newport. Its huge bay is noted for its oyster population. As one drives east up the Yaquina Valley, the first town encountered is Toledo, with its lumber and pulp mills.

As the crow flies, 3 miles east of Toledo lies a cluster of about a dozen buildings known as Elk City, but the river spends 10 miles meandering from one town to the other. The town's most notable structure was once a covered bridge that was built in 1922. The bridge was closed in 1980, and while plans were being made to restore it, a windstorm blew it into the river in 1981. The town still has some history, however. The store was built in 1865; it is the oldest commercial structure in Lincoln County, but it closed a few years ago.

This trip paddles the 10.5-mile distance from this forgotten hamlet to its modern industrial neighbor, Toledo. The tide reaches all the way to Elk City, so the paddler can expect little or no aid from the current. This is a long trip for a pair of novice paddlers, especially if the wind and tide are not cooperating. A county boat ramp at Cannon Quarry Park, about halfway between the two towns, would be a good ending point for those desiring a shorter trip. (The upper half of this trip is the more scenic section.)

From US Highway 101 at Newport, drive east on US Highway 20, and follow US Highway 20 Business into Toledo. Turn right onto Main Street and follow it as it becomes Butler Bridge Road. Following the signs to the airport,

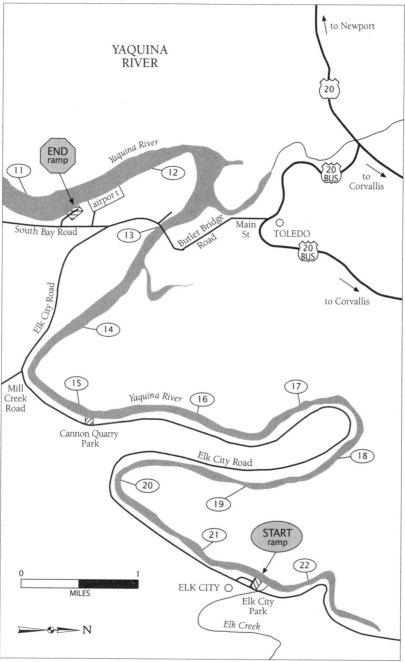

cross the bridge and eventually turn right onto South Bay Road. Just past the airport, turn right to a modern public boat ramp where you can leave your extra car.

Return to Butler Bridge Road (now Elk City Road), turn right, and follow it about 8 miles east to Elk City. Elk City Park and its boat ramp are just upstream from the cluster of buildings that make up the tiny town.

As is obvious from the sketch map, the river channel is a unique series of undulations of increasing size. Paddlers should have little difficulty determining their location on this section of the Yaquina. Because most of the travel is either due north or due south, just remember how many U-turns you have made. Just to be safe, though, carry a compass. After passing heavily industrialized Toledo, the river takes a sharp turn to the south. The modern boat ramp is on the left bank, just south of the airport.

74 Siltcoos River

Location: South of Florence
Distance: 5 miles
Time: 4 hours
Maps: USGS Florence, Tahkenitch Creek, and Goose Pasture 7.5"
Season: Year-round, but best September 15 to March 15
Rating: A (with one easy portage) (Warning: Do not paddle below rivermile 0.5)

The Siltcoos River is one of the shortest rivers in Oregon. It travels just 3 miles from Siltcoos Lake to the Pacific Ocean. Yet it is one of the prettiest paddle trips on the central Oregon coast, passing from a large coastal lake through a Sitka spruce forest and through the Oregon Dunes National Recreational Area to the Pacific. This trip can be paddled as a pleasant day's outing, or (in some seasons) as an overnight camping trip. If you're planning on camping, obtain a free camping permit at most Forest Service campgrounds or at the Oregon Dunes visitor center in Reedsport, phone (541) 271-3611.

The area near the mouth of the Siltcoos River is designated as protected habit for the western snowy plover, a bird whose population has been declining in recent years. In that area, boaters are not permitted to get out of their boats during nesting season from March 15 to September 15 each year. If you're planning to camp, or would like to stroll around in the dunes, plan this trip outside of that time period. Dogs are prohibited year-round.

Also plan this trip according to the tides because the lower section of the river is influenced by the tide. The tidal current is often weak, but low tide may make the lower river too shallow for paddling. In general, try to reach the lower section of the river at approximately high tide, or (even better)

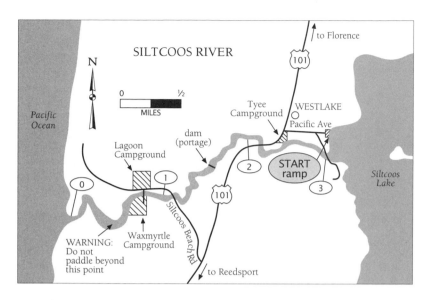

somewhat before high tide, so that the incoming flow will help you paddle back upstream.

Start this trip by driving south from Florence about 6 miles on US Highway 101, then turn left onto Pacific Avenue, at a sign pointing to Tyee Campground and Westlake. Continue east on Pacific Avenue 0.2 miles to the boat ramp. Launch here and paddle south 0.2 miles to the narrow entrance to the river, marked by a cement bridge. The river is easy to miss. It's at the back of the same bay on which the boat ramp is located; don't paddle around the point to the south.

The river is perfectly flat as it passes several homes and a Forest Service campground and then flows under US Highway 101. The banks are generally steep and lined with tall trees. After about 1.5 miles from the boat ramp, a cement dam blocks the river, but a nifty portage has been constructed on the north side of the dam, complete with plastic strips on which to slide your canoe or kayak.

Below the dam, the river is subject to the influence of the tide, although the influence is generally slight. After passing under two more bridges, and passing two more Forest Service campgrounds, the landscape quickly flattens out, and soon the spruce forest gives way to shore pines, which give way to marshes and sand dunes, the habitat of the snowy plover. From March 15 to September 15, boaters are not allowed out of their boats below about rivermile 0.7.

The river then passes through two pronounced curves and quickly becomes shallow. In fact, it is usually too shallow to permit paddlers to get closer than about a half-mile from the ocean, which is just as well because the ocean is unsafe for paddlers except those accustomed to dealing with surf.

Camping is not allowed on the beach, but it is permitted behind the fore-dunes, the low grassy dunes about a quarter mile back from the ocean. Camping is not permitted within 200 feet of the river, and fires are not permitted unless the campers are equipped with a shovel and a bucket. The area north of the river is popular with noisy dune buggies, but the roar of the ocean nearly drowns them out.

Portaging the dam on the Siltcoos River

appendix

Map Sources

Distribution Division, National Ocean Survey, Riverdale, MD 20840. For ordering NOAA charts listed in this book, go to *www.noaa.gov/charts. html.*

Oregon Parks and Recreation Department, 1115 Commercial Street Northeast, Salem, OR 97310-1001; *www.egov.oregon.gov/OPRD/index. shtml.*

U.S. Geological Survey, Box 25286 Federal Center, Denver, CO 80225. For ordering USGS topographic maps listed in this book, go to *www.topomaps. usgs.gov.*

Paddling Clubs

Cascade Canoe Club, 3025 Harris Street, Eugene, OR 97405; (503) 345-5115; *http://canoe.freeshell.org/.* For both flatwater and whitewater paddlers.

Lower Columbia Canoe Club, 17005 Northwest Meadowgrass Drive, Beaverton, OR 97006; *www.l-ccc.org.* For both flatwater and whitewater canoe paddlers.

Oregon Ocean Paddling Society, P.O. Box 69641, Portland, OR 97239; *www. oopskayak.org.* This is a sea kayak club, for flatwater kayak touring on both salt water and fresh water.

Southwest Washington Canoe Club, P.O. Box 714, Kelso, Washington 98626. For flatwater and whitewater paddling.

Willamette Kayak and Canoe Club, P.O. Box 1062, Corvallis, OR 97339; *www.wkcc.org.* Primarily a whitewater club.

Mailing Lists

Several Internet mailing lists for paddlers have been established by paddling clubs and others. Some require membership in the organization in order to participate in their list. Here are a few mailing lists for Oregon paddlers:

lccc@yahoogroups.com (Lower Columbia Canoe Club)
oopskayak@googlegroups.com (Oregon Ocean Paddling Society)
pdxseakayaker@yahoogroups.com
scappoosebaypaddlingassociation@yahoogroups.com
bendpaddler@yahoogroups.com (Paddlers of Central Oregon)
pdxrecreationalkayaker@yahoogroups.com

Weather Forecasts

National Weather Service, *www.wrh.noaa.gov/Portland.*

River Level Information
River levels are often printed in daily newspapers, usually in the weather section or the sports statistics section.

National Weather Service, (503) 261-9246, *www.waterdata.usgs.gov/or/nwis/current/?type=flow* or *www.nwrfc.noaa.gov.*

Tides
Tide tables are available at nautical and sporting goods stores, or look in your daily newspaper, or go to *www.saltwatertides.com.*

Public Agencies

The parks, boat ramps, and other access points described in this book are maintained by various government agencies, which can be contacted for more detailed information or updates.

Columbia River Gorge National Scenic Area, Headquarters, 902 Wasco Avenue, Suite 200, Hood River, OR 97031; (541) 386-2333; *www.fs.fed.us/r6/columbia.*

Clark County, Washington, Parks Department, (360) 696-8171; *www.co.clark.wa.us/parks/index.html.*

Julia Butler Hansen National Wildlife Refuge, Highway 1, Box 376C, Cathlamet, WA 98612; (360) 795-4915.

Lewis and Clark National Wildlife Refuge, Highway 1, Box 376C, Cathlamet, WA 98612; (360) 795-4915.

Mount St. Helens National Volcanic Monument, Headquarters, (360) 247-3900; *www.fs.fed.us/gpnf/mshnvm.*

Mount St. Helens National Volcanic Monument, Visitor Center, (360) 274-2100.

Mount St. Helens National Volcanic Monument, Coldwater Ridge Visitor Center, (360) 274-2131.

Oregon Department of Fish and Wildlife, (503) 229-5403; *www.dfw.state.or.us.*

Oregon State Marine Board, 435 Commercial Street Northeast, Salem, OR 97310, or PO Box 14145, Salem, OR 97309-5065; (503) 378-8587. Many of their publications are available on their website, *www.boatoregon.com.*

Oregon State Parks and Recreation Department, Headquarters, 1115 Commercial Street Northeast, Salem, OR 97310-1001; (503) 378-6305 or (800) 233-3306; *www.egov.oregon.gov/OPRD/index.shtml.*

Oregon State Parks and Recreation Department, Portland Office, 3554 Southeast 82nd Avenue, Portland, OR 97266; (503) 238-7488.

Ridgefield National Wildlife Refuge, (360) 887-4106.

Sauvie Island Wildlife Area, (503) 621-3488.

Washington Department of Fish and Wildlife, Headquarters, 600 Capital Way North, Olympia, WA 98501; (360) 902-2200; *www.wdfw.wa.gov/.*

Washington Department of Fish and Wildlife, Region 5 (Southwest Washington), 5405 Northeast Hazel Dell Avenue, Vancouver, WA 98663; (360) 696-6211.

Washington Department of Natural Resources, Southwest Region, P.O. Box 280, Castle Rock, WA 98611; (360) 577-2025; *www.wa.gov/dnr.*

Washington State Parks and Recreation Commission, Headquarters, 7150 Cleanwater Lane, P.O. Box 42650, Olympia, WA 98504-2650; (360) 902-8500.

Washington Interagency Committee for Outdoor Education, 1111 Washington Street Southeast, PO Box 40917, Olympia, WA 98504-0917; (360) 902-3000. This agency maintains a detailed list of Washington boat ramps on its website at *www.iac.wa.gov/maps/default.asp.*

Washington State Parks and Recreation Commission, Southwest Regional Office, 11838 Tilley Road South, Olympia, WA 98512; (360) 753-7143.

Washington State Shellfish Laboratory, Nahcotta, Washington; (360) 665-4166. For information on Long Island and Willapa Bay.

Willamette Falls Locks, (503) 656-3381.

Willapa National Wildlife Refuge, (360) 484-3482.

Other Organizations

Columbia Riverkeeper, 724 Oak Street, Hood River, OR 97031; (541) 387-3030; *www.columbiariverkeeper.org.*

Lower Columbia River Water Trail, *www.columbiawatertrail.org.*

Tualatin Riverkeepers, 12360 Southwest Main Street, Tigard, OR 97223; (503) 620-7507; *www.tualatinriverkeepers.org.*

Willamette Riverkeeper, 49 Southeast Clay, Portland, OR 97214; (503) 223-6418; *www.willamette-riverkeeper.org.*

Willamette Water Trail, *www.willamettewatertrail.org.*

Other Useful Websites

Many of the websites maintained by local paddling clubs list links to other websites useful to paddlers. The clubs are listed above.

U.S. Forest Service

Deschutes National Forest

Headquarters, (541) 388-2715.

Bend Ranger District, (541) 388-5664.

Crescent Ranger District, (541) 433-2234.

Fort Rock Ranger District, (541) 388-5664.

Sisters Ranger District, (541) 549-2111.

Gifford Pinchot National Forest, Washington

Headquarters, (503) 285-9823 or (360) 891-5000; *www.fs.fed.us.gpnf.*

Mount Adams Ranger District, Trout Lake, (509) 395-3400.

Cowlitz Valley Ranger District, (360) 497-1100 (formerly Randle Ranger District).

Mount Hood National Forest
Headquarters, (503) 668-1700.
Barlow Ranger District, (541) 467-2291.
Clackamas River Ranger District, (503) 630-4256.
Hood River Ranger District, (541) 352-6002.
Zigzag Ranger District, (503) 622-3191.
Willamette National Forest
Headquarters, (541) 465-6521.
Blue River Ranger District, (541) 822-3317.
Detroit Ranger District, (503) 854-3366.
Lowell Ranger District, (541) 937-2129.
McKenzie Ranger District, (541) 822-3381.
Oakridge Ranger District, (541) 782-2291.
Rigdon Ranger District, (541) 782-2283.
Sweet Home Ranger District, (541) 367-5168.

Waldo Lake (Trip 34)

index

about the author

Philip N. Jones, a Portland attorney, has been exploring the waters of the Northwest by canoe and kayak for more than thirty years. An avid cyclist, climber, and photographer, he is the coauthor of *Bicycling the Backroads of Northwest Oregon*, published by The Mountaineers Books.

Pat Riley

THE MOUNTAINEERS, founded in 1906, is a nonprofit outdoor activity and conservation club, whose mission is "to explore, study, preserve, and enjoy the natural beauty of the outdoors. . . . " Based in Seattle, Washington, the club is now one of the largest such organizations in the United States, with seven branches throughout Washington State.

The Mountaineers sponsors both classes and year-round outdoor activities in the Pacific Northwest, which include hiking, mountain climbing, ski-touring, snowshoeing, bicycling, camping, kayaking, nature study, sailing, and adventure travel. The club's conservation division supports environmental causes through educational activities, sponsoring legislation, and presenting informational programs.All club activities are led by skilled, experienced instructors, who are dedicated to promoting safe and responsible enjoyment and preservation of the outdoors.

If you would like to participate in these organized outdoor activities or the club's programs, consider a membership in The Mountaineers. For information and an application, write or call The Mountaineers, Club Headquarters, 7700 Sand Point Way NE, Seattle, WA 98115; 206-521-6001. You can also visit the club's website at *www.mountaineers.org* or contact The Mountaineers via email at *clubmail@mountaineers.org*.

The Mountaineers Books, an active, nonprofit publishing program of the club, produces guidebooks, instructional texts, historical works, natural history guides, and works on environmental conservation. All books produced by The Mountaineers Books fulfill the club's mission.

Send or call for our catalog of more than 500 outdoor titles:

The Mountaineers Books
1001 SW Klickitat Way, Suite 201
Seattle, WA 98134
800-553-4453
mbooks@mountaineersbooks.org
www.mountaineersbooks.org

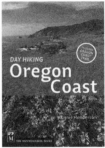